CHANGING WITNESS

Michael Warner is a historian with the History Staff of the Central Intelligence Agency. He is the editor of *The CIA Under Harry Truman* and holds a doctorate in history from the University of Chicago. Mr. Warner lives with his family near Washington, D.C.

CHANGING WITNESS

Catholic Bishops and Public Policy,
1917–1994

Michael Warner

Foreword by
George Weigel

ETHICS AND PUBLIC POLICY CENTER
WASHINGTON, D.C.

WILLIAM B. EERDMANS PUBLISHING COMPANY
GRAND RAPIDS, MICHIGAN / CAMBRIDGE, U.K.

Copyright © 1995 by the Ethics and Public Policy Center
1015 Fifteenth St. N.W., Washington, D.C. 20005

Published jointly 1995 by the Ethics and Public Policy Center and
Wm. B. Eerdmans Publishing Co.
255 Jefferson Ave. S.E., Grand Rapids, Mich. 49503 /
P. O. Box 163, Cambridge, CB3 9PU U.K.

Printed in the United States of America

Library of Congress Cataloging-in-Publication Data

Warner, Michael.
Changing Witness: Catholic bishops and public policy, 1917-1994 /
Michael Warner; foreword by George Weigel.
p.   cm.
Includes index.
ISBN 8028-4071-X (paper: alk. paper)
1. Catholic Church United States — History — 20th century.
2. Catholic Church. National Conference of Catholic Bishops.
3. United States Catholic Conference.
4. Sociology, Christian (Catholic)   I. Title.
BX1406.2.W37   1995
261.8'0'822 — dc20   95-20780
                                                      CIP

To Dorothy

Contents

Contents

Acknowledgments

T his book is the culmination of eight years of work dating back to my doctoral studies at the University of Chicago. In that time, many people have assisted and encouraged me in ways large and small, and this study has benefited from their efforts. A few of them especially earned my gratitude. The University of Chicago's Martin Marty, Barry Karl, Nathan Tarcov, along with James V. Schall, S.J., of Georgetown University, oversaw the foundations of this work. Msgr. George Higgins, Philip Costopoulos, and Vincent Vaccaro were kind enough to read portions of my drafts. Scott Koch and Gerald K. Haines raised my spirits at a crucial moment. George Weigel and Robert Royal of the Ethics and Public Policy Center offered innumerable suggestions, and stuck with me to the end. Special thanks to Mary Hittinger and Jacqui Stark for their editorial help. Finally, I wish to thank the Catholic University of America and the Catholic Theological Union in Chicago, which greatly assisted my research by extending me special access to their collections.

MICHAEL WARNER
December 1994

Foreword

George Weigel

Contemporary studies of the National Conference of Catholic Bishops and its public policy arm, the United States Catholic Conference, have been dominated by political scientists and sociologists. And no doubt the number-crunchers and the management theorists can teach us something about the political activism of America's Catholic hierarchy. Michael Warner, however, believes that the history of the NCCB-USCC (and its predecessor, the old National Catholic Welfare Conference) is best understood not as a story of structures, but as a history of ideas.

That will strike some observers as impossibly old hat. But I think Dr. Warner is on to something; indeed, I think he's on to something important. That "ideas have consequences" has become one of the hoariest of analytic clichés. But Richard Weaver's aphorism nonetheless conveys a large truth—a truth nicely illustrated by this study. For we cannot understand, much less intelligently evaluate, the public policy of the American Catholic bishops unless we wrestle with the intellectual changes that have rippled through Catholicism in America over the past two generations.

The centrality of *ideas* in grappling with a distinctive organization like the NCCB-USCC should be obvious. The bishops, after all, are

---

George Weigel is president of the Ethics and Public Policy Center, Washington, D.C.

religious leaders who do things differently than the standard policy analyst or lobbyist. When addressing an issue of the common weal, the bishops are presumed to deliberate in the light of a body of thought —a body of *ideas*—which is itself the result of an authoritative doctrinal tradition interacting with millennia of human experience and reflection. Understanding the foundational ideas and the conceptual frameworks behind the bishops' policy prescriptions is thus indispensable to understanding and evaluating those prescriptions. In considering the NCCB-USCC and its effects on American public life, the first question is not, Do the bishops have the votes? The first question is, or should be, Do the bishops have the arguments?

The degree to which the U.S. bishops' conference has in fact collectively and consistently carried the wisdom of the Catholic tradition into the American public square is, to put it gently, a matter of some dispute. The bishops themselves insist regularly, even antiphonally, that they come before the country, the Congress, and the officials of the Executive Branch as "pastors and teachers." Michael Warner thinks that claim has often been less-than-self-evidently clear. But their critics, their supporters, and the bishops themselves are all agreed that the NCCB-USCC is not, and ought not be, just one more Washington lobby. And all parties to the present debate over Catholicism as a "public Church" (the term was coined by Martin Marty, Michael Warner's advisor at the University of Chicago) seem to concur that were the NCCB-USCC ever to become just another lobby, it would have—in biblical terms—traded its birthright for a mess of pottage.

The Catholic struggle to be a "public Church" in modern America is a struggle that is, first and foremost—on Michael Warner's telling of the tale—an exercise in theology, in the self-understanding of the Church as a religious body. This struggle has taken place in a valley between two towering peaks.

The first peak was formed by the heroic efforts of Popes Leo XIII and Pius XI to bring classic Catholic understandings of the human person, society, history, and destiny to bear on the singular economic, social, and political problems of late modernity: on the world created by the Industrial Revolution, the collapse of the traditional social order in Europe, and the rise of totalitarianism in its various forms. On the death of Pius IX in 1878, enlightened opinion held that with the demise of the Papal States and the reduction of the pope to a "prisoner of the Vatican," the Catholic Church had ceased to count for much in world affairs. Leo XIII and Pius XI believed to the contrary that the Church had far greater weapons than the halberds of the Swiss Guards who grace the Vatican. According to these two great popes, the Church could exercise enormous influence through the power of ideas and moral persuasion. History has subsequently vindicated that conviction. The vision of the just society sketched by Leo XIII in the encyclical *Rerum Novarum* proved remarkably prescient in its analysis of the impossibility of socialism, and in its teaching that the *human person* is the beginning and the end of reflection on society. Pius XI's vigorous condemnation of totalitarianism, and his defense of the organic communities of civil society, embodied in the "principle of subsidiarity," laid the groundwork on which a generation of Catholic activists helped rebuild a shattered Europe in the aftermath of World War II. The Christian personalism of Leo XIII and Pius XI also anticipated (and, in some respects, helped make possible) the post-war international human rights movement, which has had such a tremendous impact on world politics.

But for all their prescience, the social teaching of Leo XIII and Pius XI was, from one angle of vision, rather reactive: it was forged in response to economic, social, and political developments that had taken place outside the Church and, in some important instances, *against* the Church. In that sense, the social doctrine of Leo XIII and Pius XI involved what a sportswriter would call "catch-up ball": a Church that many of the architects of modernity (especially in western Europe) had considered essentially anti-modern, even reactionary, was responding to an agenda set by others. To be sure, that response often probed more deeply into the philosophical depths of the modern project than many of modernity's most vociferous anti-clerical defenders; but that does not alter the fact that Catholic social doctrine in its formative period developed, in no small part, as an answer to questions that were being pressed by other institutions and actors on the world stage.

At the second mountain—the social teaching of Pope John Paul II, understood as the authoritative interpretation of the social teaching of the Second Vatican Council—we find ourselves in a dramatically different position. For John Paul II has been consistently *ahead* of the contemporary argument about the right-ordering of society: a post-modern pope, if you will. John Paul II's critics (from the ecclesiastical and political portside) often accuse him of living in another century. They're right, but they've got the wrong century in mind, thinking as they do of the nineteenth or eighteenth. In fact, John Paul is living in the twenty-first century, in a manner of speaking, and has been for some time.

Thus John Paul's insistence on religious freedom as the first of human rights and the foundation of any meaningful scheme of "rights" may have sounded, to some ears, like Polish special pleading in the days when the Soviet empire held sway over east central Europe. But with the fall of the Berlin Wall, the collapse of the political alignments of the Cold War, and the rise of ethnic, national, and religious strife around the world, the pope's teaching on the priority of religious freedom is revealed for what it has always been—a defense of the inherent and inalienable dignity of the human person against any attempt to reduce that personhood to an object of manipulation or destruction.

Moreover, the pope's teaching (in the encyclical *Veritatis Splendor*) that basic human rights and duties can be discerned, cross-culturally, through a disciplined reflection on human nature and human action is not a matter of Catholicism defending a sectarian philosophical position. In the fullest sense, it is a defense of the very possibility of a universal moral discourse—and thus a defense of the very possibility of the world conversing coherently and constructively about its future. That such a conversation is the only alternative to a Hobbesian world in which all are at war with all is conveyed with grim regularity, and in living (and dying) color, by our television news every night.

The pope has also insisted on a substantive moral core to politics and economics, and stressed the moral culture of civil society as the essential foundation for democracies and market economies that serve the ends of human flourishing: emphases that now look very much like a sketch of the key public issues of twenty-first century life in virtually every human society. Whether the venue is Milwaukee or Port-au-Prince, Johannesburg or Kraków, the priority of civil society, the imperative of nurturing genuine freedom amidst the siren-songs of license, and the need to strengthen those free associations of men and women that form the sinews and ligaments of the body politic are increasingly recognized as issues of profound importance for developed and developing societies alike.

Finally, on a related front, John Paul II's defense of the dignity of human life from conception until natural death has long since escaped the "Catholic ghetto" to which its critics have tried to confine it. Billions of men and women throughout the world recognize that the technological manipulation of human reproduction, the intrusion of coercive government into family planning and parenthood, and all the other ugly artifacts of the "Brave New World" that Aldous Huxley so chillingly (and aptly) described, threaten our very humanity. Many of those men and women, of varied religious convictions, races, and nationalities—to the amazement of those who thought secularization the inevitable (and imminently desirable) complement to modernization—are now looking to the Bishop of Rome for international moral leadership in the face of an encroaching culture of death.

What has happened to the American Church "in the valley" between the towering peaks of Popes Leo XIII and Pius XI, on the one hand, and of Pope John Paul II, on the other? That is the terrain Michael Warner explores: the change in the official social witness of the Catholic Church in the United States in the days when Catholic bishops, intellectuals, activists, and bureaucrats grew restless with (and even dismissive of) the patrimony of Leo XIII and Pius XI, but before the Church in America had even begun to internalize the radically future-oriented social doctrine of John Paul II. According to Warner, what happened is not an altogether happy story. For as the Church travelled through the valley, it jettisoned some traditional but still serviceable, philosophical and theological equipment while adopting many of the social, economic, and political tenets of secular liberalism, including a preference for statist approaches to social welfare policy and a dovish view of international affairs. Some will disagree with that analysis. I happen to think Dr. Warner correct in his suggestion that modern Catholic social doctrine ought not be understood as providing clear and direct justifications for the Nanny State or for a functionally pacifist approach to world affairs. But even those who draw different "prudential judgments" (as the jargon has it) from the principles of Catholic social doctrine ought to ponder Michael Warner's critique of what happened to American Catholicism, intellectually, during its time "in the valley."

Unlike other analysts of the NCCB-USCC, Dr. Warner understands that the bishops' conference cannot be forced onto the Procrustean bed of left-wing, right-wing political analysis. For the joker in the deck, to vary the metaphor, has been the consistent, and in my view, heroic and prophetic resistance of the Church's leadership to the abortion license as defined by *Roe* v. *Wade*. But even that commitment, as Warner shows, was the source of no little contention within the NCCB-USCC dyad, as the bishops struggled to stay "in play" in a political environment where their deepest moral commitment was publicly supported by the Republican Party, while their policy preferences on virtually every other issue of consequence aligned them with moderate to liberal Democrats.

The standard account of this seeming dichotomy (purveyed most vigorously by NCCB-USCC staff members and their acolytes in the Catholic press) is that the bishops are actually radical centrists whose positions are based on a theological analysis that transcends partisan fashions; the alternative (and to my mind, more persuasive) explanation is that the generally "progressive" reputation of the conference has been tarnished, in some quarters, by the bishops' firm opposition to abortion-on-demand, and more recently, to euthanasia. However one parses this out, the contentiousness within the conference itself, and among the conference staff, over the place of the right-to-life agenda in the social witness of the Church suggests another intellectual problem in the recent history of the NCCB and USCC, a problem implied by Michael Warner's analysis. And that was the judgment, seemingly made early in the post–Vatican II years, that the social witness of the Church would be neither seen nor heard by the faithful or the public at large unless the moral principles the bishops wished to teach were "illustrated" by concrete legislative and regulatory applications across the full range of domestic and foreign policy issues.

That strategy—which might be called Comprehensive Prescriptiveness—is surely due for re-examination. The bishops' descent into the minutiae of domestic and foreign policy (which included, memorably, a judgment on the advisability of U.S. funding for the "soft loan window" of the World Bank) has not deepened American public understanding of the moral principles of Catholic social doctrine; it has, rather, distracted attention from those principles, as the bishops' conference has become yet another "player" in the policy game. The stress on policy prescription has also magnified the role of the bishops' staff as representatives of "the Church" in the United States, a phenomenon presaged by the Washington political activism of many liberal Protestant denominations over the past forty years. That such activism has paralleled the disaffection of large numbers of congregants from their churches and the general demographic collapse of mainline-oldline Protestantism is surely a cautionary tale.

But the real problem, at the level of ideas to which Dr. Warner constantly directs our attention, is that Comprehensive Prescriptiveness suggests that the principles of Catholic social doctrine can produce "prudential judgments" on innumerable issues. But that is not what the tradition of modern Catholic social thought says about itself. Indeed, the encyclical tradition from Leo XIII through John Paul II will yield nothing as minutely detailed as any document issued by the NCCB or USCC in any given American electoral season. Some will also find in Comprehensive Prescriptiveness an unfortunate clericalism. Have the bishops, by virtue of their office as "pastors and teachers," been vouchsafed a special insight into the technicalities of public policy? But that would seem to contradict the clear teaching of the Second Vatican Council, whose *Decree on the Apostolate of the Laity* (*Apostolicam Actuositatem*) taught that, in public affairs, "it is . . . the laity more than others [who] are the channels of Christian wisdom" (par. 14).

Once again, the example set by Pope John Paul II is instructive. Both John Paul's supporters and critics acknowledge the pope's singularly decisive role in shaping the debate at the 1994 World Conference on Population and Development, held in Cairo. And John Paul did this, not by proposing an alternative draft to the final document of the conference, but by preaching twelve brief homilies during his public audiences in June, July, and August 1994, in which he clearly and persuasively articulated the Church's moral vision of human dignity, human sexuality, and the central role of the family in the development of human society. To be sure, the results at Cairo depended on the energetic diplomatic efforts of the Holy See's delegation to the conference; but their effective work in the trenches of international politics was only possible because of the pope's moral witness as "pastor and teacher" of the human family. There is a profound lesson here for all those involved in the operation of the NCCB and USCC.

Critics—even friendly critics—of the "changing witness" of the U.S. Catholic bishops in the public policy arena are regularly charged with the sin of "privatizing" the faith. Michael Warner's study should help put that charge to rest. Dr. Warner understands that the Church *must* be a "public Church" if it is to fulfill the Lord's mandate to be a light to the nations. The issue is not *whether* Catholicism in America should speak to the great political question, first specified by Aristotle: "How *ought* we to live together?" The question is *how* that witness is articulated. In a country beginning to understand the moral roots of its gravest social problems, does the Church bring into the public square the ancient wisdom of Christian orthodoxy, as mediated through the prism of modern Catholic social doctrine? Is the Church genuinely counter-cultural, in that it applies the two-edged sword of the gospel to all of our cultural pretensions, including our pretenses to political infallibility? Is the Church, in its public witness, *ahead* of the usual liberal and conservative barricades? Is the Church unmistakably, unapologetically, assertively *Catholic* when its pastors enter the American public square?

Michael Warner, it seems to me, devoutly wishes that the answer to all these questions be "Yes." His study, written from within the household of faith by a devoted son of the Church, will help make it more likely that we can give that affirmative answer in the future.

1

Introduction:
Changing Witness

American life in this century has been shaped by two world wars,
a dozen or so "police actions," economic depression and prosperity, and accelerated technological and social change. Beginning the
century as an international naif, the United States has become the
world's leading power. America has seen enormous material growth
as the state has expanded into areas once deemed private or the province of other, mediating institutions. In addition, the generations that
came of age after World War II have experienced a radical transformation of social attitudes. Americans have rejected racial segregation,
discovered environmentalism, and tolerated a tectonic shift in sexual
mores as the once preeminent Protestant elites have abdicated their
long reign over the nation's cultural institutions.

Some of these changes have been welcomed, others have been
profoundly disturbing. Not surprisingly, the last thirty years have seen
a realignment of American social and political thought. The previously
tolerant secularism of political liberals has hardened, and new tech-
nologies have bolstered the liberal faith in historical progress. Both
the political left and right have, since the 1960s, challenged the reign-
ing liberalism. A new, non-Marxist, left confronts the old faith in
progress and reform, while a new right fights the exclusion of religion
and religious values from the public sphere.

In the background stand America's Roman Catholic bishops, diligently, and often very publicly, witnessing to Christian doctrine and
principles of social order; they have labored to translate that witness
into policy recommendations in the hope of providing a common

1

language to discuss common concerns. These efforts have sometimes been more eclectic than those of America's more systematic social thinkers. The bishops are not concerned over the receptivity of the American regime to teleological arguments and values; they have assumed for generations that the regime is receptive. And unlike some elements, the bishops seem confident that gradual reform is the only way to change the United States for the better.

The impact of the Roman Catholic Church in America and on American life should not be underestimated: It is the largest private institution in the nation. Since 1919, the Catholic bishops have worked collectively through the National Catholic Welfare Council (NCWC), and from 1967 through two parallel (if not strictly identical) organizations, the National Conference of Catholic Bishops (NCCB), a canonical body established by church law, and the United States Catholic Conference (USCC), the bishops' civil arm. They have addressed America's problems and possibilities, as well as the changing ways in which Americans have thought of themselves, their world, and their God. The statements issued by the American Catholic bishops over the last seventy-odd years have discussed virtually every important and controversial aspect of national life. These statements, moreover, are placed within the context of Christian morality and philosophy, which themselves participate in the highest traditions of Western learning.

Observers agree, however, that over the years the style and substance of the bishops' teachings on social matters have changed dramatically. Indeed, a statement from 1962 has a tone and orientation markedly different from almost anything published only a decade or so later. It suffices to mention here two of the most controversial statements in the history of the Catholic Church in America: the National Conference of Catholic Bishops' pastoral letters "The Challenge of Peace" (1983) and "Economic Justice for All" (1986). Both sparked heated argument among American Catholics and garnered wide attention from the secular media.

Most people cannot identify precisely what has changed in the bishops' public witness. They note only the Church's higher profile —for good and ill—with the national news media. In fact, the American bishops *have* assumed a new and more public role as social activists, although the Catholic Church in America has a long history of participation in national life and concern for social justice—in the past met mostly through education and a wide range of charitable works. But most journalists and commentators, unmindful of that history, have either praised the bishops for their "new" concern or criticized them for their sudden "obsession" with politics.

While avowedly Catholic observers are somewhat better informed, their assessments are often colored by their political preferences. Catholics who see themselves as religiously "conservative" tend to be politically conservative as well; they have accused the bishops of abandoning traditional Catholicism and placing the Church at the service of leftist ideology. This charge is consistently denied by the bishops and their spokesmen, who cite, with an air of patient exasperation, the gospel verses and papal statements that exhort Christians to work for justice and peace. On the other side, "progressive" Catholics invoke the spirit of Vatican II and the obligation of the Church to make itself relevant to modern needs and problems. These Catholics are happier with the bishops' new social activism but seem only dimly aware of its origins. Some casually assume that the American Church discovered the outside world sometime during the Second Vatican Council, roughly around 1965; that America's bishops never challenged political authority before that time; and that contemporary critics of the bishops' activism are ideological tools of plutocracy.

The groves of academe, from which we might expect more sophisticated explanations of Catholic social teaching, often yield only more subtle misconceptions. Most academic students of the bishops and their social teaching hardly mind, and often endorse, the appropriation of Church statements (and their own writings) in support of progressive revisionism. More reliable scholars have neglected to consider the alteration of Catholic social thought in conjunction with changes in society brought about by the recent revolution in morals and mores. Historical studies of the bishops and the American Church in the twentieth century usually fail to relate social and economic life in the United States to pontifical social teaching, while studies of the social activism of American Catholics often treat the bishops' collective activities and statements only as a facet of the broader effort of the Church as a whole in America. A few scholars (most notably Thomas J. Reese, S.J., and Timothy A. Byrnes) have taken a more promising path by studying the bishops' conference itself, but in doing so, they have usually focused on the bishops as political actors rather than as social thinkers. J. Brian Benestad and Kenneth R. Overberg have examined some of the bishops' social statements of the 1960s and 1970s. I cover a much longer span, but if I see any farther than these authors, it is only because I stand on their shoulders.

SOME BACKGROUND

While the Catholic Church holds and teaches the Bible as the revealed word of God, the Church knows well that the Bible is not a handbook of rules for contemporary political decision-making. The Old Testament offers the Covenant and the Decalogue, as well as detailed ceremonial and juridical prescriptions; in the New Testament, Jesus urges his followers to keep the commandments. But neither the Mosaic Law nor the Sermon on the Mount show us how to organize and administer a polity. The gospels do not spell out how to establish a legislature, how to regulate securities markets, or how to finance road-building projects. The New Testament draws no "poverty line" like that defined by economists and social workers.[1] Indeed, a strictly literal interpretation of the New Testament might incline Christians to social apathy; if Christ Himself did not bother with politics and social reform, why should we?

Such literalism, however, has never been part of the Catholic faith, which has always believed that compassion must be guided by doctrine; that some process of translation must intervene between the gospel command of love and the citizen's daily civic duty. Throughout history, the Church has concerned itself with delineating the boundaries of moral practice in society. The Vatican has urged Christians to practice spiritual and material charity toward their neighbors, and has indicated when Christians must refrain from cooperating in harmful policies. The phrase so often used in this context is "social justice." The new *Catechism of the Catholic Church* explains that "society ensures social justice when it provides the conditions that allow associations or individuals to obtain what is their due, according to their nature and their vocation. . . . Social justice can be obtained only in respecting the transcendent dignity of man" (1928-29). Human dignity is ultimately fulfilled in man's vocation to "divine beatitude" (1700), and entails certain rights which are prior to society: "It is the Church's role to remind men of good will of these rights and to distinguish them from unwarranted or false claims" (1930).[2]

The Church is a hierarchical institution, and even the bishops of the industrialized, urbanized, and secularized United States have followed papal teachings in applying the gospel to American life. Over the last hundred years, the popes have provided such guidance to the world, and to Catholics in particular, by publishing a series of authoritative essays, called encyclical letters, on modern society. The first and most famous of these was Leo XIII's *Rerum Novarum* (1891), which subsequent papal epistles have elaborated and developed.

The Natural Law Tradition

Catholic social thought—as embodied in papal encyclicals—has generally incorporated the notion of natural law—following the methods and spirit of St. Thomas Aquinas—as the participation of human beings in the divine law. God has given guidelines of conduct which can be apprehended by human reason and which are also contained in fuller measure in Divine Revelation.[3] In *Rerum Novarum,* Pope Leo XIII sought to help men and women understand their place in the cosmos and their duty to God (indeed, the rendering of what is due to the other—to God and to neighbor—is how the Church has traditionally defined justice). *Rerum Novarum* affirms that the ultimate destiny of human beings is not this world, but rather the life to come in union with God.[4]

Still, humanity must live and labor on this earth, and God has granted us reason and freedom so that we might discover the truths, intermediate and ultimate, about life and creation. All such understanding is incomplete and even unbalanced without the additional light of Revelation. The Holy Spirit keeps this God-given wisdom alive in the Church. The workings of human reason, guided by this wisdom, can discern the ways in which we as individuals and as societies should proceed to establish just laws and social order.[5] Leo's presentation and application of the natural law teaching has been reiterated and developed by subsequent pontiffs and the Church at large.[6]

The Second Vatican Council, for instance, in the *Declaration on Religious Freedom,* incorporated the traditional teaching that the wisdom of the Church is a light even for societies of many creeds and no established Christian church, like the United States. Discussing the role of government in the lives of citizens, the *Declaration* explains that the state must allow the citizenry the free exercise of religion, in part to ensure that "society itself may profit by the moral qualities of justice and peace which have their origin in men's faithfulness to God and to His holy will" (6). This statement suggests that all religions, if they respect the fundamental rights of mankind, perform at least some social good by guiding the consciences of their adherents. The *Declaration* makes clear, however, that true knowledge of God and His will can be received in its fullness only from the Church. To the gospel is due "in great measure the fact that in the course of time men have come more widely to recognize their dignity as persons" (12).[7]

Critique of Modernity

Beginning with Leo XIII, Catholic social teaching has presented a sophisticated critique of modernity and its ideologies. For instance, Leo defended the common good against the centralizing, egalitarian, and individualist tendencies of the nineteenth and twentieth centuries. In *Rerum Novarum,* Leo not only stood against socialism, Marxism, and all utopianisms, but also against the radical laissez-faire capitalism of his time. The current pontiff, John Paul II, has further insisted that Catholic social teaching is not a *via media* between liberal individualism and socialist collectivism, but instead is an independent social philosophy.[8]

The popes have recognized that the Enlightenment and the Industrial Revolution, while bringing mankind freedom from much illness and material want, have created a new dependence on social and economic structures that, while developed and overseen by human beings, can be just as remorseless and arbitrary as brute nature. Although material progress has transformed our world, popes since Leo XIII have said this progress is incomplete; it has relieved some difficulties of human existence while exacerbating others. Rome has not accepted this ironic twist of modernity as uncorrectable. Instead, the Church has rejected the notion that human nature itself has somehow been changed by technology and industrialization; that traditional ideas and norms have been rendered unworkable by mass production or the nuclear menace. It has also rejected the modern attack on Christianity's claim to teach the truth about man and God. The popes have insisted that, while secular ideologies may offer some valuable insights about modern life, the true cure for modern ills is moral and spiritual, entailing a recognition of human limitations and obedience to God's laws.

The insights of papal social teaching regarding the principles of the social order have long proved more cogent than papal discussions of the creation and distribution of wealth and the furthering of human accomplishments. The popes of earlier generations were in part responding to the economic issues of their day. To Leo XIII and Pius XI, the Industrial Revolution had seemingly solved the problem of creating wealth, whereas the problems involved in its more equitable distribution were still controversial and dangerous. Nevertheless, these popes had plenty to say, in a general sense, about human labor and its right and wrong uses, as did succeeding pontiffs.

Over the last generation, however, two trends have drawn particular papal attention. First, while certain problems of distribution in both the developed and developing nations have remained, the spread of socialism in the Third World retarded economic growth and threw the difficulties of creating wealth into greater relief. Second, during the same period, what the popes regarded as truly pernicious ideas about human freedom have spread around the world, especially Western notions that sexual license is vital to human happiness and that personal growth requires freedom from moral absolutes.

True Social Progress

In contrast to these notions, Catholic social doctrine proclaims that true social progress is both objective and subjective. Material progress is desirable because, as an objective fact, a more accomplished and prosperous society can help human beings live longer and happier lives. True progress is also subjective, affecting the human subject in his personal attainment of truth and piety, and in his relations with others. Progress can only be considered successful if it encourages people to develop and express their likeness to God individually and in corporate bodies. Social progress fulfills this second goal only if it enhances both the moral and material life in conformity with the

nature of man and his ultimate end. Morality and economic development always affect one another, and must be improved concurrently
to avoid harming individuals and ultimately society itself.

The English Jesuit Rodger Charles has noted that the Second Vatican Council's *Declaration on Religious Freedom* wonderfully condenses
the Catholic understanding of the relation of the individual to society
and the state. The *Declaration* argues that man must follow his conscience in freedom because men "are both impelled by their nature
and bound by a moral obligation to seek the truth, especially religious
truth" (2).[9] Charles notes that "the standard for man in his moral life
is God's eternal law, objective and universal." Although conscience is
influenced by its historical context, it can and must be cultivated and
conformed to the objective moral law. Human beings are created to
serve God in communion with their fellows. Following Vatican II,
Charles says that the duty of law is to provide for the "common good,"
making "ordinances . . . with regard to the needs of all men, not only
those of believers." Nonetheless, the laws of governments must be
"judged by the moral law, revealed and natural," and they must provide for the exercise of religion and for lives of virtue and piety.[10] But
this is all the state can do to lead people to God; education, the Church,
and a freely given personal effort must do the rest.

Charles's insight suggests another: at the core of papal social doctrine is an overriding concern for the cultivation of consciences. Accordingly, the Vatican has stated that concerning Catholic social action,
political and economic activities are the province of the laity, who are
responsible for evangelizing the world through the ordinary spheres
of human activity. The popes have also consistently suggested that
Christianity is important more for the supernatural help it provides
—both in winning converts and in refining the souls of Christians—
than for any increase in material welfare that occurs through its agency.

AMERICAN ADJUSTMENTS

For three-quarters of a century, America's Catholic bishops have been
custodians of and contributors to a growing body of Catholic social
and political commentary. The bishops have stood in relation to papal
social teaching somewhat as the pope and magisterium of the Catholic

Church stand in relation to Scripture and Tradition; just as the duty of the pope and magisterium is to preserve, teach, and interpret faithfully and authoritatively the deposit of faith as transmitted by Tradition and Scripture, so too the bishops must faithfully transmit papal pronouncements on faith and morals to the souls in their charge. Likewise they must transmit the principles of the just social order to the faithful and to all other concerned citizens.

A shift in the social teachings of the Catholic Church in America, however, has occurred over the last generation—however ambiguous and confusing it may sometimes seem. In 1982, Bishop Thomas J. Gumbleton of Detroit explained the episcopacy's new role as social theorists and activists: the Church's former reliance upon what Gumbleton called certain "timeless and unchanging [ethical] norms" had been overthrown during the tumult of the 1960s. According to Gumbleton, the Second Vatican Council urged Catholics to go back out into the world; the Vietnam War and the civil rights revolution forced the faithful to reinterpret their social and political attitudes. The Church, or at least its progressive elements, performed this reinterpretation with the help of ideas conceived by Latin American scholars and activists—the adherents of "liberation theology"—who indirectly taught their North American cousins how to read Scripture as a critical and ever-developing call for political action.[11]

Against the proponents of the older natural law tradition, Bishop Gumbleton and other American theorists argued that the natural law vision of an organic society guided by the Church's wisdom was anachronistic, ahistorical, and in no way indispensable to Church teaching. Another American prelate who enunciated the new social teaching of the American episcopacy was Archbishop Rembert Weakland of Milwaukee, who credited Latin American theologians with helping to bring the American Catholic Church into the "postmodern" age. In 1989, at the University of Notre Dame, Weakland addressed a conference on liberation theology, where he explained that "post-modernism" had recognized the folly of the Enlightenment's hope that unaided human reason "would be able to create a perfect world." Although the archbishop observed that the American church was not completely rid of its infatuation with "the liberalism of the Enlightenment," he noted that recent pastoral letters of the nation's bishops recognized the "ultimate absurdity of rational solutions." He praised the NCCB's pastoral letter "The Challenge of Peace" for showing "how absurd the rational solution can be when it leads to holding itself and the world hostage by nuclear deterrence." Weakland also attacked the selfishness of bourgeois life in America, saying that the Church has been fighting "the extreme personalism of U.S. society with a deeper understanding of the common good." He lauded the subsequent NCCB pastoral letter "Economic Justice For All" for showing a way out of the "mechanized, clocklike concept of the marketplace," toward a more participatory society.[12]

Archbishop Weakland was walking a fine line here, indirectly answering critics of the bishops' social teaching on his left and on his right. He wanted to say that the new social teaching of the Church was something fresh and different and good because it attacked political and social conservatism. But he did not want to imply that the bishops were bent on a radical course, or that they had jettisoned traditional Catholic teaching—and with it the ground of their own authority.

Natural Law and the "Biblical" Ethic

How superior was the new American social analytic to the traditional teaching that it supplanted? Archbishop Weakland's own examples perhaps revealed more than he intended. "Economic Justice for All," ironically, illustrated the difficulties the bishops faced in moving from the Church's natural law tradition of social teaching toward a "post-modern" perspective that related Scripture directly to modern problems. In separating itself from past documents, American and pontifical, which were concerned with a strict definition of rights and duties, the economic pastoral stated that "biblical justice" was concerned "with the rightness of the human condition before God and within society." "Central to the biblical presentation of justice," the bishops asserted, "is that the justice of a community is measured by its treatment of the powerless in society, most often described as the widow, the orphan, the poor, and the stranger" (38). The pastoral drew upon this idea in urging citizens to judge America by its treatment of the poor, and to evaluate America's allocation of income, wealth and power "in light of its effects on persons whose basic material needs are unmet" (70).[13]

The notion that any attainment of justice should be measured primarily by society's treatment of the poor rested on a slim body of scriptural evidence. A key passage in "Economic Justice for All" stated: "the Law, the Prophets, and the Wisdom literature of the Old Testament all show deep concern for the proper treatment of such people" (38). The note accompanying this passage cited several Old Testament passages, virtually all of which discuss the obligation of the individual believer—but not of society or the state—to render justice and give alms to neighbors and those afflicted by poverty or distress.[14]

"Economic Justice for All" was drafted under the supervision of Archbishop Weakland—a fact that illuminates the problem with claims of bishops like Weakland and Gumbleton for the innovative but scripturally grounded achievements of the new social teaching. In fact, Weakland himself admitted that there were few scriptural warrants for even key documents like the pastoral letter on the economy. In 1983, Archbishop Weakland told the NCCB that his drafting committee was finding it difficult to square traditional social doctrine with Scripture. "So much of the social teaching of the church of the last century," he explained, "has been derived from the natural law theory and the committee must wrestle with its relationship to the Gospel vision."[15] Two years later Weakland complained that the committee was grappling with a related problem, noting that "the problems of the relationship between Scripture and moral discourse have not been completely thought through by moral theologians today." This situation hampered his committee from consistently applying Scripture to modern life. Weakland admitted the source of these difficulties: "Perhaps," he mused, "some of these weaknesses come from the loss of a uniform and universally accepted philosophical framework for such a consistent interpretation."[16] In the end, however, Archbishop Weakland believed "Economic Justice for All" had done a credible job of reconciling natural law and the "biblical" perspective.

A CHANGING WITNESS

In the late 1960s, the public witness of the Catholic Church in America, through its social teachings, shifted from a basis in the natural law tradition, as embraced by Leo XIII, to a Scripture-based ethic, promoted since by bishops such as Thomas Gumbleton, Rembert Weakland, and others. Despite the episcopacy's declared biblical perspective and their exercise of the traditional authority of their episcopal office, however, one unfortunate effect of the new biblical ethic has been the dilution of episcopal authority and the moral force of the gospel in American public life. The American Catholic hierarchy has adopted a more public role and voice, and engaged in public arguments over details of public policy—as well as articulating principles of social order and justice grounded in the Church's tradition. The bishops have consequently labored to distinguish the statements of the Church from mere policy preferences vested in religious rhetoric. How successful they have been in distinguishing themselves from the pronouncements of a hundred other interest groups remains to be examined.

The bishops and their staff, of course, rarely have the time they might like to study the Church Fathers and great theologians, and to draw neat distinctions between doctrine, principle, and practice. George Santayana could have been describing the Catholic Church when he noted that "the workings of the great institutions are mainly the result of a vast mass of routine, petty malice, self-interest, carelessness and sheer mistakes. Only a residual fraction is thought." While American episcopal judgments have often been issued in response to general trends or under the pressure of specific events, they also reflect the strengths and shortcomings of the procedures of the conference itself. To an even greater degree, conference social statements have mirrored the concerns and desires of the individual bishops and staffers involved in their production, and of other interested Catholics both inside and outside the bishops' conference and its secretariat. On more than one occasion, those Catholics have sought to expand the envelope of Catholic social thought and to generate innovative and even controversial applications of Church doctrine.

The larger social and historical context of the Catholic church in American life has also shaped episcopal social teaching. For instance, the American bishops have studiously refrained from endorsing candidates for public office, understanding that the price of prophecy is too high if it endangers the Church's tax exemption. In responding to national and world events, Catholic social statements frequently incorporate the fears and hopes of their time as much as they apply the gospel. Various scholars have recounted the particular effects of the social and political debates of the 1960s on the contemporary American Catholic Church. With acknowledgments to them, this study takes a harder and closer look at the intellectual and ideological influences on the Church and its social teaching. This said, I offer no apologies for my effort to understand the American bishops and their advisors as they have understood themselves. This volume focuses on ideas and their expression, confident in the truth of the common notion that ideas make a difference and that what is expressed may transcend the circumstances of its expression.

The vastness of this subject requires a little oversimplification for the sake of a coherent overview. Many historical episodes, and not a few institutions and relationships, are thus omitted, or mentioned only in passing. This is not a history of the National Catholic Welfare Conference or the National Conference of Catholic Bishops and the United States Catholic Conference, but rather the story of how competing factions and ideas have shaped and influenced the social teaching of the American bishops. It is not a complete, systematized chronicle, but instead an interpretive essay. The place I begin is Rome, because before making their social pronouncements, the American bishops have either taken their cue from the pope or gauged their distance from him.

2

Foundations of Catholic Social
Thought: 1891-1930

The Church has long stood at the crossroads of politics and moral
reform. Since Roman times, Christianity and clergymen have
wielded political influence, preserving literacy and culture after the
fall of the empire, quite literally civilizing most of Europe. Despite its
two-millennial history of missionary and educational activities, the
Church began to develop a body of official social teachings only in
the nineteenth century. Indeed, before the Industrial Revolution, few
saw the need for an explicit response to the ordering of economies,
governments, and politics. The class and economic structure of
Christendom for centuries had remained fairly stable. Political and
civil authority were regarded as deriving from God; economies were
based on agriculture, and the various crafts and trades preserved ancient patterns well into the eighteenth and even the nineteenth centuries. Political structures maintained the hierarchical patterns of
society. While no single theoretical system emerged within the Church
either to describe or criticize the social order, Catholic thinkers and
scholars over the centuries studied their societies and demarcated the
relation of the church, the state, and the bounds of justice among
peoples and institutions.

When the political and economic revolutions of the eighteenth and
nineteenth centuries began to dissolve the traditional patterns of
society, the Church confronted something entirely new — the rise of
liberalism and the emergence of industrialization and mass society,
phenomena which began on the Continent but which spread across
the globe. Liberalism, capitalism, and democracy in Europe brought

manifest material benefits but also unsettled and uprooted millions of people and became a matter of no small perplexity for the Catholic Church and its popes.

Remembering with horror the Church's trials during the French Revolution, the Holy See sought desperately to retain the Papal States in the face of the nineteenth century drive for Italian unification. Popes through Pius IX (1846-1878) believed that the continued existence of the Papal States would guarantee the temporal and political independence of the papacy, and that should they be forfeit, the pope would become the thrall of the Italian nation or some other European power. To escape the terror of the revolutionaries and the anti-clericalism of even comparatively moderate European democrats, successive popes uncomfortably allied themselves with absolute monarchy. (At the time, Rome paid little heed to the distant, Protestant experiment with democracy in the United States.) Not until after the Church lost the Papal States to Italy in 1870 did the Holy See resign itself to finding some *modus vivendi* with the democratic, egalitarian system of thought called liberalism.[1]

ANTECEDENTS

Catholics in Europe and America, meanwhile, had already begun to ponder how the Church could address the new political and economic ideas. Many of these Catholics desired social reform not as an end in itself, but rather as a source of new protections for the millions of souls disturbed by radical and secular ideologies and uprooted from their traditional ways by capitalism and industrialization.

About mid-century, Catholic intellectuals discerned a way to respond to liberalism and capitalism within an orthodox moral and theological framework. One of the most prominent of these social thinkers was Germany's Bishop Wilhelm Ketteler. In the 1840s he offered a Catholic social solution, opposed to socialism and economic liberalism, that would defend both private property and the state's duty to intervene to protect the emerging proletariat. Another was the Italian Jesuit Luigi Taparelli d'Azeglio, theorist of natural rights and a teacher of the young Gioacchino Pecci, later Pope Leo XIII (1878-1903).[2] Their ideas and those of like-minded thinkers gradually spread across the industrializing world. Clergymen such as James Cardinal Gibbons in the United States and Henry Cardinal Manning in England defended labor's right to organize, and other Catholics warned that the Church was in danger of losing the working classes to socialism—as had occurred in France.[3]

Restoring Thomism

The last pontiff of the nineteenth century, Leo XIII, was to produce a cogent social doctrine, according to the principles of the natural law philosophy of the thirteenth century scholar and saint, Thomas Aquinas. Aquinas had developed the affinities between Christianity and the newly rediscovered teachings of Aristotle. Although Thomist social thought had not been forgotten by the Church, it lay neglected for two hundred years during the Enlightenment while philosophers and scientists demolished Aristotelian natural science.

Leo ended this neglect, restoring Thomas and his disciples to their former prominence in Catholic intellectual life. By the last half of the nineteenth century, the Enlightenment itself lay in ruins, and Catholic thinkers noticed that Thomas Aquinas's project had survived the overthrow of Aristotelian science more or less intact. Leo's 1879 encyclical *Aeterni Patris (On the Restoration of Christian Philosophy, According to the Mind of St. Thomas)* praised Thomism and cited its teachings as a foundation for Catholic thought.[4] In 1891 Leo took matters further with the publication of his encyclical letter *On the Condition of Workers,* better known today by its Latin title *Rerum Novarum. Rerum Novarum,* along with *Aeterni Patris,* marked the rehabilitation of Thomism and a remarkable effort to discern Christian norms of justice for industrializing societies.

The philosophical school that Leo XIII refurbished looks strange to modern eyes, even though many of its terms (essence, substance, form, etc.) have become so thoroughly integrated into our vocabulary that we use them constantly without realizing their origins. Thomism was one "school" of the scholasticism that dominated Western intellectual life for a millennium. Scholasticism had appropriated the methods and concerns of Classical Greek philosophy (particularly Plato and Aristotle), but had put these pagan tools to the service of Christian theology and cosmology. Scholasticism was thus a philoso-

phy, a theology, and a dialectical method. The Schoolmen assumed
that forms (or ideas) have a real, transcendent existence independent
of human life and knowledge. This assumption gave rise to the perennial Scholastic debates over how it was that forms and essences
manifested themselves (if at all) in God's creation.

St. Thomas Aquinas presented strikingly innovative answers to
these questions, and his branch of Scholastic thought is today the only
one left as a living discipline. Thomism also systematized knowledge
of objects (including ourselves) by measuring their various degrees of
perfection, according to the norms observed for each species. All such
degrees are, according to Thomas, really participation in the orders of
nature and-or grace. Man participates through reason in the law of
nature that God created. (Christians, additionally, participate in
another order of grace.) The Thomistic observer measures society by
its degree of ordered participation in God's divine law, which is also
manifested in the natural law.

RERUM NOVARUM

Coming from what many regarded as one of the world's most reactionary institutions, *Rerum Novarum* astounded observers with its co-
gency and heartfelt concern for the working class. Protestant theologian Abraham Kuyper was taken aback:

> It must be admitted to our shame that the Roman Catholics are far
> ahead of us in their study of the social question. Indeed, very far
> ahead. . . . The action of the Roman Catholics should spur us
> Protestants to show more dynamism. . . . The Encyclical of
> Leo XIII gives the principles which are common to all Christians,
> and which we share with our Roman Catholic compatriots.[5]

Certainly nothing in the era had taken "a deeper hold on the public
mind" than the conflict between capital and labor. *Rerum Novarum*
opened by addressing this central question of the industrializing
world. Evidence of that conflict abounded "in the changed relations
between masters and workmen; in the enormous fortunes of some
few individuals, [in] the utter poverty of the masses," and in "the
prevailing moral degeneracy" (1). Leo noted that workers had been

gradually subjected to the "hardheartedness of employers and the greed of unchecked competition." The traditional crafts and guilds had been abolished and no new protections put in their place. Laws and public institutions had "set aside the ancient religion," and a small number of rich men had laid "upon the teeming masses of the laboring poor a yoke little better than that of slavery itself." Given the wide-spread ills, "some opportune remedy" had to "be found quickly for the misery and wretchedness pressing so unjustly on the majority of the working class" (3).

Having listed the evils of unbridled capitalism, Leo prophesied that socialism would worsen the situation, injuring workers, families, and society itself. Socialism was bad philosophy and bad economics. Leo denied the Marxist thesis that social classes are naturally hostile to one another, and countered that nature's law requires labor and capital to dwell in harmony. Leo forecast the general impoverishment that so-cialism would bring to all of society—a prophecy whose truth is all too apparent in the struggling economies of the former Soviet Union. The working man who is robbed of the "liberty of disposing of his wages," said Leo, is also robbed of "all hope and possibility of increas-ing his resources and bettering his condition" (5). Under socialism, Leo predicted, "the sources of wealth themselves would run dry, for no one would have any interest in exerting his talents or his industry." Socialism's dream of equality "would be in reality the leveling down of all to a like condition of misery and degradation" (15).

A Natural Hierarchy

These condemnations of socialism and laissez-faire capitalism pre-pared the ground for Leo's vision, which he raised on the classical and Christian idea that society should be ordered according to the natural hierarchy of the ends of human activity. Leo consciously echoed the Greek notion that society is analogous to the human body, as well as the Pauline notion that the Church, like a body, "is one though it has many parts."[6] Like the human organism, the body politic relies on an "inequality" of functional groupings to maintain itself and flourish.[7] The various needs of societies—food, shelter, clothing, education, governance—create natural divisions of labor along functional lines, with all citizens theoretically working for the common good. Citizens deserve recompense from their community in proportion to their contributions to its welfare; each group has some claim to the fruits of the society it has helped to build.[8]

Leo followed Aquinas and Aristotle in believing that justice required each profession or trade be compensated in proportion to its contribution to the common good. Leo approved of this inequality, explaining that some citizens, such as those "who make the laws or administer justice," perform functions that most nearly affect "the general interest of the community" (34). These persons accordingly merit a greater per capita share of the society's wealth and honors. This understanding of distributive justice defended an inequality of incomes, but it did not imply that those men and women who perform different tasks have lesser dignity, or that the laws of morality permit a society to neglect those unable to contribute to the commonweal.

Leo XIII may sound like Adam Smith in positing a natural order that springs from people simply going about their daily business, but the resemblance is limited. Leo emphatically opposed classical liberalism, arguing that the human dignity of the worker transcends the importance of profit—itself only a partial measure of the good of economic intercourse. Man's "true worth and nobility" reside not in material well-being, but in "moral qualities . . . in virtue" (24). In the Catholic tradition, labor is not just another commodity. Productive activity should serve—or at least not injure—the totality of human needs, which include cultural and spiritual attainments as well as bodily sustenance and material comfort. Leo insisted that employers respect the spiritual well-being of their workers, including their "religious duties," and not expose them to corrupting influences or vices that could lead a worker "to neglect his home and family, or to squander his earnings." Neither were employers to "misuse men as though they were things in the pursuit of gain, or to value them solely for their physical powers, [which would be] truly shameful and inhuman" (20).

Leo discusses work largely in the context of the family, calling it a "most sacred law of nature that a father should provide food and all necessaries for those whom he has begotten." In fact, Leo posits the family—not the individual or the state or polity—as the primeval social entity. Private property is a "right" of individuals "in accordance with the law of nature," but he adds that this "right . . . must belong to a man in his capacity of head of a family," (13) and is "even stronger . . . in relation to man's social and domestic obligations" (12).

Leo also understands work as *personal* and necessary. It is "personal," "inasmuch as the force which acts is bound up with the personality and is the exclusive property of him who acts"; it is "necessary" because man, commanded by nature, must preserve his life (44). Leo advocated freely set wages sufficient "to support a frugal and well behaved wage-earner" (45). On fair wages workers could support their families and acquire property through savings. Wealth would increase and its distribution gradually become more equitable. With a growing economy and the extremes of wealth and poverty ameliorated, people would "cling to the country in which they were born, for no one would exchange his country for a foreign land if his own afforded him the means of living a decent and happy life." These gains could only accrue, however, if the citizenry's means were not "exhausted by excessive taxation" (47).

The relations of capital and labor are also of primary concern to the state. The state should protect its laborers, for "it is only by the labor of working men that States grow rich" (34). Not only do the workers need protection, however; the public should be protected from disorderly strikes and from those workers who would happily "seize upon that which belongs to another" or "incite their fellows to acts of violence" (38). The state has an additional and special duty to ensure its policies do not harm the poor. Wealthy citizens can usually make the best of bad policies and laws, but "the mass of the poor have no resources of their own to fall back upon" (37).

The State and Societies

The encyclicals of the Leonine papacy, as Russell Hittinger has noted, assume the state is in the traditional form of the "classical or medieval *civitas.*" In fact, says Hittinger, Leo "typically treated the state as a kind of prodigal child of Christendom that needed to be summoned once again by the Holy See to its proper responsibilities, albeit in the face of certain modern crises."[9] To what norms and responsibilities was Leo recalling the errant states of his time? First, all activities of the state were to "serve the common good," which includes "public well-being and private prosperity." The state itself must be "conformable in its institutions to right reason and natural law"; only states that observe "moral rule" will thrive and prosper (32). The "body politic" (society as a whole) must also be concerned with the providing of temporal goods—"those material and external helps, 'the use of which,'" says Leo quoting Thomas Aquinas, "'is necessary to virtuous action'" (34). Distributive justice, wherein each citizen receives his due, should be an especial concern of public officials. The well-governed commonwealth thrives through everything that "makes the citizens better and happier" (32).

The state, however, is limited by the natural hierarchy of ends; it should not seek to do everything for its citizens. "The state must not absorb the individual or the family"; "both should be allowed free and untrammeled action so far as is consistent with the common good and the interests of others" (35). Leo asserts the rights of the family against the state, for the family is a true society and "older than any State" by virtue of its end, which is the transmission of life (12). Like the state, the family is a society with its own authority (in this case "paternal" and parental) that "can be neither abolished nor absorbed by the State." The state can address a "grave disturbance of mutual rights" within the family, but "nature" forbids state intrusion beyond certain limits (14). The state likewise may not forbid the formation of "private societies" which are in accord with good morals, justice, and the general welfare of society (51).

Leo articulates the traditional hierarchy of powers and conception of authority when he says "laws only bind when they are in accordance with right reason, and, hence, with the eternal law of God" (52). And he bluntly states—in a document that sounds many warnings against "the spirit of revolutionary change"—that if citizens and families, "on entering into association and fellowship, were to experience hindrance in a commonwealth instead of help, and were to find their rights attacked instead of being upheld, society would rightly be an object of detestation rather than of desire" (1, 13).

The Role of the Church

Leo viewed the human condition with gritty realism: "to suffer and to endure . . . is the lot of humanity; let them strive as they may, no strength and no artifice will ever succeed in banishing from human life the ills and troubles which beset it." Those who argue otherwise, observed Leo with prescient accuracy, will foster "evils worse than the present" (18). As the whole of *Rerum Novarum* demonstrates, Leo and the Church were hardly indifferent to the temporal miseries of the modern situation. Nor was the Leonine Church indifferent to the spiritual darkness and misery of modern man.

Leo posited the Church as a wellspring of truth, charity and amity. The Church's God-given wisdom supplements and completes the truth about human nature and natural law as discernable to human reason. The Church not only reveals the way of eternal life, but it has a special role in society: proper understanding and right evaluation of temporal matters is impossible "without taking into consideration the life to come." Without "the idea of futurity," human thought loses "the very notion of what is good and right" and finds too late that "the whole scheme of the universe" has become "a dark and unfathomable mystery" (21). Man's ultimate end and permanent home is not this earth, but the life to come.

Accordingly, man can only achieve his ultimate goal of salvation by following in the "blood-stained footsteps of his Savior" (21). Because the end of the Church is higher than that of the state, the Church must be allowed independence. The root ills which beset modern society have no real solution apart from the remedies prescribed by the Church: the "salutary teachings" and sacraments, which "alone can reach the innermost heart and conscience," and which "bring men to act from a motive of duty, to control their passions and appetites [and] to love God and their fellow men" (26). If "human society is to be healed, now, no other way can it be healed save by a return to Christian life and Christian institutions" (27).

If granted its independence, the Church secures temporal as well as spiritual benefits for society: "Christian morality . . . leads of itself to temporal prosperity. . . ." (28). Further, the Church ameliorates social tensions by reminding the wealthy of their social and spiritual obligations, and the poor that "in God's sight poverty is no disgrace" (23): true dignity is found in virtue (24). But if work and want are mankind's eternal companions, the Church helps men endure through mutual charity and works of mercy, examples of which abound in the many religious societies and institutions founded by the Church for the relief of the poor (28-30).

The amity which the Church can engender in society derives from the radical equality of all before God. Leo recalls that "all have alike the same last end, which is God Himself," and that "the blessings of nature and gifts of grace belong to the whole human race . . . and that from none except the unworthy is withheld the inheritance of the kingdom of Heaven." From obedience to Christian teachings flow friendship and brotherly love, which ease the problems encountered in even the most just societies (25). Of course, says Leo, "no one is commanded to distribute to others that which is required for his own needs and those of his household," but once necessities and propriety have been met, "it becomes a duty to give to the indigent out of what remains" (22). Such charity dampens the pride of the rich and moderates the desires of the poor, helping all classes to "join hands in friendly concord" (24).

Leo defends the irreplaceable role of Christian charity against those who would substitute in its place "a system of relief organized by the State": state-mandated alms-giving is not virtuous, and state-sponsored relief efforts always lack some measure of compassion (30). *Rerum Novarum* concludes with an encomium to the highest of the theological virtues, Charity—the mistress and queen of the virtues and the motive and blessing of all the Church's efforts—which will increase "as her liberty of action is more unfettered" (63).

Rerum Novarum encompassed all the major themes that have defined Catholic social teaching over the last century. Thomistic in its philosophical assumptions, it contained the seeds of the modern Catholic view of human dignity, including its theological basis and social character. Although the encyclical focused on the condition of labor and did not present a full-fledged social philosophy, *Rerum Novarum* announced the Church as a newly powerful and cogent voice against the miseries, evils, utopianisms, and ideologies of the age. It became the touchstone of later papal social teaching, and a starting point for and measure of serious reflection by other Christian and Catholic thinkers. Catholic scholars soon universalized its injunctions to fashion rules of social order applicable not just to the industrializing West but to the world.

IMPLEMENTING THE ENCYCLICAL IN AMERICA

American Catholics became aware of *Rerum Novarum* only gradually and at the instigation of a handful of Catholic intellectuals. The nation's bishops issued no collective response to the encyclical. They had begun meeting as a national hierarchy in 1852, but their collective statements, usually issued as a pastoral letter, rarely touched social issues as such before the twentieth century. The bishops' inattention left the field open to the laity and a few concerned priests. Even before Leo's encyclical, American Catholic thinkers such as Father Edward McGlynn and journalist George Dering Wolff had challenged Victorian assumptions by arguing that poverty did not always stem from moral failure, but often lay in unjust circumstances beyond the control of the poor. *Rerum Novarum* supported this line of thinking and showed reform-minded Catholics the possibility of social action based on principles that were neither collectivist nor individualist. Indeed, around the turn of the century, Catholic colleges in America began establishing programs to study social justice, and both academics and clergymen became interested in social action.[10]

Progressive Era Catholics recognized that the proponents of socialism were their main intellectual competitors for the hearts and the minds of the working class. The first years of the twentieth century marked socialism's high tide in America. Socialist mayors ran cities like Milwaukee, and Socialist Party candidate Eugene Debs pulled 6 per cent of the popular vote in the 1912 presidential election. Catholic thinkers staunchly opposed the materialist core of socialism while laying plans to co-opt its appeal. One of the leaders of the Catholic response to socialism was Father John A. Ryan, then teaching at St. Paul Seminary in Minnesota. He urged Catholics to promote a "living wage" that would guarantee working men their fair share of the nation's wealth. Ryan also emphasized the need for reform legislation, in conjunction with works of charity and attention to the moral life.[11] He and others, such as Fathers Peter Dietz and William Kerby, helped disseminate the teachings of *Rerum Novarum* throughout the Catholic community in the United States.

This growing Catholic social movement received scant attention from the American hierarchy until World War I—a watershed event for American Catholicism. Upon America's declaration of war against

Germany in April 1917, the nation's senior prelate, James Cardinal Gibbons of Baltimore, assured President Wilson that Catholic resources would be mobilized behind the war effort. The bishops accordingly formed the National Catholic War Council, based in Washington, D.C., to coordinate Church-sponsored service and relief activities.[12] The war was soon over, but the bishops pondered its causes and the problems of the peace to come. Commentators and organizations representing various facets of American society issued statements urging the nation to reform its laws and institutions so as not to "lose" the peace. The Administrative Committee of the National Catholic War Council joined this chorus with a document of its own — the "Program of Social Reconstruction," published February 12, 1919.

"Program of Social Reconstruction"

The "Program of Social Reconstruction" remains the best-known of the bishops' pre-Vatican II statements, in part because its tone and specific economic and political recommendations set the pattern for American episcopal social commentary for some forty years. The document had been outlined, at the urging of the War Council, by the council's Father John O'Grady.[13] Visiting the already well-known Father John Ryan, by then at Catholic University, he serendipitously saw on Ryan's desk notes for a speech on social reform that Ryan had intended to give to a Knights of Columbus event in Kentucky. The two men hastily reshaped the speech into a statement and presented it to the War Council's Administrative Committee. The committee did not issue the document as a collective effort, but released it below the signatures of the committee's four prelates.[14]

The "Program" was "a jungle of disorganization," according to Ryan's biographer, Francis Broderick, but its impact has lasted decades.[15] The foreword of the "Program" warned somberly that "the only safeguard of peace is social justice and a contented people." The "Program" began by reviewing several recent European and American proposals for social reconstruction, reiterating the Church's rejection — in conformity with *Rerum Novarum* — of any "radical reforms, leading ultimately to complete socialism" (4). The bishops then emphasized that their proposals and applications were "an adaptation" of the "principles and traditional teaching" on charity and justice of the

Catholic Church. The bishops noted that, unlike Europe, the United States did not need to rebuild a war-ravaged economy; they therefore outlined only "desirable and also obtainable" reforms, as well as "a few general principles which should become a guide to more distant developments" (13).[16]

Modest Proposals

The bishops addressed two types of reform measures: those needed to move the nation from a war-footing to peacetime production, and long-term measures aimed at economic justice and improvement of social conditions. In the short term, the "Program" urged federal and state intervention to help resettle citizens released from military service and war work. Long-term reforms included a list of familiar Progressive Era nostrums: minimum-wage requirements and social insurance legislation in the states, vocational education, support for workers' rights to unionize, and the abolition of child labor. Despite the comparative daring of their call for federal and state intervention, the bishops emphasized individual responsibility, arguing that "all forms of State insurance should be regarded as a lesser evil" and as "temporary." The ideal was "a condition in which all the workers would themselves have the income and the responsibility of providing for all the needs and contingencies of life" (25).

The "Program of Social Reconstruction" mentioned "ultimate aims" and the need for a philosophic foundation in treating of social justice, but it discussed neither. Instead, the document simply observed that "the present industrial system is destined to last for a long time in its main outlines." It was unlikely that collectivism would supplant private ownership. Socialism, the bishops held, would bring bureaucracy, tyranny, "social inefficiency and decadence," and "the helplessness of the individual as a factor in the ordering of his own life" (34). By comparison, capitalism looked good, but the bishops noted that it had its own faults: inefficiency and waste in production and distribution, "insufficient incomes for the great majority" of wage-earners, and "unnecessarily large incomes" for a minority of privileged capitalists (35). However, progressive taxation, anti-trust actions, higher wages and, above all, a Christian spirit in both laborer and employer would correct these ills.

THE NATIONAL CATHOLIC WELFARE COUNCIL

After the war, Cardinal Gibbons wished to preserve the gains in organization and access to policymakers achieved by the War Council.[17] Influenced by Catholic social reformers, he also wanted to establish a vehicle for expressing the social concerns of the Church. Gibbons soon persuaded his fellow bishops. In February 1919 (the month the "Program of Social Reconstruction" was published), the American bishops assembled at the Catholic University of America in Washington, D.C., to celebrate the Golden Jubilee of Gibbons's episcopal consecration. The papal delegate to the affair expressed the wish of Pope Benedict XV (1914-1922) that the American episcopacy establish a national office for the promotion of Catholic interests; the bishops quickly concurred.[18] They organized their new National Catholic Welfare Council (NCWC) along the same lines as the War Council. The NCWC began operations in December, 1919, with Paulist Father John Burke as its first general secretary.[19]

The formation of the National Catholic Welfare Council was announced in September 1919 in the bishops' first collective pastoral letter since the Baltimore Plenary Council of 1884. Composed by Catholic scholars and titled simply "Pastoral Letter," it did even more than the "Program of Social Reconstruction" to lay the theoretical foundation of American Catholic social analysis for the next half century.[20]

In social matters, the pastoral reiterated *Rerum Novarum*, adding considerably more religious content and adjusting Leo's language and tone for an American audience. Like *Rerum Novarum*, the bishops' statement assumed that man's freely willed conformity to the true and the good is the only sure path to real progress. Despite the recent and great achievements of science, culture, and industry, technical and scientific advances had a dark side: "unlimited freedom of thought"; "the growing relaxation of moral restraint"; and a "craving for excitement and its reckless gratification." The bishops tied the "swifter and wider" destruction of World War I to scientific progress, and observed a new danger: that a secularized, ideological, and expedient education could now be used "as the strongest means of attacking the public weal" (90-93).[21]

According to the "Pastoral Letter," the root cause of this tragic misdirection and misuse of man's talents was secularism—the expulsion of God from daily life and the ultimate valuing of the "human and transitory." As a consequence, "the law of morals is regarded as a mere convention," and conscience only as a higher form "of animal instinct" (102). The state is enthroned in the place of God, and becomes "the sovereign ruler in human affairs." In such a society, social thought espouses the notion that "the really decisive factor in human affairs is force" (101). Echoing the natural law argument of *Rerum Novarum,* the "Pastoral Letter" said the only remedy for these ills was to recognize God as the source of justice, as the author of our being, and the beginning and end of human existence. Human worth, dignity, and true liberty is found in obedience to what "God commands, whatever the world may think or say" (104).

The "Program of Social Reconstruction" and the "Pastoral Letter" wedded economic progressivism with social conservatism. Both statements attacked modern errors, particularly secularism, that denied the true principles of social order. Both rejected secularism's awful children—collectivism and individualism. The documents criticized American society, made politically moderate recommendations, and emphasized the duty of all citizens to lead upright lives and to take responsibility for themselves and their neighbors. The authority and logic of papal social teachings, based on the natural law, served as the basis for social commentary in these two American documents.

Whose Conference?

The concept of a bishops' council and secretariat that would speak out on social issues proved to be controversial. Disputes over the authority of the new organization added drama to the council's early years. Fearing the council would usurp the authority of local bishops in violation of canon law, episcopal traditionalists like William Cardinal O'Connell of Boston and Bishop Charles McDonnell of Brooklyn led a minority of the bishops in an ecclesiastical guerrilla campaign to discredit the Welfare Council. McDonnell went so far as to hint that a papal communique endorsing the planned organization was a forgery.[22] After the council began operations, several bishops secretly complained to Rome; Pope Benedict XV responded by threatening to ban the NCWC if his American brethren did not clarify its functions.

Although Benedict died in January 1922 before the issue was resolved, his successor, Pius XI (1922-1939), signed a decree dissolving the NCWC shortly thereafter, saying that the decision had been made by Benedict just before his death. (William Teeling suggests that documents "purporting to cover" this decree must have been surreptitiously placed among Benedict's papers before they were examined by the new pope.)[23]

The matter did not end there, however. Pius's decree crystallized episcopal support for the NCWC, and the Americans sent to Rome a delegation carrying a petition signed by two-thirds of the nation's bishops. The majority's representatives pleaded with the Vatican to reverse its decision, arguing that the Welfare Council had already done much good and that non-Catholics would be confirmed in their view of the Church as an autocracy if the papal order remained standing. After lengthy consideration, the Vatican's Sacred Consistorial Congregation revoked the decree in June 1922. In return for the repeal, the American bishops agreed to several significant limitations on their new organization: membership in the NCWC would be voluntary; the organization would have no entrée into a diocese unless invited by the local ordinary; NCWC decisions would have no force of law; and the organization's name would be changed.[24] At their annual gathering the following autumn, the bishops implemented these changes and rechristened their secretariat the National Catholic Welfare Conference—emphasizing the fact that the body had no plenary or binding power of law, as had been implied by the term "council."[25]

Over the years, these conditions influenced the content of the bishops' social teaching and the mode of its presentation. Because the Vatican mandated optional membership, the NCWC secretariat remained relatively small and fairly responsive to local dioceses, who were more its customers than its members. NCWC social commentary thus remained focused on issues of immediate interest to American Catholics and less likely to engage the bishops as a group in partisan controversy over political issues.

The Social Action Department

Even before the NCWC was on sure footing, its secretariat in Washington, D.C., had settled down to work. Through the secretariat, the American bishops disseminated their commentary and suggestions on social questions and organized and coordinated Catholic efforts regarding the same. The secretariat published episcopal statements, oversaw press and lobbying activities, and coordinated the activities of Catholic welfare agencies. Its technical designation as the National Catholic Welfare Conference, Inc., was supposed to distinguish it as the civil arm of the bishops' canonical organization, the National Catholic Welfare Conference, but in practice the distinction between the NCWC and the NCWC, Inc., quickly blurred and the two were interchangeably referred to as the NCWC.

Within the NCWC's secretariat, the Social Action Department served as the headquarters for the promulgation and application of the principles enunciated in papal encyclicals and American episcopal statements. As early as 1918, Father John Burke, soon to head the bishops' secretariat, had recognized that the key to influencing national policy in Washington, D.C., was making one's views on an issue known long before any relevant legislation came to a vote.[26] Officials in Washington seemed to agree; President Warren Harding was the first of several presidents to find the NCWC a useful barometer of Catholic opinion.[27] Much of this work of information and influence was done by the Social Action Department. From 1920 to 1968, the year of its dissolution, the department was run successively by four priests—John A. Ryan, Raymond McGowan, and George Higgins, with the assistance of John F. Cronin. These men exercised a quiet but crucial influence over the composition of the bishops' statements and their translation into social action.

The Progressive Thomist, John A. Ryan

Father John A. Ryan, the first and most controversial director of the Social Action Department, served longest as its chief—from 1920 to 1945. Already fifty by the time the bishops formed the NCWC in 1919, Ryan was blunt and scholarly in his manner. His career and personality combined unwavering obedience to the Church with an outspoken zeal for the rights of "the working man." A born polemicist who was usually happy to dish back what he received, Ryan was a little more patient with critics whom he deemed sincerely interested in social justice.[28]

Ryan took his inspiration from *Rerum Novarum* and, ultimately, from its Thomistic philosophy.[29] He believed that society was "some sort of organism," and that many of Aquinas's teachings on social life were "still pertinent because they were based upon the eternal laws of justice." Included were teachings "concerning property, its uses and its duties, the just price and trade."[30] Ryan believed that many souls could be saved through economic progress and that good morality and good economics were ultimately in harmony.[31] Years before John Maynard Keynes's famous General Theory, Ryan warned that the nation's economic health depended on businessmen paying workers a fair share of the product of industry. Ryan called this a "living wage," one which provided not only subsistence but allowed the worker and his family to save and to enjoy some of the fruits of culture.[32] Finally, he believed that virtue was indispensable to social progress. He attacked contraception, for example, and testified before Congress about the harmful effects of artificial birth control on individuals, families, and society itself.[33] One analyst of Ryan's thought has suggested that it was Ryan's natural law "grounding" that gave him the independence to pick and choose among Progressive Era proposals, promoting only those which promised "a greater approximation of full justice."[34]

Given his authorship of the rather daring "Program of Social Reconstruction" and his support for progressive and liberal causes and candidates, it is not surprising that the epithet "socialist" dogged Ryan throughout his public life. Officials of Catholic University, for instance, refused more than one contribution offered on the condition that the university fire Professor Ryan. But Ryan was not a socialist, and his ideas, while often caricatured, were thoughtful and complex. He carefully defined his own political position by debating and criticizing socialists and even fellow Progressives, reminding them that Christianity's aim in promoting social welfare was the salvation of souls.[35] Nor was he a pacifist. Although he worked with peace groups and once urged Congress to divert funds earmarked for battleships to social problems, he also criticized pacifists and defended the traditional just-war theory.[36] Ryan attacked Mussolini's fascism, and had no patience with apologists for repressive anti-Catholic regimes in Spain, Russia and Mexico.[37] He rejected socialism and capitalist individualism because both demoted human dignity; the former explicitly denied it, while the latter refused to recognize it.[38]

The contrast between Ryan's positions on birth control and Prohibition reveals the structure of his thought. Ryan cautiously supported Prohibition when the Volstead Act took effect in 1921, but soon decided that forcing abstinence on the entire population merely turned good citizens toward crime while enriching gangsters and crooked officials. Ryan concluded that the nation's mass defiance of Prohibition rendered the Volstead Act invalid and non-binding on the consciences of the faithful. Ryan eventually denounced Prohibition as a puritanical and impertinent invasion of privacy. At the same time, Ryan saw nothing incongruous about defending the Church's duty and right to insist on strict enforcement of the increasingly flouted laws banning the sale of birth-control devices. Birth control was intrinsically evil, according to the natural law and the lights of the Church, but whiskey was not.[39] The natural law's prohibition of contraception apparently served as the hinge of the argument; Ryan believed the state must never abet or condone, either by statute or by lax enforcement, that which is intrinsically evil.

Despite the fact that the secretariat answered to a handful of senior prelates, everyone concerned knew that the NCWC could, at least in theory, be denied entrée into individual dioceses if it became too controversial. The bishops of the NCWC's executive board were sensitive to occasional accusations that the Social Action Department had overstepped its authority and was putting words in the bishops' mouths. For instance, barely two years after Rome reluctantly granted a reformed NCWC a new lease on life, Ryan found himself at the center of a new controversy within the Church. Ryan and the NCWC had spoken in favor of the amendment proposed by Senator Thomas J. Walsh (D-Mont.) to restrict child labor—a bill opposed by some Catholics who, though no less opposed to child labor, feared the legislation's centralizing tendencies. William Cardinal O'Connell of Boston felt provoked by Ryan's stand and complained to the priest's superiors. Although Ryan was never in any real danger of being disciplined for his activism, he took care from then on to stay out of Cardinal O'Connell's way.[40]

Ryan received another warning in 1925 from the Social Action Department's episcopal chairman, Bishop Peter J. Muldoon of Rockford, Illinois. Although the Social Action Department was already allied with several non-Catholic religious groups for the promotion of certain policies, Muldoon told Ryan not to provoke criticism by a too-close cooperation with Protestants.[41] Staff members such as Ryan sometimes advocated policies they knew would anger some Catholics, but during his tenure, Ryan especially took pains to ensure that his positions flowed from the logic of the social encyclicals, and he also tried to avoid giving offense to certain powerful bishops.[42] Ryan's biographer Francis Broderick noted that Ryan "normally stayed clear of belligerent phrasing, confident that even an unpopular statement avoided giving offense if phrased precisely, moderately, courteously."[43]

Ryan's Colleagues

Ryan's principal assistant was Father Raymond McGowan, who ran the Social Action Department for nine years after Ryan's death. Before 1945, Fr. McGowan had the undistinguished labor of turning Fr. Ryan's inspirations into practical initiatives and managing the day-to-day affairs of the department. The two priests worked well together, differing at times on matters of emphasis but not much over general policy. McGowan paid more attention to structural and moral reform than Ryan did.[44] He also organized activities that won national recognition for the department, such as its investigations of labor disputes in the 1920s and its Catholic Conference on Industrial Problems, which brought capital and labor together to discuss joint concerns.[45] McGowan was unsung, but not invisible, and, like Ryan, he occasionally took fire from unhappy bishops. For instance, in 1936 he was abruptly exiled to a rural Maryland parish at the command of Baltimore Archbishop Michael J. Curley. Msgr. Ryan quickly interceded, however, and McGowan returned to Washington.[46]

NCWC General Secretary John Burke also influenced the social and political statements of the conference until his death in 1936, although his duties as chief of the secretariat usually precluded him from taking a hand in the day-to-day affairs of the Social Action Department. He added a note of wariness regarding the place and role of government. In an early NCWC statement, published just three years after the reputedly interventionist "Program of Social Reconstruction," Father Burke, through the Administrative Committee, warned that federal assistance to state and local governments could be prodigal and un-democratic.[47] The NCWC also held a similarly jaundiced view of military spending in the 1920s; Burke argued that an "armed peace" was hardly better than war in its waste and debasement of the nation's moral and intellectual life.[48] Burke's specific distrust of federal power extended to matters of foreign policy as well. In 1929, for example, when the American occupation government in Haiti drew the ire of the island's bishops, Burke persuaded President Herbert Hoover to appoint Catholics to the Haitian governing commission, a step that gradually eased the confrontation.[49]

The Social Action Department and the secretariat itself learned to move slowly and cautiously in the politically conservative 1920s. Through the decade, John Ryan's mixture of progressive activism and restrained rhetoric defined the NCWC's approach to social issues. *Rerum Novarum* had been published a generation earlier, but the American bishops had lacked a means of collectively implementing its prescriptions until the formation of the NCWC after World War I. Even then, the principles in their 1920 "Pastoral Letter" were clear but rather abstract. Likewise, the specifics in the bishops' "Program of Social Reconstruction" were really too narrow to form the basis of a comprehensive political program. The secretariat thus had plenty of leeway, at least in theory, and Ryan was inclined to use it to the hilt, engaging his Social Action Department on a wide range of issues. At the same time, however, the controversies over the NCWC and Ryan himself created a sense of caution within the secretariat. While relatively secure after 1922, the secretariat and its staffers were not committed to any explicit program of social goals and political tasks. The early 1930s would provide the NCWC with both the program and the spur for a burst of Catholic action.

3

A Narrow Mandate:
1931-1960

The social teaching of the National Catholic Welfare Conference, which matured in the 1930s and remained largely unchanged for three decades, was greatly influenced by Pope Pius XI's encyclical *Quadragesimo Anno* (1931). *Quadragesimo Anno* provided the NCWC and its Social Action Department a narrow mandate to promulgate social doctrine, and provided a relatively detailed social blueprint that, because of its pontifical origin, was immune to the sort of questioning many Catholics had directed at NCWC documents in the 1920s. The encyclical presented Msgr. John A. Ryan and his successors an opportunity to prove their orthodoxy in the face of criticism from Catholic conservatives by keeping their ideas and proposals close to the letter of *Quadragesimo Anno*. Unfortunately for the Social Action Department, the encyclical's policy suggestions (as opposed to its statements of principle) were not easily translatable to American conditions, laws, and institutions.

QUADRAGESIMO ANNO

With an ever-deepening economic depression in Europe and the United States, and the specter of new gains for European communists and fascists, Pope Pius XI commemorated the fortieth anniversary of *Rerum Novarum* with an encyclical addressing social and economic developments since the turn of the century. *Quadragesimo Anno* (*On the Reconstruction of the Social Order*) represented the most ambitious papal attempt to apply natural law guidelines to specific institutions under modern conditions. In it, Pius paid homage to *Rerum Novarum,* calling it the "Magna Charta" of the social order. But while *Rerum Novarum* had described the emerging features of the modern crisis, it did not explore the origins of modernity as such.

In *Quadragesimo Anno,* Pius XI reconsidered the older social order, which, while not perfect, had "met in a certain measure the requirements of right reason, considering the conditions and needs of the time." This order perished during the Enlightenment "because men, hardened by too much love of self, refused to open the order to the increasing masses as they should have done," and because "deceived by allurements of a false freedom and other errors, they became impatient of every authority and sought to reject every form of control" (97).[1] Further, the Enlightenment's alluring promise that liberation from ignorance would guarantee economic and social progress did not prove universally valid.

Rationalism—the replacement of God with reason and the elevation of material prosperity as the primary goal of human endeavor—took root just as "a new form of economy [was] bursting forth." This rationalism gave "free rein" to human appetites, and was itself codified in the social philosophy of classical liberalism (133). Liberal individualism undermined society's mediating associations, leaving "virtually only individuals and the State" (78). Greed led the rich to treat their workers "like mere tools" (135). The state itself became "a slave, surrendered and delivered to the passions and greed of men," and international relations were distorted by imperialisms of nationality and finance (109).

Pius turned his attention next to the evolution of rationalism's younger child, socialism, which had developed significantly during the forty years since *Rerum Novarum.* Socialism had split into two camps, both of which were "fundamentally contrary to Christian truth." One branch had mutated into communism, stirring up "class warfare and absolute extermination of private ownership" while wreaking "horrible slaughter and destruction" through Europe and Asia (111-12). The other, moderate socialism, appeared to be moving toward Christian social teachings. Indeed, some Catholics wondered "whether the principles of Christian truth [could] perhaps be also modified . . . so as to meet socialism half-way" (116). But this, said Pius, was impossible. Socialism contradicted Christianity by teaching that "human association has been instituted for the sake of material advantage alone" (118). Pius encouraged "those who wish[ed] to be apostles among socialists . . . to profess Christian truth whole and entire" (116). Those who truly sought the goals of Catholic social teaching had "no reason to become socialists" (115).

The Principle of Subsidiarity

Pius XI made his most enduring contribution to the Catholic understanding of the social order when he clarified Leo's comments on the natural limits of governmental authority. The state, he explained, should follow the principle of "subsidiary function," even though "many things which were done by small associations in former times cannot be done now save by large associations." Subsidiarity requires that each sector of society remain within the sphere and authority that is natural to it: i.e., that families, associations, corporations, and governments concentrate on doing what they alone do most usefully and best. The principle of subsidiarity, in modernity, was especially important in relation to the proper bounds of state power. Arrogating to government too large a share of social responsibility harms the state and citizenry; many state efforts would be wasteful, while the initiatives of individuals and non-governmental institutions would be wrongly circumscribed. "[I]t is an injustice and . . . a grave evil . . . to assign to a greater and higher association what lesser and subordinate organizations can do" (79).

Pius, however, did not advocate a weak state. His principle of subsidiarity respected the "natural" balance between the extremes of statism and governmental inaction. Adherence to subsidiarity allows the state to "more freely, powerfully, and effectively do all those things that belong to it alone because it alone can do them" (80). Nor need the state follow any specific political model. In the context of his proposed "Industries and Professions" scheme, Pius amplified Leo's teaching that "men are free to choose whatever form [of government] they please, provided that proper regard is had for the requirements of justice and of the common good" (86).

"Industries and Professions"

Pius XI tempered his condemnations of modern thought and economic practices with positive proposals for reforming the social order. Pius was deeply concerned over the clash between a largely laissez-faire capitalism and a labor force closed off from ownership and social and economic betterment. *Quadragesimo Anno* noted that the "so-called labor market" had separated men "into two divisions, as into battle lines" (83). Pius sought means of uniting people and groups across the class divide, which he believed he had found in the ideas of German Jesuit theorists such as Heinrich Pesch and his student, Oswald von Nell-Breuning (who drafted *Quadragesimo Anno*).[2]

Pius followed Pesch and Nell-Bruening in suggesting that new "Industries and Professions," by emulating medieval guilds in organizing and fostering the various arts, professions, and trades, could foster social unity. These new guilds would be "well ordered members of the social body," in which both employers and employees worked for the common good; each would establish its own system of governance and allow workers to strike and employers to protect themselves (82-87). Although the passing similarity between this proposal and some syndicalist aspects of Mussolini's fascism has been noted, Pius rejected fascism as a social model.[3] Indeed, *Quadragesimo Anno* devoted as much space explaining how to limit the potential harm that might be done by the Industries and Professions plan as it did in presenting the idea in the first place.

A mere description of Pius XI's Industries and Professions scheme suffices to debunk the suitability of the proposal. Indeed, no one ever paid the idea much more than lip service. The degree of political and economic liberty required to establish the Industries and Professions would not have been acceptable to the command economies of Eastern and Central Europe. Even during the depression, many nations were developing market structures and social welfare sectors that calmed industrial and class conflict and attempted to meet the alarming social crisis of the time. Subsequent papal social encyclicals have especially praised *Quadragesimo Anno* for its explication of the principle of subsidiarity, while passing over the Industries and Professions scheme in polite silence. In America, however, *Quadragesimo Anno*—including its Industries and Professions proposal—would reign supreme for thirty years in statements by the National Catholic Welfare Conference as Rome's definitive word on modern economic problems.

THE SOCIAL ACTION DEPARTMENT

The social teaching of the American bishops and their staff before 1960 was based on the guiding principles of the Thomistic natural law philosophy of *Quadragesimo Anno* and remained remarkably consistent in addressing new issues through decades of great political change. After Catholic immigration ebbed in the 1920s, the social status and political aspirations of American Catholics rose in tandem with their incomes and education. In the midst of this transformation, the bishops criticized modern ideologies, offered political prescriptions on domestic matters that transcended the platforms of the Democrats and the Republicans, and urged joint action by Catholics and all Americans of good will. Political liberalism and social conservatism were the hallmarks of the NCWC's Social Action Department. The American hierarchy would voice its support for unions or economic justice and, in the next breath, denounce secularism, centralization, and the debauchery of contemporary morals. This willingness to criticize American society and work for reform coincided, moreover, with a fairly clear division of labor between clergy and laity. The bishops generally limited their collective remarks to statements of principle, while the Social Action Department commented on legislation and events, and organized more socially active lay groups.

Perceptive observers noted at the time, however, that the natural law theory underlying the NCWC's social statements could be used to condone various competing policy alternatives without actually engaging in the politically risky task of choosing among them.[4] Indeed, conference policy preferences tended to be rather vague and detached. For both theoretical and practical reasons, moreover, the bishops confined their remarks on world affairs to broad statements of principle. Not only was the Social Action Department too small to track and comment knowledgeably on most international issues, the bishops were reluctant to raise questions about Catholic patriotism, especially by criticizing U.S. foreign policy.

The NCWC was one of the most effective religious lobbies in Washington, D.C., despite the studied ambiguity of its policy stands. A 1951 study of religious lobbies by Luke Ebersole noted several ways the NCWC and other Catholic organizations differed from other religious lobbies. From their decades of experience, Catholic groups were remarkably familiar with the legislative histories of various issues. For example, the NCWC had followed Social Security legislation since its proposal in 1934; by the late 1940s, Catholic lobbyists wielded encyclopedic knowledge of the subject. The NCWC and other Catholic groups also tracked the administration of new laws and criticized federal agencies for any improper implementation of them. Finally, the high profile of Catholic clergymen and publications, combined with the efforts of the NCWC, usually ensured that Catholic lawmakers knew the "Catholic" position on various issues.[5]

Much of the NCWC's modest success can be traced to the Social Action Department. This small office, operating on a shoestring budget, formulated social statements and directed several NCWC initiatives, wielding disproportionate influence among the bishops despite the air of precariousness that hung over it for many years.[6] Colleagues and successors of Father John Ryan at the Social Action Department were in some respects almost as influential as he, although they were neither as partisan nor as controversial. Preferring to work quietly with private groups and to emphasize moral and intellectual formation, they were less interested than Ryan in promoting direct governmental action to advance social justice.

The "Right Reverend New Dealer"

For twenty-five years Father John A. Ryan was the chief organizer and guiding theorist of the Social Action Department. As much as anyone, he systematized and disseminated the bishops' social teaching. Ryan personally introduced this teaching to hundreds of priests, several of whom went on to become bishops. Indeed, it was in large part due to his efforts that papal social teachings—rather than the radicalism of Dorothy Day or the traditionalism of many German-American Catholics—became the norm of American Catholic social thought by 1945. If not uncritically accepted by all American Catholics, these teachings were at least widely known and used as a touch-stone to assay Catholic activism.

Instructed and encouraged by *Quadragesimo Anno,* the American bishops and their secretariat in the 1930s began issuing more frequent and detailed statements of their own. Pius's encyclical was an unexpected, almost personal vindication of Ryan's life work and his long participation in politics. Ryan had joined the union fight for social legislation in Minnesota during Teddy Roosevelt's administration; he had campaigned for Progressive presidential candidate Robert M. LaFollette in 1924, and for the Democrat presidential nominee, the Catholic Al Smith in 1928. In May 1931, anticipating that *Quadragesimo Anno* would be a straightforward commemoration of *Rerum Novarum,* Ryan had visited the Manhattan office of the *New York Times* to hear the encyclical broadcast by shortwave radio from the Vatican. He was surprised and deeply gratified by what he heard. *Quadragesimo Anno* not only commemorated *Rerum Novarum,* but went beyond it to endorse many of the ideas that Ryan had personally promoted for three decades, including social justice, the living wage, and new forms of cooperation among workers and industrialists.[7]

Ryan enjoyed another vindication of sorts in the election of Franklin D. Roosevelt as president. Now in his sixties, Ryan surely recognized his last chance to influence a progressively minded administration to enact the sort of reforms advocated in the bishops' 1919 "Program of Social Reconstruction." Roosevelt had quoted from Pius XI's encyclical *Quadragesimo Anno* in the 1932 campaign, and after his election, he met genially on several occasions with NCWC General Secretary Father John Burke.[8] Father (soon to be Monsignor) Ryan adored FDR. Not only was Ryan a vocal defender of the New Deal —particularly of its short-lived National Recovery Administration— he became one of its minor architects by virtue of his service on several Roosevelt administration committees. It was not without justice that the popular but eccentric Father Charles Coughlin (the "radio priest") unkindly dubbed Ryan "the Right Reverend New Dealer."[9] Indeed, Ryan delivered a controversial radio address shortly before the 1936 election in which he implicitly endorsed the re-election of President Roosevelt and indirectly derided Republicans as "those timid Tories who see Communism just around the corner—where, by the way, prosperity was lurking from 1929 to 1933."[10] Several months later

Ryan gave the benediction at FDR's second inaugural.[11] Ryan's active and sometimes divisive political partisanship came to an end in 1940, however, after Burke's successor as NCWC General Secretary, Bishop Michael J. Ready, prohibited personnel of the National Catholic Welfare Conference from taking part in that year's presidential campaign, a prohibition thenceforth observed.[12]

After Ryan

After Ryan's death in 1945, Father Raymond McGowan ran the Social Action Department for nine years. His understudy, Father George Higgins, the "labor priest," had joined the department as an assistant director during World War II, and took over on McGowan's death in 1954. He continued his predecessors' tradition of labor activism even after the Social Action Department was restructured in 1968, and he held several posts in the new United States Catholic Conference (USCC) into the 1980s. Higgins did some rethinking of NCWC policies, although he never broke from them completely. In his "Yardstick" column for the National Catholic News Service, for example, he frequently touted the Industry Council Plan, the NCWC's version of Pius XI's proposed corporatist reconstruction of society. By 1957 Higgins seemed to realize that post-war prosperity had dated many of the bishops' economic proposals (such as the council plan). In one "Yardstick" column, he quoted an unnamed "visitor" who remarked, "It's hard for people to get excited about long-range reconstruction of economic life when things are going reasonably well for the majority of the population." Higgins conceded that "he probably [had] something there."[13]

Higgins's contemporary and colleague was the Sulpician priest Father John F. Cronin, who came to the department in 1946 as an assistant director, a post he held until his retirement in 1967. Cronin, who had investigated communist infiltration of unions in Baltimore, was proof that the department not only tolerated but embraced intellectual diversity. His knowledge of communist activities drew inquiries from the Federal Bureau of Investigation and Richard Nixon, then a young congressman from California. The priest shared information on accused spy Alger Hiss with Nixon and the FBI, and eventually became Nixon's friend and one of his speechwriters when the congressman moved on to the vice-presidency.[14] Cronin's contributions to the department went beyond his expertise on communism, however. His 1950 book *Catholic Social Principles* (revised and re-published as *Social Principles and Economic Life*) was a guide to the application of the papal encyclicals in the United States.[15]

Higgins and Cronin demonstrated the integrity of the Social Action Department in their reaction to the brief ascendancy of Senator Joseph McCarthy (R-Wisc.). Although many Catholics supported McCarthy, his tactics repelled others. The bishops were divided, although their annual statement of 1951 indirectly criticized the senator.[16] Fr. Cronin briefly passed information from his extensive files to the senator in the early weeks of the Tydings Committee hearings on communism in the spring of 1950, hoping that McCarthy would use the carefully researched data responsibly. It quickly became obvious that the senator had no such intentions—indeed, McCarthy probably never read the files. Cronin publicly broke with McCarthy and accused him of spreading baseless allegations.[17] Four years later, when McCarthy asked Cronin for NCWC support during the Senate debate over a motion to censure him, Cronin refused to help.[18] George Higgins was never under illusions about McCarthy. He cautioned Catholics that the Roman Catholic senator did not speak for the Church, and explained that the best way of fighting communism was through promoting social justice.[19]

The Department at Work

These four priests in the Social Action Department—Ryan, McGowan, Higgins, and Cronin, along with a handful of aides—drafted NCWC public policy statements for four decades; and they handily cited the same documents as authority for departmental initiatives.[20] The formal and informal rules of the NCWC enhanced the department's influence. The bishops' conference itself virtually never publicly addressed public policy; NCWC commentary was technically issued by the seven-member Administrative Board, although few observers understood this distinction. In the 1940s and 1950s, a handful of midwestern cardinals and archbishops such as Samuel A. Stritch of Chicago, Edward Mooney of Detroit, and John T. McNicholas of Cincinnati, controlled the Administrative Board. William E. McManus, an NCWC staffer who later became a bishop, recounted that he and Higgins would "lobby" these influential prelates in Washington at annual NCWC meetings. The Administrative Board then "put the finishing touches" on draft statements and presented them at the bishops' meetings. With church business usually filling the agenda, proposed statements on public affairs rarely saw debate.[21] The Social Action Department never had completely free rein, of course, but for years it exercised substantial influence over episcopal social statements. By the end of the 1950s, however, it was clear that the social prescriptions of the American Church were growing stale, with no significant development after 1940. The ideas of Msgr. Higgins and Fr. Cronin were aging along with them, and neither man was training a successor.

TEACHING AND ACTION IN AMERICA

The statements on social matters by the American hierarchy from 1931 through 1960 incorporated the Thomistic natural law principles that were the foundation of the papal encyclicals *Rerum Novarum* and *Quadragesimo Anno*. The NCWC, while addressing the particular circumstances of the American situation and advocating certain kinds of social reform, never lost sight of the primary teaching mission of the Catholic Church: to bring men to salvation through Jesus Christ. Virtue, morality, and the dangers of secularism and other ideologies, remained the focus of the bishops' statements through this period.

"A Statement on Man's Dignity" (1953) retained the logic of the NCWC's 1920 "Pastoral Letter" while updating its language. Firmly rooted in the Thomistic tradition, the letter addresses man's knowledge of his place in the cosmos by intellect, and the ultimate fulfillment of his longings in God through a "self-determining will capable of choosing wisely within the framework of law" (7). Human dignity, said the bishops, springs from three sources: man's creation by God, his nature as a creature endowed with reason and will, and his destiny to be redeemed by Christ. Human dignity can only be preserved through free conformity to God's will; indeed, man has often effaced his dignity by enslaving himself to his appetites or to erroneous ideas. The bishops observed that while poverty frequently fosters moral and spiritual decay, material abundance does not guarantee virtue (nor the opposite). "Man's goodness is from within," and therefore "economic and social reform, to be effective, must be preceded by personal reform" (25).[22] The NCWC offered a similar analysis in its 1958 statement, "Explosion or Backfire?":

> Economic development and progress are best promoted by *creating conditions* favorable to [man's] *highest development.* Such progress implies discipline, self-control, and the disposition to postpone present satisfactions for future gains. [Emphasis in original.][23]

Virtue is thus the key to order and progress. According to "God's Law: The Measure of Man's Conduct" (1951), morality is the correct regulation of three relationships: man to God, man to self, and man to man. The bishops noted that "right reason" had arrived at the knowledge of the existence of God, of man's creation by God, and of a sense of man's dignity and freedom. These universal insights into natural law laid the foundation for family, state, and society, and kept them in right relation. But man's understanding of these truths is partial, needing God's revelation for clarification and completion.[24]

Christianity and the Social Order

"God's Law" presented a two-tiered basis for the construction of a sound social ethic. While conceding that non-believers who follow the natural law could fashion good laws on their own, "God's Law" suggested that Christians have a deeper and fuller understanding of the good order of society. Moreover, the worldwide presence and influence of Christianity affected directly, or even indirectly, societies officially hostile or historically indifferent to the Christian faith. The key to social stability, said the bishops, is not the proportion of Christian citizens in a polity but the degree to which a society and its citizenry act on Christian moral precepts.

"God's Law" expressed the NCWC's pre-conciliar teaching on human dignity, and, like the bishops' social teaching as a whole, it left a great deal unsaid concerning the Christian contribution to a good social order. Though presumably workable when Christian ideas hold sway in state and society, the two-tiered social ethic proposed by the NCWC is more problematic in a non-Christian or post-Christian country. Even in a Christian society, the Church could easily be at variance with citizens on social issues such as birth control or the separation of church and state. How should the Church handle such issues and disagreements? Should it insist on its right and duty to interpret the natural law even to non-Catholics? Which parts of the Church (i.e., laity, priests, or bishops) should speak to questions of political order and policy, and how? In the United States, the only widely acceptable course for the bishops was to make the best possible case for the policy changes they desired while insisting that nothing in America's traditions ruled out peaceful appeals to divine law; this was the essence of the Church's oft-cited "teaching mission."[25]

The NCWC prayed that someday America might be a Catholic country in its manners and its laws. Msgr. Ryan drew fire from his secular liberal allies for frankly, albeit politely, admitting that the bishops' long-term goal was the conversion of America, the benevolent establishment of the Church, and a more Christian polity.[26] This position ultimately became untenable for the American Church when the Second Vatican Council's *Declaration on Religious Freedom* clarified Catholic teachings on religious liberty in a pluralistic society.

The frustrating slowness of such an indirect strategy was clear to American Catholics who fought the prolonged, but ultimately futile campaign against the liberalization of laws regulating (or even prohibiting) artificial birth control. Following World War I, the NCWC found fewer and fewer supporters outside the Church for its argument that birth control was a grave moral evil and a threat to society's foundations. Thrown on the defensive by the tireless efforts of Margaret Sanger and other birth-control crusaders, the NCWC had either to defend every existing legal barrier to the practice or accept tactical retreats that might give public relations momentum to Sanger and her allies. The bishops opted for the former course (over the objections of more than a few priests and lay people), and NCWC General Secretary John Burke spent years urging federal officials to close down birth-control clinics and to preserve postal regulations banning the distribution of information about birth control through the mail.[27]

Economics and Social Stability

NCWC economic and political recommendations were also derived from traditional Catholic morality and the philosophy of natural law elaborated in *Rerum Novarum* and *Quadragesimo Anno*. According to the bishops, lasting social stability was the product of an organic social order in which each level of reality—the physical, the social, and the spiritual —was in harmony with its own particular norms. Society comprised groups or classes (as a body contains various organs), each performing some function for the good of all. If one group oppressed another, society would sicken. The bishops expressed these principles in dozens of statements issued between the 1930s and the early 1960s.

NCWC discussions of industrial relations illustrated the bishops' view that the most important social classes were capital and labor. The rights of labor and capital to wages and profit were conditioned by their respective services to the common good.[28] Echoing Leo XIII and Pius XI, the bishops noted that both classes had imbibed false principles, with the evil consequence of class conflict. As the most powerful segment of society, government was obligated to uphold the principle of subsidiarity by maintaining a balance among the classes and staying within its own proper sphere. Individualist liberals wanted to restrict the state to the role of social umpire, while collectivists would have government shackle individuals in an elaborate system of economic planning:

> Until the organic nature of society is again recognized and reestablished through vocational groups or guilds, either one of two things must happen. The state must assume all responsibility, that is, become an absolute economic dictatorship or else the individual remains helpless, defenseless, and completely overpowered by those who enjoy economic supremacy. (56)[29]

Despite these unequivocal sentiments about what was good and just for the social order, the bishops' statements rarely prescribed policy and program details for reconstructing American society. Douglas Seaton, for example, has noted that the bishops and their advisers remained more than a little vague about the ways of determining just returns for labor and industry.[30] The NCWC spent more than two decades advocating the creation of "industry councils" to regulate the nation's economic life without ever specifying how such organizations would have enough authority to do good and enough civic virtue to refrain from harm. The bishops' reticence surely stemmed from their firm belief that such particulars belonged to the laity, but it is still difficult to understand how non-Catholics—who held the balance of political and economic power in America—would be inspired by such arid theorizing.

The Root of the Problem: Secularism

When it came to identifying the source of modern problems, the bishops clearly blamed intellectual error and moral failings, rather than technological development or class conflict. Their lengthy pastoral letter, "Statement on Church and Social Order" (1940), echoed *Quadragesimo Anno* in blaming modern forms of oppression on erroneous social principles. But justice alone could not heal society. The bishops noted that even in the best societies, Christianity was needed to foster brotherly love.

Moral reform was seen to be prerequisite to true economic reform. Like Leo XIII and Pius XI, the American hierarchy believed that sin (in both its original and garden varieties) lay at the root of modern social evils. The Church's most powerful cure for modern ills was to instill within individuals virtue, and, most importantly, a spirit of charity. "Church and Social Order" stated that the only remedy for social and economic ills was a return to the gospel and a recognition of God as the origin and end of creation. Only then would citizens act with the benevolence and love that encourages souls to bear one another's burdens. Without adherence to Christian principles, the labors of economic institutions would be sterile and divisive.

If God is the proper end of all creation and human activity, then denial of this fact leads to pernicious and oppressive falsehoods. The American bishops stressed this over and over again. Their 1947 "Statement on Secularism" explained that ignorance of God's role in human life and of humanity's place in creation led to unstable morals, poor education, the debasement of family life, greed and socialism in economics, totalitarianism and war abroad, and the imperiling of democracy at home:

> Secularism holds out no valid promise of better things for our country or for the world. During our own lives, it has been the bridge between a decayed devotion to Christian culture and the revolutionary forces which have brought on what is perhaps the gravest crisis in all history. (15)

Worse still, secularism eroded the possibility of setting things aright:

> The moral regeneration which is recognized as absolutely necessary for the building of a better world must begin by bringing the individual back to God and to an awareness of his responsibility to God. This, secularism, of its very nature, cannot do. (3)[31]

CATHOLIC PATRIOTISM AND FOREIGN POLICY

The concern with secularism and secularist persecution of the faith overseas guided the bishops' commentary on foreign affairs. By and large, the NCWC rarely looked beyond America's borders unless to condemn secularist assaults in a world seemingly gone mad. The few NCWC statements on foreign policy generally endorsed American diplomacy, in part because the bishops wanted to show skeptical Protestants that American Catholics were as patriotic as anyone else. This desire had a rational basis. The bishops and their advisers never felt quite secure in an America still influenced by anti-Catholic prejudice. They were shocked and saddened, for example, by the wave of anti-Catholic bigotry that opposed the presidential candidacy of Democrat Al Smith in 1928.[32] The rare criticisms of American foreign policy that the NCWC permitted itself arose from the bishops' solicitude for the worldwide interests of the Church.

The bishops' concern with secularism extended to its offspring—communism—and the bishops campaigned vigorously against it. As early as 1924, for example, the American bishops denounced Soviet repression of the Church.[33] While the NCWC consistently urged Catholics to work with all men of good will in the arduous task of reforming society, they warned the faithful to choose their allies with care. For example, the 1937 "Statement on Social Problems" indicted a "sizable army of communist propagandists among left-wing professors, teachers and intellectuals," and noted that "many of the promoters of organizations calling themselves peace and youth movements, sponsors of stage and screen entertainment, and so-called crusaders for democracy" often wittingly or unwittingly served communist ends (6-7).[34] The bishops likewise responded to the plight of the Church during the Spanish Civil War, publicizing the persecution of Catholics by the pro-communist government. They declared that irreligion and atheism, whatever be their changing cloak, are things with which bishops may not temporize. Pitiable indeed is the fact that many men, right-minded and honest, have fallen victims to the misshapen news which has been given the world about the Church in Spain. (4)[35]

The bishops also kept a wary eye on Mexico. Neither communism nor fascism but a century-old "anti-Christian tyranny" plagued that nation. The NCWC condemned the persecution of the Church by Mexican authorities, and Father Burke mediated in an effort to soften their policies. Although the NCWC ruled out support for U.S. military intervention in Mexican affairs, it did call for all Americans to protest Mexico's trampling of the principles of religious freedom enshrined in the American founding.[36]

Totalitarian Regimes

Totalitarian regimes drew the NCWC's greatest ire. No charges of being un-American would attach to the bishops' heartfelt criticism of Hitler and Stalin. The bishops repeatedly expressed their outrage at the "satanic resourcefulness of the leaders of modern paganism" in Nazi Germany. As early as 1936, the American Church had founded a private Catholic committee to aid German refugees, and, a year later, the bishops publicly denounced the Nazi campaign "to eliminate religion" and knowledge of God.[37] In 1942, though still ignorant of the horrors of Germany's concentration camps, the American hierarchy expressed "a deep sense of revulsion against the cruel indignities heaped upon the Jews."[38]

The Soviet Union received almost uniformly harsh treatment from the NCWC. In the 1930s, Father Burke, on behalf of the NCWC, quietly urged the Roosevelt administration to withhold diplomatic recognition from the USSR. Burke did not press the issue, however, and explained to a State Department official that the bishops did not want to make a public issue of a primarily political matter.[39] But unlike many in Washington during the World War II alliance with Moscow, the NCWC never allowed itself to hope for a gentler Stalin. In late 1944 the NCWC attacked Nazi Germany in words that were almost certainly meant for Stalin's ears as well: "The ideology of a nation in its internal life is a concern of the international community.... Surely our generation should know that tyranny in any nation menaces world peace" (14).[40] And in November 1945, the American bishops denounced the Soviet Cold War strategy as "ruthlessly setting up helpless puppet states" in Eastern Europe.[41] Moscow's deceits, they said a year later, had split the victorious wartime alliance and widened "the cleavage between nations."[42]

The bishops' stance moderated little after Stalin's death. The 1959 "Statement on Freedom and Peace" identified communism as the foremost obstacle to peace, followed by nationalism and poverty. Nevertheless, the bishops urged that American "preoccupation with communism" not deter efforts to develop the Third World (19). Communism would be conquered, they added, only when Christians proclaimed freedom under the principles of God's law. Statesmen should continue their "often disheartening quest for peace, reductions in armament, and the introduction of the rule of law into the society of nations," but they should remember that "appeasement in such matters leads only to the peace of the conquered" (24).[43]

THE DEBATE OVER NATURAL LAW

In the first decades of the twentieth century, the Catholic Church in America embraced and implemented the wish of Leo XIII and his successors that Thomistic scholasticism be made the philosophical and theological touchstone of Catholic educational and religious institutions. Following World War II, the spread of totalitarian ideologies and the enormity of the atrocities committed by Stalin and Hitler had compelled a rethinking of the grounds of morality among the intellectuals and academics of Europe and America. Even non-Catholic thinkers, such as Leo Strauss and Mortimer Adler, wondered if mankind could not discern some universal basis for morality immune to ideology or subjectivism. Thomism seemed an attractive alternative to Pragmatism, the influential American philosophical system that to some thinkers seemed to have left American progressives and liberals susceptible to the blandishments of communism before World War II.

The natural law offered such a basis—one made all the more attractive by the cogent philosophical exposition and social commentary of Catholic scholars such as Étienne Gilson and Jacques Maritain. Thomism also received a respectful hearing in the United States because of the efforts of American Catholics such as John Courtney Murray, who argued in a long series of writings, which culminated in *We Hold These Truths* (1960), that the roots of the American regime were firmly planted in the soil of the Christian natural law tradition. These developments marked the high point of Thomism in the United States in both its academic and social applications.

Ironically, the widespread interest in natural law among non-Catholics coincided with an increasing concern among Catholic intellectuals that Thomism had been rendered obsolete by modern science and philosophy. For instance, the Thomistic notion of real essences had never been scientific—in an empirical sense—and it stood in lonely opposition to the entire, subject-oriented emphasis of philosophy since the Enlightenment. This conspicuous isolation was too much for some Catholic scholars to tolerate.

With the growth of lay Catholic social action inspired by Pius XI's *Quadragesimo Anno* in the 1930s and 1940s, there also arose a new and critical way of looking at the Church's role in the pluralist society of America. Lay groups (some sponsored by the NCWC) began to implement the social teaching of the Church in their workplaces and communities. These "emerging laymen," as the Catholic writer Donald J. Thorman later called them, tended to be politically liberal and constructively anti-communist in an age when American conservatism was more a temperament than a set of principles. Frustrated with the lethargic traditionalism of many clergy and the seeming passivity of mainstream Catholic piety, liberal Catholic laymen also began to criticize the American Church's campaign to impose Catholic moral standards on non-Catholics—particularly the clergy's repeated efforts to shore up America's crumbling legal restrictions on birth control and pornography. Liberal Catholics after World War II began to denounce such efforts as divisive and tangential to society's real problems.[44]

These Catholic liberals of the 1940s and 1950s felt themselves a breed apart within the American Church. Garry Wills has noted that they found intellectual and aesthetic inspiration from a broad spectrum of prominent French Catholic thinkers such as Charles Péguy, Cardinal Suhard, Jacques Maritain, and Teilhard de Chardin.[45] Although these Frenchmen shared little besides a Catholic education and a spirit of innovation, their writings awakened liberal American Catholics to the Catholic intellectual revival across the Atlantic and introduced them to recent, non-Christian ideas. Impatience with Thomism combined with the liberal criticism of Church social action created a powerful undercurrent of dissatisfaction and restlessness among American Catholic priests, religious, and scholars.

A gradual but real shift in attitudes occurred within a significant and learned segment of the American Church. Looking back from the mid-1960s, Daniel Callahan noted that "textbook scholasticism," about a decade earlier, was being replaced in Catholic intellectual circles by personalism and existentialism.[46] Callahan's observation confirmed that of William Oliver Martin, who reported in 1959 that some Catholic intellectuals had concluded that Thomism was a "closed" system that had been superseded by contemporary European philosophical developments.[47]

Breaking the Links

Explicit criticism of natural law theory from within the Church was inevitable. Protestant critics were never lacking; in 1953, for instance, the Protestant theologian Reinhold Niebuhr, writing in the Catholic magazine *Commonweal,* described the natural law as "that rigid intrusion of stoic or Aristotelian rationalism into the more dynamic ethic of Biblical religion." He called it "a source of tension between Catholics and non-Catholics."[48] Four months later *Commonweal* carried a remarkably similar critique by Catholic layman Edward A. Marciniak, an officer of Chicago's Catholic Labor Alliance. Marciniak argued that the task of social reform was so vast that no real progress was possible "without the unstinting cooperation" of all men of good will. Catholicism offered natural law as a unifying force, he acknowledged, and experience partially supported this view, but ecumenical cooperation needed to be expanded:

> Our bond of unity with non-Catholics is not the Natural Law— censorship, gambling, government-in-education, birth control, divorce, prohibition, for example, are things that generate the greatest disagreement. On the other hand, we have found common

ground with other men of good will in the tension of preventing a race riot, in the heartaches of providing homes for the poor, in helping displaced persons and migratory workers, and in the daily comradeship of social action.[49]

The NCWC's tentative explanation of the links between revelation and natural law, especially regarding sexual morality, only encouraged doubts about Thomism's utility for Catholic activists. As we shall see, the vituperative attack by American Catholic intellectuals and theologians on Paul VI's 1968 encyclical *Humanae Vitae* raises the question of what the American bishops could do to convince Catholics of the validity of natural law and the authority of the Church, and this as the nation was buffeted by social and cultural upheaval.

4

Vatican II and a New Theology

Pope John XXIII startled the Catholic world in January 1959 when he called for an ecumenical council. Since the first ecumenical council in Jerusalem in A.D. 50 (the conclave described in chapter fifteen of Acts), most councils had been convened to address some doctrinal or ecclesiastical crisis or threat. John's council, however, had a more ambitious goal. The Church over the last decades had been "transformed and renewed," and was eager to show the modern world "the vivifying and perennial energies of the Gospel," declared John on Christmas Day, 1961.[1] "As a religious organization," explains John Kobler, the Church "had kept up with the times socially, intellectually and spiritually. From a merely internal point of view, there was really no need for any 'updating' *(aggiornamento)*."[2] John XXIII wanted the Church to reach out to mankind in an age of rapid developments in technology and society. The Council Fathers expressed Pope John's concern and inspiration in their first "message" (in October 1962) from the Council itself, stressing the universal need for social justice, and, more particularly, for peace:

> The world is still far from the desired peace because of threats arising from the very progress of science, marvelous though it be, but not always responsive to the higher law of morality. Our prayer is that in the midst of this world there may radiate the light of our great hope in Jesus Christ, our only Savior.[3]

Vatican II was "an invitation to dialogue" explains Kobler; an expression and assessment of the Church "in her natural religious attitude,"

57

made in hopes of prompting non-Catholics to share their own experiences "as a way to the building of friendship and peace."[4]

JOHANNINE OPTIMISM

John's two social encyclicals—*Mater et Magistra* (*Christianity and Social Progress*) in 1961 and *Pacem in Terris* (*Peace on Earth*) in 1963—helped lay the foundation for the council's deeper and more comprehensive reflections on modern times. These encyclicals should be read as guides and supplements to the work of the Second Vatican Council (1962-65), particularly in three major areas: John's defense of the natural social order, his endorsement of modern political institutions, and his development of the Catholic view of international relations.

Since the promulgation of *Quadragesimo Anno* in 1931 by Pius XI in the midst of the Great Depression, the world had seen a second world war and the rebirth of Western Europe. John XXIII felt the need to update several aspects of pontifical social teaching. John abandoned Pius XI's proposal to emulate pre-industrial guilds, and he muted *Quadragesimo Anno*'s attack on collectivism.[5] The conflict between labor and capital had cooled since the 1930s, and, with the death of Stalin, Communism seemed as if it might be entering a new phase. The expanded role of the modern state looked to be permanent and problematic. John's encyclicals bowed to these new realities while defending the theoretical core of Pius XI's attacks on statism. Echoing the concerns of his predecessors, John insisted that all elements of society should adhere to the principle of subsidiarity, balancing the powers of individuals, associations, and government, because tyranny ensues "where personal initiative is lacking" (57).[6]

John also encouraged Catholics to cooperate with all men of good will in the reform of society. While Catholics should not compromise in matters of faith or morals, they should also avoid confusing "the error as such and the person who falls into error" (158).[7] Rather than demonizing their opponents, Catholics should remain alert to the possibility of cooperating with or even converting individual followers of modern ideologies. In a passage widely interpreted as easing the Church's critique of moderate socialism, John asserted that even false philosophies often held certain insights and admirable features. Above

all, Catholic advocates for justice were to remember that lasting reforms could not be forced; gradual change "is the law of nature," and
institutions should be reformed "slowly and deliberately from within"
(162).

Democracy and Development

Any consideration of political reform naturally raises the issue of
the proper direction and goals of reform. John XXIII went further
than his predecessors by explicitly endorsing modern notions of political equality and democratic governance. *Pacem in Terris* noted the
worldwide spread of the beneficial conviction "that all men are equal
by reason of their natural dignity" (44). The working classes had
gradually won greater influence in economic and public affairs, and
women were taking greater part in public life. All over the world,
peoples were attaining standards of living and liberties hitherto enjoyed only in the West. This could only lead, John implied, to a spread
of democratic institutions. "A natural consequence of men's dignity
is unquestionably their right to take an active part in government,
though their degree of participation will necessarily depend on the
stage of development reached by the political community of which
they are members" (73). Departing from his predecessors, John even
outlined the proper form of the state, which should embody the classic
three-fold division of powers: legislative, executive, and judicial.
Furthermore, each nation should draft certain declarations of its
juridical intent: a charter of fundamental rights, a constitution pre-
scribing clear rules for the people's designation of public officials, and
a statement defining the relations between government and citizens
"in terms of rights and duties" (77).[8]

Decolonization in the 1950s had focused the world's attention on
the problems and prospects of the former colonies. In *Mater et Magistra*
John held that the unequal development of nations threatened human
and Christian solidarity, and that rich nations should offer their poorer
neighbors training and capital. In urging the developed nations to help
the developing world, John invoked Christ's exhortation to charity
and quoted the First Epistle of John: "He that hath the substance of
this world and shall see his brother in need and shall shut up his
bowels from him; how doth the charity of God abide in him?" (159).[9]

Pope John cautioned developed countries against dominating recipient nations. He feared that aid would foster materialism and endanger the ancient awareness of higher values often preserved in less-developed countries. *Pacem in Terris* also noted that certain problems had become global in scope, defying national efforts to solve them. In light of this situation, while applauding the United Nations, John hinted at misgivings concerning its Universal Declaration of Human Rights. He also complained ambiguously that the UN's structure and "means" were not yet equal to its task.

"GAUDIUM ET SPES"

The Second Vatican Council met for four autumns between 1962 and 1965, producing several documents that profoundly influenced the social teaching of the American Catholic Church.[10] The most important of these was *Gaudium et Spes* (*Pastoral Constitution on the Church in the Modern World*), issued in December 1965. This document was the only "pastoral" constitution produced by the council. Unlike the council's fifteen other documents (generally doctrinal in their content and primarily meant for Catholic audiences), *Gaudium et Spes* addressed all peoples in explaining the right order of human activity and the relation of the Church to the world. *Gaudium et Spes* was simultaneously more comprehensive and more accessible than most of the papal encyclicals that preceded and followed it; consequently this document has been a primary source for Catholic social thinkers over the last generation.

The Phenomenological Method

Before examining *Gaudium et Spes,* it is important to understand the philosophical method—phenomenology—employed by the council. Since its formulation in the early twentieth century by the German mathematician and philosopher Edmund Husserl, phenomenology has been used and criticized by every major school of Continental philosophy. Husserl conceived of it as a means of transcending "the crisis of the sciences"; a way of avoiding the sterile alternatives of scientific reductionism or of some form of psychological or his-

toricist subjectivism. His slogan was "back to the things themselves."
In practice, that meant close scrutiny of the dialogic processes by
which the mind observes the world. As a method, phenomenology
has yielded startling insights about how we "know" our world, the
things within it, and ultimately ourselves and each other. Phenomenological concepts are not as familiar to Americans as they are to
Europeans, but they have gained a certain recognition here through
one of phenomenology's offspring—existentialism. Phenomenological methods, however, do not necessarily have to incorporate the
rejection by existentialism (and Husserl) of ontological certainty.
Indeed, Catholic thinkers in Germany, France, and the Low Countries, such as Max Scheler, had by 1960 made phenomenological
methods and ideas well known within theological circles.[11]

John XXIII and the Council Fathers, though mostly trained in
Scholasticism and Thomism, adopted the phenomenological method
in the council's first session in 1961, taking to heart Leo Cardinal
Suenens's plea to view people in life, not in abstract relations. Vatican II implicitly rejected Husserl's belief that metaphysical certainty
is impossible, and placed phenomenology in the context of traditional
Church teaching. In doing this, the Council Fathers "relinquished"
Scholasticism, but they did so for the purpose of inviting the world
to a dialogue.[12] Something of the council's method and purpose can
be glimpsed in the optimism of John XXIII:

> For [John XXIII] the truth was concretized, knowledge of truth
> grows in the 'veracity' of mutual human relationships. . . . Truth
> is no longer a merely possessed, guarded, and authoritatively inter-
> preted objective *Depositum;* truth occurs rather in the freedom of
> mankind as a social process of truth finding.[13]

Whatever the "social process of truth finding," *Gaudium et Spes*
boldly asserts the vanity and futility of all human striving not ultimately directed toward the Redeemer, Jesus Christ. As evidence of
this, the Council Fathers pointed to the strange and alarming paradox
of modernity itself—this "new stage" of history triggered by human
intelligence and creativity. Wealthier than ever and striving for unity
and freedom, mankind was also afflicted by lingering poverty, strife,
and "new forms of social and psychological slavery," which threatened
humanity's achievements (4). These changes were "part of a broader

and deeper revolution," in which modern thought was "increasingly based on the mathematical and natural sciences and on those dealing with man himself." Mankind had "passed from a rather static concept of reality to a more dynamic, evolutionary one" (5). Science had helped cleanse religion of "a magical view of the world," but had also encouraged a widespread denial of God, abandonment of religion, and imprudent criticism of formerly accepted values (7). Many people wanted freedom and a more equitable distribution of the fruits of culture, but many of those same people possessed unbalanced intellects, trained to technical expertise but philosophically confused and morally stunted. All of these developments, however, become intelligible to the light of faith, for "beneath all changes there are many realities which do not change and which have their ultimate foundation in Christ, who is the same yesterday and today, yes and forever" (10).

The vision of *Gaudium et Spes* is fully developed in its presentation of the Church's teaching on human dignity. Man's dignity is derived from his creation by God, by his intellectual participation in the Divine Mind, and by his obedience to God's law in the society of other men. But man does not always recognize God as his beginning and end; soon after his creation, he chose to serve "the creature rather than the Creator," directing his activity toward base and sordid ends. Man is a "weak and sinful being" (10), "out of harmony with himself, with others, and with all created things" (13). Only through the Holy Spirit can he find "the light and the strength to measure up to his supreme destiny" (10). Dignity demands that man preserve the right order among reason, will, and appetite. He must recognize in himself an immortal soul and subjugate the "rebellious stirrings in his body," forbidding it to "serve the evil inclinations of his heart" (14). Because man can be swayed by external *and* internal coercion, he must free himself from "all captivity to passion" (17).

Culture and the Laity

The discussion of culture in *Gaudium et Spes* makes clear the meaning of the council's openness to the new "dynamic, evolutionary" ways of modern thought. Culture comprises "all those factors by which man refines and unfolds his manifold spiritual and bodily qualities"; it is man's social matrix. Life's "historical and social aspect" has created a plurality of cultures, sometimes even within a single society (53). With an increased consciousness of history, men are increasingly aware that they are the "artisans and authors of the culture of their community" (55). Because the purpose and goal of culture is the perfection of man and society, culture should operate within the objective norms of morality. By acknowledging that human understanding is shaped by history, *Gaudium et Spes* hoped to create a modern, scientific context for the ancient notion that the Church, with the help of the Holy Spirit, is to read and judge "the signs of the times."

Gaudium et Spes also explained the respective roles of clergy and laity in promoting social reform. The Church as a whole reserves the right to initiate charitable activities "on behalf of all men," especially for the benefit of the needy when circumstances demand action (42). But secular activities belong "properly though not exclusively to laymen," who are to become more learned in their particular fields and "penetrate the world with a Christian spirit." They are to draw "spiritual light" from their pastors, but not to imagine that clergymen have either the mission or the expertise to prescribe concrete solutions for every problem. Indeed, in those common situations where Church teaching could accept any one of several proposed solutions, the Christian people should remember that no one has the authority "to appropriate the Church's authority for his opinion." The clergy are to establish an evangelistic dialogue with all men and "wipe out every ground of division, so that the whole human race may be brought into the unity of the family of God" (43).

"Dignitatis Humanae"

Where *Gaudium et Spes* had sketched the modern dilemma and the truth of the central role of Jesus Christ in history, Vatican II's *Dignitatis Humanae* (*Declaration on Religious Freedom*) explained the importance of human dignity and freedom in responding to the truth and resolving the conflicts of modernity. The two documents were issued by the council on the same day—December 7, 1965—and should be read as complementary parts of a coherent teaching. The *Declaration* implicitly renounced the old notion that "error has no rights" and explicitly affirmed that religious freedom should be preserved even where the Catholic faith is established by law. All men have a right to religious freedom because, without freedom, they cannot attain their dignity—that is, the willing performance of their duties to God, family, and neighbor. Religious freedom is to be curtailed "only when and in so far as necessary": "society has the right to defend itself against possible abuses committed on pretext of freedom of religion" (7). Government should allow people to exercise their religious freedom so that they might fulfill their duties to God, and that "society itself may profit by the moral qualities of justice and peace," which stem from faith (6).[14]

Freedom, however, is not a sufficient condition for dignity because it permits, but does not obtain, the substance of dignity: that people seek truth and serve God. *Dignitatis Humanae* notes that many seem inclined "to use the name of freedom as the pretext for refusing to submit to authority and for making light of the duty of obedience" (8). People have used religious freedom irresponsibly and even to harm others. Society has the right and the duty to safeguard the religious freedom of its citizens through acknowledging the office of parents in educating children in piety and virtue, and by means of juridical norms "in conformity with the objective moral order" (5, 7). Catholic social teaching thus understands dignity as the constellation of mental and physical freedoms required by every human being to fulfill his duty to know and to serve God.

Pope John XXIII and the Second Vatican Council renovated Catholic social teaching while keeping it firmly based on the foundation laid by Leo XIII and Pius XI. John's encyclicals and the social documents of Vatican II expressed the Church's teaching in the modern vocabulary of "dignity," "rights," and "development." Some Catholics believed this shift in terminology gave the Church new flexibility in dealing with contemporary dilemmas, and they wanted to extend that flexibility radically. Even before the close of Vatican II, some American Catholics urged Church leaders to conform their political and moral statements to secularized conceptions of individual rights and social development. But others within the American Church disagreed, and disturbing arguments soon arose among Catholics over the Church's ability to accommodate itself to the modern world.

THE BATTLE OVER NATURAL LAW

The controversy that erupted within the American Church over artificial birth control in the early 1960s fundamentally changed the internal debate over natural law. The nation's bishops had long waged a determined rear guard action to slow the liberalization of restrictions on artificial contraceptives. In the early 1960s, as many prominent lay and clerical Catholics tired of the struggle, a cadre of liberal Catholic intellectuals, inspired by Vatican II's openness to new concepts and expressions, began publicly to dispute the Church's ban on artificial birth control.

The turn in the argument raised the stakes and the decibel level of the debate over natural law. American Catholics had in the past disagreed about the wisdom of forcing the natural law on non-Catholics; now they began to argue among themselves over the very existence of the natural law as a norm for human conduct. Traditionalists based their case against birth control on the natural law and suggested that critics were less than orthodox. Critics were convinced of the need to modernize Catholic moral teaching. They questioned their opponents' premises, arguing that Thomistic natural law was not an integral part of Catholicism but rather a medieval anachronism that alienated Catholics from modern thought. The Church had no authority to promulgate infallible teachings based solely upon such philosophical speculations. Natural law, they claimed, dictated no ban on artificial birth control. Indeed, natural law, properly understood, urged mankind to utilize the fruits of rational inquiry when these fruits—in the form of scientific knowledge—made life safer and easier. According to these critics, the Church's futile campaign against public acceptance of contraception provided *prima facia* evidence of the inapplicability of a Thomistic ethic to a pluralistic society under modern conditions.

Modernizing Natural Law

Loyola University Scripture scholar John L. McKenzie, S.J., for one, argued that natural law was not implied by the Gospels, nor did Christian social analysis have any need of an ethical system that supplemented Scripture. McKenzie charged that such a system gave

Christians a way to rationalize their evasion of the scriptural duty to love all mankind. They had been doing so for centuries, he suggested: "One may adduce as open to discussion the Christian ethics of the possession and use of wealth, of the ownership of slaves, of the just war, of external and internal politics, of sex, and most recently of Christian segregation."[15] McKenzie was joined by Michael Novak, a seminary-trained layman active in the Democratic party and a leader in this campaign to replace traditional moral norms with more flexible guides to ethics. Novak's first book decried the "Latin scholastic" mentality in Rome, where logical pedantry had replaced philosophical inquiry, and in the United States, where deference to ecclesial authority had stifled social concern.[16]

Several of these critics tried to preserve a modernized version of natural law, one purged of its "essentialist" (i.e., Thomistic) elements but still somehow distinct from mere antinomianism. These renovators of natural law sometimes described their alternative versions in language that evoked—for those unschooled in the distinctions between the sometimes contradictory goals of thinkers using phenomenological insights—the phenomenological vocabulary of Vatican II. Robert O. Johann, for instance, said human nature is not a static condition but rather a work in progress, in which reason's openness to "Being" allows mankind to interpret and rearrange data in light of man's own "ideal." The morally right, he contended, "is not what conforms to determinate nature but what conforms to the dictates of a reason enlisted in love's service."[17] Leslie Dewart and Michael Novak separately declared that the right moral order cannot be deduced from ideas but must be determined empirically. "A man's doing must be consistent with his knowing," said Novak. To be truly empirical, the search for a more human order should include all men of good will, with the goodness of their will measured by their willingness to engage in a critical, communal dialogue.[18] These authors postulated a natural law constituted not by the immanent imperatives of man's God-given nature but by nature's command to respond "rationally" to changing circumstances. Catholic critics of Thomistic natural law admonished man to form his conscience rationally, but seemed to doubt the existence of an objective foundation on which and by which to form his conscience.

This critique of the natural law was not new, but rarely had it been voiced in the American Catholic Church before 1960. It soon altered American Catholic philosophy and theology. At mid-decade, the members of the American Catholic Philosophical Association (ACPA) judged Thomism exhausted. The ACPA spent two consecutive annual conventions discussing this development. ACPA president Ernan McMullin doubtless spoke for many at the association's 1967 convention when he attributed the collapse of confidence in Thomism to the rigidity with which it had been taught in America since Pope Leo XIII established it as Catholicism's quasi-official philosophy. Aquinas had long been an intellectual crutch for many Catholic scholars, McMullin explained, but when Vatican II had seemingly neglected Thomistic theology, these scholars lost heart and sought philosophical inspiration in modern works.[19]

Humanae Vitae

The criticism that greeted Paul VI's encyclical letter *Humanae Vitae* (*Of Human Life*, 1968) revealed the extent of Thomism's decline among American Catholic intellectuals. Less than a year before the encyclical's publication, at a Congress of the Laity in Rome, the delegates had passed a startling resolution calling for lay "discretion" in choosing the means of family planning. The resolution tried to reframe the debate over birth control in the context of possible measures to slow what many regarded as the ominous growth of the world's population.[20] In less than a decade, liberal Catholic sentiment about birth control had moved from tolerating it among non-Catholics, to permitting it for Catholics, and actively promoting it abroad. Although Paul VI ultimately ignored the resolution, the statement expressed a logic persuasive to many Catholics: that traditional Church teaching on issues of "personal" morality was rightfully subordinate to a Christian response to inequality and poverty in the modern age.

Humanae Vitae dashed the hope of many Western Catholics that the Vatican would replace theologically based pronouncements on morality with a general ethic of social concern. Many Catholic thinkers immediately voiced their disappointment with the encyclical's reaffirmation of the Church's ban on artificial birth control. More than two hundred theologians and canon lawyers in America—the most prominent being Charles Curran and one of his teachers, Bernard Häring (a German then teaching in the United States)—issued a controversial manifesto attacking Paul VI's argument. They complained among other things that *Humanae Vitae* was "based on an inadequate concept of natural law" that ignored "the multiple forms of natural law theory."[21] This public dissent was merely the tip of the iceberg; many American Catholics had expected Rome to endorse contraception, and their disappointment still echoes in the American Church.

Though the American hierarchy defended the pope's much-awaited encyclical when it appeared in July 1968, and again that November in their pastoral letter, "Human Life in Our Day," the bishops did not attack the sexual revolution of the 1960s head on. Indeed, the last time the American hierarchy collectively devoted an entire statement to decrying the social effects of contraception as well as urging the federal government to stop promoting the practice was in 1966.[22] "Human Life in Our Day" was so concerned with answering theological criticisms of *Humanae Vitae* that the bishops passed on this opportunity to reiterate the NCWC's teaching that contraception promoted vice and undermined society's foundations.[23]

The Effect on Social Doctrine

The collective retreat of American Catholicism from Thomism as a philosophical template naturally precipitated a sharp decline in confidence in the social teachings based on natural law. Several years before *Humanae Vitae*, American Catholic observers had begun to criticize the social action of the Church as outmoded and inordinately fearful of harmful ideologies. For example, the editors of *Commonweal* criticized the bishops' 1963 statement "Bonds of Union" for blaming racism on secularism and materialism: "there have been too many God-fearing segregationists and too many agnostic integrationists to make this explanation plausible." Such airy theorizing, *Commonweal* charged, gave little sustenance to the courageous Catholics and non-Catholics struggling for civil rights.[24] Father Peter Riga of Buffalo, N.Y., argued in *Today* magazine that American Catholics had neglected racism and other social problems while salving their consciences by supporting schools and charities. He blamed this apathy in part on a fear of communism and "seminary training for a world of the 16th century instead of the 20th."[25] Historian David J. O'Brien later summarized such complaints about "the apparent inadequacy of republican [viz. natural law] categories in the face of spiraling problems of violence and injustice":

> In John Courtney Murray's [and, by implication, the NCWC's] advanced version of the republican tradition, natural law ethics provided no leverage for bringing about the kingdom of God, only for establishing minimal levels of decency. Neither did it provide an emotionally compelling ground for resistance to evil.[26]

During the 1960s, the Catholic academy in America abandoned its allegiance to the older notion of the organic society embodied in earlier papal encyclicals. Speaking at the Catholic Economic Association's 1969 convention, Richard L. Porter, S.J., of Oklahoma State, surveyed the teaching of "social economics" at the nation's best-known Catholic colleges. Only five of the thirteen institutions he queried still offered courses that applied the traditional Catholic social teaching to economic problems, and even they seemed embarrassed by such classes in their catalogues. "Although I had known that the 'encyclicals course' had been on the decline for some years," Porter commented, "I was somewhat shocked at the extent of the decline." He suspected the primary cause of this phenomenon was that "there was no real basis for treating human conduct in a way parallel with economic method" after the abandonment of the natural law approach.[27]

A NEW PARADIGM

No thought exists in an intellectual vacuum. Liberal Catholics concerned with social reform had already questioned the Thomism of the NCWC, and their questioning had taken the shape of a philosophical attitude. They concluded that the Church's old ways of thinking no longer worked in the modern world. Just as John XXIII had bowed to the changing conditions of production and abandoned some of Pius XI's tired economic prescriptions, they argued the Church had to replace traditional scruples and mores devised for pre-industrial life if it was going to keep up with what was then called the Space Age. In particular, modernizing Catholics believed that the Church now consisted of two rival factions: traditionalists, who believed that salvation was primarily personal, and reformers (with whom the modernizers identified), who held that Jesus cared little for ritual but demanded that his disciples help their neighbors.[28]

The origins of the new social teaching—sometimes called "Political Theology"—predated Vatican II. Phenomenology had gradually revolutionized Continental dogmatic theology, and by the 1960s it had begun to affect social and moral thinking in America as well. Some European theologians and intellectuals, trained in the new philosophy and appreciating the way in which existentialism had put phenomenological concepts to work for radical political and social movements, turned a critical eye to the documents of Vatican II. According to theologian John A. Coleman, European Catholic intellectuals promoted a new social teaching in reaction to the Second Vatican Council:

> Some theologians found the *Pastoral Constitution on the Church in the Modern World* overly optimistic in its assessment of modern liberal society and too willing to adopt a cooperative rather than a critical prophetic stance. They feared that cooperation might mean, once again, cooptation. While accepting much of the council's new emphases, *a new political theology reversed some of its trends* [emphasis added].[29]

The ground was well-prepared, and new theologians were ready and waiting when the birth control controversy and Vatican II seemingly created for American Catholics the need for a new conception of modern man.

The New Kingdom

The most significant contribution the new Political Theology made to social thought was its proposition that, because men can be known only by their mutual dealings, salvation must be social. The kingdom of God is not merely eschatological; it is "breaking through" into human history and calls all men to help build a more just society here and now. Theologian Avery Dulles explains that the adherents of this new "secular dialogic" argued that the primary mission of the Church is to assist all peoples to experience the gospel values of peace, justice, and reconciliation.[30] Some theologians had already shifted their focus from an eternal moral code to scrutinizing the "signs of the times" — that is, viewing actual conditions and conflicts with the help of both secular expertise and Scripture (read in a fresh way to discern its meaning for the modern age).[31] New social prescriptions would spring from this method of seeking God's will.

In contrast to Vatican II's *Gaudium et Spes,* which stressed the intellectual roots of modernity's ills, the new thinkers blamed them on the allegedly rigid patterns of inequality that had marked contemporary societies. The German theologian Bernard Häring—himself a major influence on American theologians—observed that modern modes of production and social intercourse had vanquished the traditional, patriarchal structures of familial and communal life. The collapse of traditional structures, said Häring, had liberated mankind in many ways. But it had also created a cold and impersonal social climate in which many people understandably sought love and companionship only within their narrow personal relationships to the neglect of larger societal and political concerns. Häring termed this neglect "apathy." Even worse, in his view, was the tendency of some of these lonely people to romanticize the vestiges of the patriarchal past. The new social thinking directed the Church to resist these pulls toward apathy and reaction by adopting a "prophetic" role—a critical posture rather than a social doctrine—to highlight the conflicts and injustices that impede justice and salvation.[32]

Although claiming to study the "signs of the times," none of these new theologians showed much interest in seeking God's will in the bourgeois ethos of capitalism and individualism that dominated the historical moment in Europe and North America. Instead, their first step was to jettison the Thomistic conception of justice. Justice, said the new thinkers, could no longer be conceptualized as the correct ordering of social relations or personal faculties. Since people could be known only by how they treated one another (and not by the norms of a fanciful natural law), justice was to be understood as the act of perpetually redressing inequitable interpersonal relations, or "structures," especially where those resulted in relative disadvantage or poverty for individuals or social groups.[33]

Overdue for Change

After Vatican II, American Catholics took these new ideas about justice and the Church's role in society and added a few twists of their own. The council's phenomenological vocabulary was unfamiliar to American ears trained in Thomistic concepts and accustomed to dealing with the positivist or pragmatic philosophical assumptions of secular academia. Paradoxically, American Catholic intellectuals who were *not* Thomist in orientation were more likely than not to have some interest in, and affinity for, Continental phenomenology. This combination of a knowledgeable minority and a largely untutored majority in American Catholic intellectual circles allowed phenomenology to sweep almost all before it in a few short years. Thomism remains a vital force among some American Catholic scholars, but it is far from the ubiquitous presence it was in Catholic intellectual life in 1960.

The notion that God constantly reveals himself through secular events altered the way in which the Church in America—or at least its intellectual elite—understood its teaching mission and its need to cooperate with non-Christians. *Gaudium et Spes* had defined the Church's teaching mission to the world as reflecting the light of the "divine life" over all the earth by acts of mercy and justice, and endowing the daily activity of men "with a deeper meaning and importance" (40). The ink was hardly dry on *Gaudium et Spes,* however, when many American Catholic thinkers quietly set aside the council's trust in the Church's God-given wisdom. They adopted instead the notion that Catholics should seek grounds for cooperation with all people of "good will"—even those advocating divergent and erroneous views of peace and freedom—in addressing situations of conflict and injustice.[34]

Some American Catholics reassessed the Church's traditional teachings on "personal" (i.e., sexual) morality and judged them flawed in theory and problematic in practice. These interpreters had a specific ax to grind; they misinterpreted the council's message as a warrant to liberalize the Church's ban of artificial birth control. Catholics involved in social action, whatever their individual views on birth control, felt that stressing chastity, for example, provided only an indirect remedy for social ills and often hindered ecumenical social action. The new belief that the Word of God was revealing itself through

secular events, combined with philosophical doubts about the existence of any eternal moral code, led Catholic social thinkers in the
United States to conclude that the hard questions of sexual morality,
among non-Catholics and Catholics, were better left to the individual
conscience.

Taken together, these ideas persuaded many Catholics that the
social teaching of the American Church was overdue for change.
Many clergymen acted upon the notion that salvation was social—
and therefore at least partly political—by becoming directly involved
in political matters. The call by the "political theologians" for the
Church to adopt a socially prophetic stance swiftly led to a preference
for state intervention, with the Church, particularly the clergy, playing
the role of prophetic advocate and lobbyist. Finally, the desire to
cooperate with all potential allies in social reform resulted in the
Church muting its "divisive" teachings on sexual morality.

Not all American Catholics accepted these ideas. Nevertheless, the
cumulative weight of the new conception of the Church's social role
tended to pull the resolution of the American debate toward the
"prophetic" mission and to foreclose any restoration of the earlier,
Thomistic social teaching. This reconsideration of the Church's impact on society tended to be quite critical of established episcopal
practices. After 1970, the Thomistic concepts that remained in the
social teaching of the American bishops would survive only as isolated
vestiges, useful to the bishops and their advisers on various issues but
no longer forming a coherent whole.

5

The Liberal Moment

As the Second Vatican Council convened in 1961, America's bishops and the nation's intellectual and political leaders shared a general optimism about society and a faith in what moderate social reform could achieve. In retrospect, this was the liberal moment in both society and the Church. As Daniel Callahan noted, "Papal social thought, ecumenism, internationalism and social justice were becoming accepted parts of the American Catholic consensus."[1] But liberalism now meant something different from what it had a century earlier. The new liberalism—and the old—defended private property, freedom of conscience, and equality for all in laws enacted by representative legislatures. A new liberalism was emerging, however, that saw strict legal equality as meaningless if, as Anatole France famously quipped, the law forbids the rich as well as the poor to sleep under bridges. Liberals now deemed equality something for government to promote; indeed, the state's new duty to promote equality eventually overcame the traditional liberal fear of statism. By endorsing liberal ideas for ecclesial and liturgical reform, John XXIII and the Second Vatican Council had routed the complacent triumphalism allegedly responsible for the apathy of clergy and laity toward social justice. In the American Church, this revolution in theory presaged changes in organization and personnel in the bishops' conference and its secretariat. The Second Vatican Council and disillusionment with natural law theory, coupled with the quest for a new social analytic, spurred the overhaul of the National Catholic Welfare Conference.

75

REFORMING THE NCWC

One of the most important recommendations of Vatican II—which would reshape the life of the Roman Catholic Church in the years to come—was that national episcopal conferences be formed and invested with a certain juridical authority. The council document *Christus Dominus* (*Decree on the Pastoral Office of Bishops in the Church,* 1965) advocated the creation of "certain offices" for "the service of all or many dioceses of a determined region or nation" (42). It also asked that bishops (at least as individual prelates) teach "the ways by which are to be solved the very grave questions concerning the ownership, increase, and just distribution of material goods, peace and war, and brotherly relations among all peoples" (12). Taken together, these passages not only encouraged, but according to some, mandated the establishment of national conferences and secretariats that could assist bishops in forming and promulgating Catholic social policy.[2]

Anticipating the recommendations of *Christus Dominus,* the American bishops resolved in 1964 to reform the NCWC. A committee to study the secretariat first met in April 1965, and a subsequent article in the *National Catholic Reporter* detailed the debate that arose, both inside and outside the hierarchy, over the extent to which the NCWC should be reshaped. Some feared that an expansion of the NCWC would foster centralization and erode diocesan initiative; they argued that a few changes to the NCWC's by-laws would suffice to strengthen the conference's authority. Others argued that the current NCWC secretariat was weak and stuck with a "clerical mentality" that ignored the views of laymen and religious. They cited the existence of separate dining rooms for clerical and lay employees at the NCWC's headquarters as one example of this bias.[3]

The more ambitious reform proposal ultimately prevailed, and the American hierarchy ratified the restructuring at its annual meeting in November 1966. The National Catholic Welfare Conference became the National Conference of Catholic Bishops (NCCB), an entity under canon law; the same bishops became the United States Catholic Conference (USCC) when commenting on public policy or acting as an entity incorporated under civil law. The bishops' conference has since used the acronyms NCCB and USCC almost interchangeably. Membership in the conference was mandatory, as was diocesan financial support; the reformed conference would be headed by an elected president, instead of *ex officio* by the nation's most senior cardinal. In transforming itself from the NCWC to the NCCB-USCC, the conference also made other important changes in its procedures, committee structure, and "organizational culture."[4]

The secretariat quickly reorganized as well. In 1968, the twenty-four separate offices carried over from the NCWC were streamlined into five departments: Communications, Christian Formation, Health Affairs, International Affairs, and Social Development. The Department of International Affairs subsumed the functions of several NCWC offices, including the old Latin America Bureau, the Office for United Nations Affairs, and the newer Secretariat for World Justice and Peace. The old Social Action Department—as well as the Family Life Bureau, the Division for Poverty Programs, and the National Catholic Rural Life Conference—became part of the Department for Social Development. The men who moved into newly created posts in these offices gave less allegiance to the natural law tradition than had their predecessors in the NCWC. Some of them believed the Thomistic-based tradition was actually a hindrance to Catholic social action. Changes in personnel and attitudes which began at the top soon extended through all the levels of the conference.

Dearden and His Lieutenants

In 1966 the bishops elected Archbishop John F. Dearden of Detroit the NCCB's first president. Dearden's election set precedents that, wittingly or not, have been followed in virtually every succeeding election. Dearden was a political liberal and a moderate reformer in ecclesial and theological matters. A former philosophy professor and a bishop since 1950, Dearden was "a leader of the so-called progressive wing of Roman Catholicism," who Church officials expected would "set a liberal tone to the future work of the Conference."[5] During his five years as president of the NCCB and USCC, he provided, according to Archbishop Francis Hurley, "intellectual stability to the excitement that was surrounding the new vision of the Church after Vatican II."[6]

Dearden most influenced the USCC through his appointments. In 1968, Dearden selected as general secretary—on the recommendation of his friend, Archbishop Paul Hallinan of Atlanta—a young, soft-spoken auxiliary bishop with a growing reputation for his skills as a diplomat and conciliator. Joseph Bernardin's main job was to implement the streamlining of the old NCWC staff structure. The new general secretary would accomplish this task and quite a bit more.[7] Bernardin believed that the Church and its teachings urgently needed modernization. Shortly after his appointment, Bernardin told the *National Catholic Reporter* that the current national crisis had created a situation in which it was no longer enough "to make statements or issue pastorals. We must come up with specific programs which we will fund."[8]

Bishop Bernardin publicly explained some of his views while speaking at the University of Bridgeport later that year. He noted that John XXIII had convened Vatican II so that the Church might address its "crisis of irrelevancy" brought on, in part, by theological rigidity left over from the Counter-Reformation. Bernardin suggested that good Pope John had meant to go considerably further with his reforms than the council actually went. Vatican II had united two opposing tendencies, according to Bernardin's hermeneutic of the council: one "scholastic and conceptualistic," the other "more biblical" and historical. Conservative resistance from the former camp, however, had made Vatican II's documents into compromise texts that could only hint at the full vision Pope John had intended to portray. Bernardin warned that conservatives' fear of the unknown threatened to halt renewal in the Church. If the movement for change lost momentum—perhaps from a refusal of traditionalist Catholics to hear those whom they considered unorthodox—there would be "tension and conflict," and the Church would lose its struggle to restore the relevance of religion to everyday life.[9] Bernardin left the USCC in late 1972, but he later served as NCCB president from 1974-77 and remains one of the most influential members of the bishops' conference.

The reforms that created the USCC from the NCWC provided for wider consultation on the public policy statements of the Church by allowing clerical, lay, and religious members to serve alongside the bishops appointed by the USCC committee chair (who was always a bishop).[10] The list of laymen and priests selected to serve on the USCC's departmental committees included advocates of the new social teaching such as Chicago's Edward Marciniak. A layman sympathetic to Bernardin's vision of reform of the American Church, Marciniak fifteen years earlier had attacked the natural-law basis of the Church's social teaching. For several years Marciniak served on the oversight committee of the USCC's Department for Social Development. In 1970 he wrote an article for *America* magazine, recording the demise of the "John A. Ryan era" of Catholic social action, and urging the bishops to develop a new strategy for social involvement that would be "free of dogmatism." The bishops, he suggested, should seek to discern how far Catholics could be led and then carry them "one step beyond their limit."[11]

THE END OF AN ERA

The Washington staff of the old NCWC also underwent a dramatic change. Social teaching and commentary, once formulated by the Social Action Department, a small office with remarkable continuity of personnel, would now be shaped by several larger offices, each of which would experience relatively rapid staff turnover. At the same time, the restructuring of the bishops' conference limited the terms of bishops elected to chair NCCB and USCC committees to three years. "A chair has little opportunity to develop expertise in his committee's area of responsibility before his term expires," explains Thomas Reese. "He can be, therefore, very dependent on staff."[12] Reese could have added that the chairs have been particularly dependent on the staff for direction and support on complex public policy issues. Had the seminaries, colleges, and universities of the American Church retained a vibrant tradition of Thomism, this reorganization might not have been accompanied by a shift in the secretariat's social and political outlook. But Thomism itself was under siege in the 1960s, and its adherents were dwindling.

The Old School

Father John F. Cronin retired from the Social Action Department in 1967. Cronin had been one of the most systematic social thinkers in the American Church, but toward the end of his tenure, his disillusionment with the results of Catholic social action helped spur the secretariat's development of a new ethic for Church social teaching. At a farewell banquet in his honor, Cronin brooded on the failures of the Church in this area. The Church, he said, had become "largely irrelevant in the lives of thirty- or forty-million poor Americans," and he noted that the Social Action Department had shrunk to a shadow of its former self.[13] A few weeks earlier, Father Cronin had remarked that the department had misguidedly treated papal social encyclicals like Scripture, drawing from them political and economic remedies alien to American life. Cronin suggested that American Catholics should have recognized that Rome wanted them to adapt papal teaching to their own circumstances.[14]

Speaking at a convention of the Catholic Economic Association after his resignation, Cronin reflected on the demise of the natural-law social teaching. He noted that since Vatican II, most moral theologians had looked for the ethical foundation of social teachings in the New Testament's command to love God and neighbor instead of in "the casuistry and narrowly conceived natural-law emphasis of traditional Catholic moralists. Theological students today are far more likely to cite [Helmut] Thielicke or [Dietrich] Bonhoeffer than St. Alphonsus Liguori."[15] Cronin did not seem displeased by this development, which implicitly questioned his life's work.

Cronin's long-time colleague Msgr. George Higgins stayed on at the USCC for more than a decade after its reorganization, but his role in forming the social thought of the secretariat dwindled. When in 1968 the Social Action Department was remade, the bishops offered Higgins a directorship of one of the secretariat's newly formed departments (accounts vary as to which). Higgins declined, opting to head the much smaller Division for Urban Life. His new post constituted recognition by the bishops that the priest had become almost an institution in himself. Largely relieved of administrative duties and given a modest expense account, Higgins acted as the bishops' freelance representative to the American labor movement. By removing himself from the secretariat's day-to-day operations and concentrating on labor issues, however, Higgins's influence over USCC social teaching waned.[16] Like Cronin, in the wake of Vatican II, Higgins questioned the sufficiency of the traditional natural law teaching. Several years later he noted that Vatican II "simply pushed aside the theology we got in our seminary days. . . . many, many people changed in those four years."[17] The council "was, by all odds, the greatest experience of my life," he told well-wishers celebrating the fiftieth anniversary of his ordination in 1990.[18]

GUARDIANS OF THE NEW TEACHING

The new guardians of the bishops' social teaching publicly stated their desire for more "relevant" ideas and programs. In June 1967, Msgr. Marvin Bordelon left a parish in Louisiana and transferred to the United States Catholic Conference, inheriting Father John Cronin's old room at the staff house. Bordelon had been hired by the USCC to implement, in the American context, the international sections of *Gaudium et Spes;* he took over the new Department of International Affairs when it was created in 1968. The bishops did not care much about world affairs, Bordelon recalled later. It was " 'my country, right or wrong.' That kind of bullshit."[19] Few if any bishops were willing to take what Bordelon considered the ultimate step toward world peace by promoting the erosion of the very concept of national sovereignty. This indifference contributed to Bordelon's decision, in late 1972, to leave the priesthood.

Before leaving the secretariat and the active priesthood, however, Msgr. Bordelon tried to raise the consciousness of American Catholics with a new theology, one which was supposed to build public interest in helping the Third World. The challenge of eradicating Third World poverty, he said, required that the Church work to form a public conscience in the West. Tragically, he noted in one article, Americans tended to limit their benevolence to America's poor. Catholicism did not help matters much, in part because Catholic theology was still too "transcendental" and insufficiently "incarnational." Alluding to the scholastic roots of the traditional social teaching, Bordelon complained that American Catholics worried too much about angels dancing on pins and not enough about getting dirty with the poor.[20]

Louis M. Colonnese

There was more than one proponent of the new social justice at the USCC. Father Louis M. Colonnese, who served as director of the

Latin America Division from 1968 to 1971, soon became one of the USCC's most vocal advocates of change. Abandoning the old liberalism of the NCWC, Colonnese was a partisan of the left-leaning "New Church." In 1969 he urged Catholics to read the signs of the times, which, he said, demonstrated "the non-static nature of the Kingdom of the Savior" and called "for a concept of mission based upon a processive rather than [an] essentialist philosophy of history." Colonnese feared that American bourgeois values might infect Latin America, and he urged missionaries from America to avoid cultural imperialism and serve the "real needs" of developing peoples. He also contended that missionaries had to realize that the Church has "no monopoly on truth or goodness" and that non-Catholics (i.e., activists and revolutionaries) who seek social justice are also instruments of God's will.[21]

Father Colonnese had a short, stormy tenure in Washington. Increasingly radicalized and abrasive even toward his allies and superiors, Colonnese was "a jackass," recalled his nominal boss, Marvin Bordelon, who blanched at Colonnese's brashness and wondered where all the money went after it reached the Latin America Division.[22] Bernardin and Bordelon finally fired Fr. Colonnese in 1971. Shortly after his dismissal, he claimed that he had been ousted because of his "ideology." "I have tried to show U.S. Catholics that the aid and trade policies of this country foster dependency and economic colonialism," Colonnese stated. "When I could not be silenced or co-opted, I was fired." General Secretary Bernardin responded by suggesting it was Father Colonnese's personality—and not his politics—that had become intolerable.[23] Indeed, the ideas that Colonnese voiced continued to influence the secretariat and some bishops after his departure.

James S. Rausch

In the long run, Father James S. Rausch proved more adaptable and more influential than Bordelon or Colonnese. In 1970, Bishop Bernardin made him the USCC's assistant general secretary, a post he held until he succeeded Bernardin as general secretary in 1973 (when he became a bishop himself). An expert on international relations, Rausch believed that recent theological and ecclesial developments had finally positioned the Church to campaign for justice; he also pushed the USCC toward a more systematic and critical analysis of U.S. foreign policy. In his foreword to Joseph Gremillion's anthology *The Gospel of Peace and Justice,* Rausch applauded what he saw as the Church's abandonment of the "exaggerated dualism which over the centuries has hampered the attempt of religion to relate to the secular order."[24] Rausch was a little more moderate than Father Colonnese and Msgr. Bordelon, but his promotion to general secretary gave their ideas and prescriptions a powerful voice in the bishops' secretariat. "Jim felt that the role of the general secretary was to lead the conference of bishops," said one former co-worker. He got along with his superiors in the NCCB and USCC (Bernardin and John Cardinal Krol of Philadelphia), although some bishops apparently thought him a little too brash and viewed his appointment as bishop of Phoenix as the proverbial kick upstairs.[25]

J. Bryan Hehir

Rausch's most important appointment at the USCC was one of his first: in 1973 he named Father J. Bryan Hehir director of the Office of International Justice and Peace. A Massachusetts native with a passion for world affairs, Hehir had been sent by the Archdiocese of Boston in 1967 to graduate school at Harvard University. While there he studied under Henry Kissinger and absorbed the ethical thought of philosopher John Rawls, but his mentor was Stanley Hoffmann, a French-born expert on international relations. Hoffmann persuaded the young priest that the Vietnam War was unjust and imbued him with a vision of the world that stressed the growing interdependence of nations and the erosion of the bipolar international order that had been dominated since 1945 by the two superpowers. Hehir's writings in *Worldview* magazine caught the eye of Msgr. Bordelon's assistant, James Jennings, who urged Hehir to apply for a position with the secretariat.[26]

A prolific writer and systematic thinker, Hehir examined all aspects of world affairs through the lens of Catholic social teaching, which he hoped to modernize into a more useful instrument for statesmen and citizens. Hehir's approach combined a respect for tradition with creativity in moving the new social teaching of the Catholic Church away from the radicalism of figures like Fr. Colonnese and back to a more pragmatic liberalism. In 1969, for example, Hehir demonstrated this balance in a review of James Douglass's *The Non-Violent Cross*. He criticized Douglass's proposal to replace the traditional strictures on war (known to Catholic scholars as the "just-war" theory) with a doctrine of non-violent resistance, and observed that, while "few would deny the need for a renovation of the [just-war] doctrine," that doctrine still supplied "a better structure for an ethic of force than Douglass's position."[27]

RACE AND POVERTY

The rethinking of Catholic social teaching and the reorganization of the bishops' conference occurred as the Church wrestled with two of the most divisive events in recent American history: the civil rights movement and the Vietnam War. Called on to exercise moral leadership in both situations, the hierarchy knew that ecclesial missteps could fracture the American Catholic community. Church leaders also realized that any course of action would be seen as extremist by some Catholics and as equivocating by others. While the bishops began drawing back from the natural-law social teaching on domestic issues, on matters of war and peace they preserved it—for a time—in the face of determined resistance from their secretariat.

In 1963, one year before the beginning of the urban race riots, the bishops issued "Racial Harmony," a pastoral letter on civil rights. As in a previous letter on the same subject—"Discrimination and Christian Conscience" (1958)—the NCWC stressed individual efforts for tolerance and moral reform.[28] Catholics, the bishops said, were bound to raise the issue of racism and justice in their daily lives. "Racial Harmony" also said that oppressed minorities were obligated to work for the common good while seeking the fullness of their own rights.[29] Following the publication of "Racial Harmony," the Social Action Department of the NCWC stepped up its civil rights activities. John Cronin assisted the Kennedy administration in this area and later helped coordinate lobbying efforts aimed at persuading Congress in favor of the Civil Rights Act of 1964.[30] Meanwhile, George Higgins badgered organized labor to put its house in order. In the NCWC's 1966 Labor Day statement, he saluted the efforts of unions to promote interracial justice but noted that many locals still discriminated. Too few unions grasped the seriousness of the race crisis, he argued. Higgins urged the labor movement to take a "ruthlessly honest look at this problem, which is largely of its own making."[31]

The bishops and their secretariat were concerned that black impatience with the slow pace of reform might explode in violence. Richard Cardinal Cushing of Boston noted that whites had "required a superhuman patience" of blacks and had then been dismayed when blacks responded with "an excess of agitation"; the next move must come from whites, he said.[32] Higgins, too, warned that the racial crisis could lead to "a national catastrophe," and cautioned blacks to avoid radicalism and utopian hopes.[33] Shortly after the Watts riots in 1965, Higgins voiced his impatience with distracting schemes such as the "international peace army" envisioned by an aide to Martin Luther King, Jr., the Rev. James Bevel. Higgins suggested that Bevel and Dr. King bivouac their army in the ruins of Watts for a few days before traipsing off to save the world. He had even less sympathy for the militants in the black-power movement, calling them racist and inflammatory.[34]

By 1966 the bishops could see progress in civil rights, but they were becoming increasingly alarmed about the persistence of poverty in America. Their pastoral letter "Race Relations and Poverty" (1966), drafted by John Cronin, conflated these two problems in a manner that soon became typical of NCCB and USCC statements. The pastoral referred to "the aggrieved of our nation"—defining them as the poor and members of minority groups such as blacks, Hispanics, and Indians—and suggested that the primary cause of their relative deprivation was prejudice (7, 11).[35]

A Paradigm Shift

"Race Relations and Poverty" embodied a definitive shift in how the American hierarchy—or at least its secretariat apparatus—viewed societal problems: a social-political analysis of individual groups replaced the understanding of human society as an organic entity under the ordering norm of the common good. The thinking of John XXIII and Vatican II had released Catholic social thinkers from the corporatist remedies suggested by Pius XI's *Quadragesimo Anno,* and the new NCCB would now experiment with different approaches. For example, poverty as such had received virtually no treatment from the NCWC's Social Action Department. Instead, Msgr. Higgins and Fr. Cronin had classified and analyzed social groups by their function in providing for the common good. The Social Action Department assumed that restructuring society along organic lines would indirectly, but decisively, diminish the incidence of poverty. By 1967, however, the bishops' advisors doubted the efficacy of this approach. Even Fr. Cronin had begun viewing social groups not according to their abilities but according to their needs.

In other respects, however, "Race Relations and Poverty" echoed the moderate tone of earlier statements. Its list of remedies reiterated calls for better schools for poor children and night classes for adults, for job opportunities and training, low-cost housing, and welfare programs that promoted family stability. The pastoral preserved the old NCWC's stress on subsidiarity, mentioning governmental intervention as one of several possible measures and adding that such intervention must occur at "appropriate levels" (14). The letter also called for dialogue to replace "shouted epithets of hate" (10).

John Cronin explained the logic of "Race Relations and Poverty" a few months later, warning that "our cities might burn" if whites failed to respond to black disillusionment. Civil-rights legislation had raised expectations, but it had not cured the inner-city poverty that caused the "riotous rage" felt by many blacks. In the consequent unrest, Cronin noted that black nationalism and white backlash fed on each other, threatening even greater violence. But Cronin seemed at a loss for solutions; his training had conditioned him to think in terms of long-term, structural imbalances, not sudden social crises. Apparently inspired by the secular media and the Community Action Program of the Johnson administration's War on Poverty, Cronin said that in some areas progress might require working outside of and in opposition to local power structures.[36]

In April 1968 the social and racial tensions of a turbulent decade were brought to a head by the assassination of Martin Luther King, Jr. A month earlier, four of the nation's most senior prelates had held an "emergency meeting" to respond to the report of President Johnson's National Commission on the Causes and Prevention of Violence, which had studied the urban riots.[37] King's murder shocked and frightened liberal Catholics; many feared that the black community had lost its last great moderate, and that the anger caused by white delay would soon boil over.[38] The NCCB's already scheduled pastoral letter on race, released three weeks after King's murder and the riots that followed, reflected this concern. Entitled "The National Race Crisis," it proclaimed: "The crisis is of a magnitude and peril far transcending any which the Church in America or the nation has previously confronted." America must act "while there is still time for collaborative peaceful solutions" because "civil protests could easily erupt into civil war" (22, 27).[39]

Downplaying Federalism and Subsidiarity

"The National Race Crisis" set the tone for many future statements by its further development of the new social teaching. A sense of crisis replaced the emphasis of earlier documents on federalism and subsidiarity. To close the gap between white America and the marginalized poor, the bishops sought to make the institutional Church an advocate for the oppressed. They urged governmental intervention to stabilize a dangerous situation. All white Americans, they said, shared in the guilt of racism and should recognize "that racist attitudes and consequent discrimination exist, not only in the hearts of men but in the fabric of their institutions" (8). The Church should work with all men of good will to "encourage, support and identify with the efforts of the poor in their search for self-determination" (19). The attribution of social guilt to that mass of allegedly apathetic and prosperous Americans who did not work directly for change would become a staple of USCC and NCCB analyses.

The following year, the bishops clarified their new approach to poverty and justice. In an astounding—and inaccurate—indictment of the NCWC, the USCC's 1969 Labor Day message declared that previous Catholic efforts, while well-intentioned, were misguided in that they had attacked the symptoms of poverty rather than its causes. The USCC proposed that the Church address the current crisis by leading a massive development effort to assist "the struggle of the poor to achieve self-determination."[40] Two months later the bishops launched just the sort of plan the Labor Day statement had called for, promising $50 million to meet "the evident need for funds designated to be used for organized groups of white and minority poor to develop economic strength and political power in their own communities."[41]

In 1970 the bishops reaffirmed these judgments with their new Campaign for Human Development. American Catholics, they said, had traditionally shown great generosity to the poor, but "in our time" the poor needed concerted action to break what Pope Paul VI called the "hellish circle" of poverty. "Poverty in the United States is a cruel anachronism today," the result of circumstances "over which the poor themselves have little or no control." The Campaign for Human Development was teaching the poor to help themselves, while educating "the non-poor" and instilling in them a new sensitivity to the problem of poverty.[42]

This new approach downplayed the traditional principle of subsidiarity. While Higgins and Cronin of the NCWC had worried about the growth of federal power, the spectacle of state and local authorities in the South resisting federally mandated efforts to end segregation changed a lot of minds in Washington, including the bishops' advisors in the USCC.[43] USCC officials became boosters of dramatically expanded federal power, claiming that the federal government was the most reliable, and sometimes the only engine of change—a conclusion the staff eventually applied to other social questions as well. One of Higgin's friends at the USCC, Father John McCarthy, told Congress in 1969 that American poverty was caused by whites who wanted a pool of servile labor. Because state and local authorities had upheld this systematic oppression, he argued, the federal government had to bypass these structures to "get straight into" areas where people desperately needed help. Don't worry about eroding the traditional federalism of the American political order, suggested Fr. McCarthy; we should not give those "state governments that had a certain role to play in producing that poverty the key to supposedly getting us out of it."[44]

Poverty Abroad

USCC officials soon began to use their new analytic in examining poverty in the Third World. Paul VI had to some extent shaped American thinking with his 1967 encyclical letter *Populorum Progressio* (*On the Development of Peoples*). Recent years had seen much economic development in Third World countries, Paul explained, but much remained to be done. Social unrest was on the rise around the globe; the restlessness of the poorer classes in developing nations had spread to countries with agricultural economies. The social tensions resulting from the clash of industrialization with traditional cultures made people vulnerable to the "deceitful promises of would-be saviors" (11). But *Populorum Progressio* stressed that true development must enhance man's intellectual and spiritual life as well as his temporal existence. Finally, the encyclical emphasized the duties of wealthy nations to foster international development—even if their citizens should have to pay higher taxes to do so.[45]

USCC staffers responded to Paul VI's call to redistribute wealth from North to South, but they never fully assimilated his teaching on the development of the human person. Whereas the NCWC had stressed the importance of evangelization in the Third World as much as, if not more than, the need for economic development, USCC statements advocated increased foreign aid.[46] During the 1960s, American Catholics had supplied missionaries and generously assisted missionary efforts to the Church in Latin America and other regions. But by 1967, Catholics such as Msgr. Ivan Illich (a priest of the New York archdiocese who was then working in Mexico) were questioning the wisdom of imposing "North American" political and ecclesial models on the southern hemisphere. Illich wanted America to send money, not missionaries.[47]

The demand for money, not missionaries, was not without critics. Richard Cardinal Cushing of Boston angrily called Illich's thesis "a colossal lie."[48] Nevertheless, the USCC's Louis Colonnese offered a remarkably similar analysis only two years later. Colonnese warned of the danger of over-confidence in bourgeois modes of thought, saying "that exportation of theological norms, cultural value judgments, historical precedents or institutionalized structures is not desired and should not be tolerated."[49]

THE VIETNAM WAR

American military involvement in Vietnam also had an impact on policymaking in the USCC, setting in motion a conflict between traditionalists, who adhered to just-war criteria for evaluating conflicts, and other Catholics who wanted to adopt a radical pacifism. Two factors would frame the debate within the Church: (1) concern about the destructiveness of modern weaponry and strategies of war; and (2) the discussion of war and peace in *Gaudium et Spes*, which upheld classic just-war doctrine, but which also called for a reconsideration of modern warfare. The Vietnam war led several influential prelates to view questions of war and peace in a different light and convinced USCC leaders that modern conflicts could not meet traditional just-war criteria.[50] These shifts occurred gradually, however, and NCCB statements on the war in the late 1960s and early 1970s consistently applied just-war criteria despite the struggle of USCC staffers and certain bishops for the Church to adopt a more critical view.

Since World War II the NCWC had supported the nation's foreign policy and tacitly endorsed every use of American arms. Not even the bloody Korean War, which cost 33,000 American combat deaths and threatened to escalate to a nuclear conflict, stirred the NCWC to formal comment. Indeed, the bishops' only collective statement on that war was a brief resolution in late 1950 broadening the Church's qualified endorsement of a peacetime draft.[51]

The conflict in Vietnam was another matter. In 1966 George Higgins drafted the bishops' first statement on the war. Citing the just-war tradition, he argued that the American war effort was justified as long as the nation's leaders sought a just peace.[52] The statement warned, however, that the government was bound to pursue every possibility of a peaceful resolution, and it urged the public to scrutinize the prosecution of the war and to protest any escalation past morally acceptable limits.[53]

Msgr. Higgins and Fr. Cronin carefully distanced the Social Action Department from Christian pacifism and the growing anti-war movement. The United States, said Higgins in 1965, "cannot possibly hope to fulfill its large share of the responsibility for reestablishing international peace unless it is prepared to the hilt for the eventuality of war."[54] In 1966, John Cronin denied that Christianity was a pacifist religion; he suggested that unilateral relaxation of America's policy of nuclear deterrence might tempt communist states to new adventurism.[55] In a 1967 address to the anti-war group Clergy and Laity Concerned about Vietnam, Cronin reminded those who accused the Johnson administration of war-mongering that religious leaders should look to the preservation of freedom in Vietnam as well as the attainment of peace. He also urged them not to forget other important issues such as halting nuclear-weapons proliferation and lessening Cold War tensions.[56]

Growing Dissent, Deliberate Ambiguity

By 1968, the bishops were surprised and alarmed by protests against their foreign-policy stand and by unprecedented criticism in Catholic journals against the same. The bishops' pastoral letter "Human Life in Our Day" showed a growing frustration with the war among the bishops—and an increasing chariness of controversy. After noting how divisive Vietnam had become among Catholics, the statement subtly cast doubt on the bishops' earlier judgment that the war effort was justified. Had the war not already violated the just-war principle of proportionality—that the means of defense must be commensurate with the threat—by creating "inhuman dimensions of suffering" and placing too great a claim on the nation's scarce resources?[57]

By invoking proportionality, the bishops implied that the government's war aims were just (presumably they would have condemned an unjust war). But the conclusion of "Human Life in Our Day"—that poverty and injustice might be more amenable to peaceful remedies than to "military efforts to counteract the subversive forces bent on their exploitation"—undermined this assumption (141). By hinting that "non-military" aid might have done more good for the Vietnamese people, the letter suggested the futility of the war effort and thereby its failure to meet just-war criteria. This ambiguity was probably intentional, as it allowed the bishops to support and criticize the war effort simultaneously at a time when strong but mutually opposed public pressures urged both courses.

The bishops defended, with more enthusiasm, the right to selective conscientious objection implied by the just-war tradition. In previous conflicts, American Catholics had been more than willing to fight for their country (only 139 Catholics received conscientious-objector status in the two world wars). Vietnam was different. By 1969 about 2,500 Catholics had become conscientious objectors, many of them seeking counsel and aid from their priests and bishops.[58] "Let's help those God-damned kids," Chicago's John Cardinal Cody allegedly told his fellow bishops.[59] Vatican II's qualified defense of conscientious objection, and the sheer number of Catholic objectors, eventually impelled the bishops to endorse "selective" objection to certain wars or military duties, such as service with nuclear weapons. "Human Life in Our Day" urged the government to tolerate selective objection and allow objectors to render alternative service to the community. It was not until October 1970, however, that the NCCB explicitly said Catholics could be conscientious objectors, whether selective or not.[60]

The Peace Movement

While the bishops stepped lightly to avoid even more controversy, the new staff of the reorganized USCC began to reorient the secretariat's peacemaking activities. In 1969, USCC staffers met with Soviet clergymen to endorse arms control, supported a "Vietnam War moratorium" in Washington, and lobbied against President Nixon's proposed anti-ballistic missile system so prominently that one congressman asked the Internal Revenue Service to revoke the USCC's tax-exempt status.[61] In addition, the USCC's Msgr. Marvin Bordelon, preferring to set his own agenda, abandoned the forty-year-old Catholic Association for International Peace (CAIP). The CAIP, formed by Fathers Ryan and McGowan in 1925 as a Catholic alternative to pacifism, more recently had defended the just-war teaching of Vatican II and generally supported the Johnson administration's policies in Vietnam. The association's aging membership had long depended on the NCWC for administrative support, and after Bordelon's withdrawal, the CAIP faded away.[62]

At roughly the same time, certain bishops began to attack directly the hierarchy's grudging support for the war effort; they argued that modern wars, as such, flouted biblical calls for peace and justice. This position reflected a widespread belief among Catholic intellectuals, such as Thomas Merton, that the reputedly pacifist message of the Gospels ought to be regarded as more authoritative than the just-war teaching. Father (soon to be congressman) Robert Drinan, for example, implicitly criticized the bishops for not condemning the Vietnam War and hinted that they should adopt the "almost pacifist attitudes of the pre-Constantine Church."[63] Bishop Thomas Gumbleton, an auxiliary bishop serving under Cardinal Dearden in Detroit, called the United States' intervention in Vietnam gravely immoral whether judged "in the light of the earliest Christian tradition on war, or according to the 'just-war' doctrine."[64]

"Human Life in Our Day" encouraged this abhorrence of modern war by recasting the argument of Vatican II's *Gaudium et Spes*. The Council Fathers had lamented the competition of the "superpowers" but had not drawn explicit distinctions between the comparative behavior of the United States and the Soviet Union. Indeed, *Gaudium et Spes* mentioned neither country. *Gaudium et Spes* treated the practical threat of communism tactfully for several reasons, among them the fact that millions of Catholics resided behind the Iron Curtain in what —in 1965—seemed to be a potentially liberalizing Eastern bloc. No one, however, could call *Gaudium et Spes* soft on communism; the pastoral repudiated atheist ideology and condemned all "lust for political domination" and "contempt for human rights" (21, 85). Everyone knew these passages referred to the communist world.

Three years later "Human Life in Our Day" took this description of the superpower competition out of its philosophical and diplomatic contexts and used it to suggest that the United States bore a large share of the blame for the Cold War. The bishops complained of "exaggerated forms of nationalism" and the international "war system," and inaccurately claimed that *Gaudium et Spes* had condemned the use of weapons of mass destruction. "Human Life in Our Day" made virtually no mention of communism or Soviet behavior, although it alluded to the Soviet invasion of Czechoslovakia in saying that "provocations in Eastern Europe" should not erode U.S. commitment to arms control. Indeed, the bishops seemed more worried that Washington would lose the opportunity for limiting nuclear arms by forging ahead with its proposed anti-ballistic missile system.

The emergence of this line of argument almost certainly helped the bishops decide in late 1971, long after mainstream opinion had soured on Vietnam, that the war effort no longer merited their endorsement. This judgment—the first serious criticism of an American military action by the nation's hierarchy—was nevertheless expressed in traditional, just-war terms. Citing its previous arguments in "Human Life in Our Day," the NCCB concluded that the destructiveness of the war had exceeded any benefits it promised.[65]

Far from quieting the controversy, the bishops' statement further emboldened Catholic critics of the war; they urged NCCB leaders to condemn American operations in Southeast Asia. The debate pitted the NCCB's new president, John Cardinal Krol, and his deputy, General Secretary Joseph Bernardin, against Bishops John Dougherty of Newark and Thomas Gumbleton (who served on the USCC International Affairs Committee and enjoyed the support of staffers at the USCC Division for World Justice and Peace). Philosophically, however, the conflict came down to an argument between those who insisted on critical scrutiny of both sides of the Vietnam War and those who implied that there was no moral defense for American intervention in the Third World.

Stop the Bombing

Organized Catholic opposition to the American bombing campaign of Vietnam coalesced in early 1972. The USCC's Marvin Bordelon argued in the January issue of *America* magazine that U.S. bombing operations (which, he claimed, killed thousands of civilians per month) violated the just-war principle of proportionality.[66] At the NCCB's biannual meeting in April, Bishop Gumbleton took a somewhat different approach. He complained that the bishops' latest condemnation of abortion was flawed because it was not accompanied by a condemnation of the bombing campaign. He argued that such inconsistency toward the taking of human life undermined the bishops' moral credibility.[67]

The debate was joined a few days later by General Secretary Bernardin, who infuriated the staff of the USCC International Affairs Committee by publicly criticizing North Vietnam's powerful "Easter offensive." Bernardin issued a statement deploring Hanoi's assault and calling for restraint by all sides.[68] His press release went out with Cardinal Krol's approval after minimal coordination with Msgr. Bordelon; in fact, Bernardin declined to include Dougherty's suggested criticism of the U.S. Air Force counterattacks against North Vietnam. USCC staffers and members of Bishop Dougherty's committee rejected the sentiments expressed in Bernardin's message; one staffer quipped that the press release could have been written by the Nixon White House.[69] More criticism of Krol and Bernardin followed over the course of the summer. In July, the National Association of Laity commended eight bishops, including Bishop Gumbleton, for opposing the war. At the same time the association censured Krol and Bernardin for "abdicating moral responsibility" in response to President Nixon's alleged escalation of the Vietnam conflict.[70]

In November 1972, Dougherty and Gumbleton finally persuaded the NCCB to issue a statement against the bombing. Gumbleton, who had demonstrated his own political commitment by endorsing the presidential candidacy of Democrat George McGovern, questioned his colleagues' courage when they shied away from explicit condemnation of the U.S. war effort. But opposition to parts of Gumbleton's proposed resolution remained, and Gumbleton's supporters ultimately agreed to replace the phrase, "war is no longer admissible as a means of settling disputes," with the milder formulation, "war is not an apt means of settling disputes."[71]

The bishops on one USCC committee went even further the following year. Though it had rejected a condemnation of President Nixon's renewed air war in December 1972, the Committee on Social Development and World Peace accused the Nixon administration in July 1973 of ordering "carpet bombing" in Cambodia, implying that American military efforts to shore up the "shaky and ineffectual government" of Cambodia in its fight against Pol Pot's communist Khmer Rouge guerrillas had caused the situation to deteriorate.[72]

By this time, USCC staff had come to view the war as part of a global pattern of American and Western interference with the self-determination of Third World peoples. James Jennings, who was Msgr. Bordelon's assistant at the Department of International Affairs, explained that poorer nations and social groups would not wait forever for justice: "Movements by minority groups in the United States are frequently attempts to achieve self-determination by casting off white domination, and are not too dissimilar from Vietnamese efforts . . . to overcome the domination of France, Japan, and, most recently, the United States."[73] This conceptual linkage between justice at home and abroad would have a profound influence on the bishops' social thought in the years ahead.

MOVING TOWARD PRAGMATIC LIBERALISM

Daniel Callahan probably spoke too soon when he declared, in 1963, that liberalism had finally won the day in Church and society.[74] The Catholic liberalism he had seen, which championed "papal social thought, ecumenism, internationalism and social justice," had indeed triumphed, at least in institutional terms. Liberal Catholics and their allies among the bishops easily took control of the new NCCB and USCC, but it was soon clear that their ideas would not sweep all before them. Indeed, most American Catholics—and more than a few bishops—proved far more cautious about social controversy and more supportive of American foreign policy than were the liberal Catholics now ensconced in the USCC. At the same time, more than a few Catholic thinkers had gone beyond liberalism to voice a radical critique of the Church's moderate stance toward America's political and social structures. One crucial victory also remained unattained: an end to the Church's allegedly morbid and divisive obsession with sexual probity. Pope Paul VI's encyclical *Humanae Vitae* proved that Rome was not going to subordinate "personal" morality to social justice, and gave new hope to Catholic traditionalists. The secretariat settled in for the long, patient work of reshaping Catholic attitudes at all levels of the Church and of resisting pressures from both radical and traditionalist critics of the bishops' conference and secretariat.

Bishop Joseph Bernardin's leadership within the NCCB and USCC over the next few years would come to symbolize both the pragmatism and the ambivalence of the new American Catholic liberalism. Although Bernardin had announced his desire to renew the Church's social teaching, his ecclesial conservatism and political caution sometimes put him at odds with reformers in the USCC. He eschewed those Catholics whom he regarded as radicals to his left (who wanted the bishops to condemn American foreign and economic policies) and to his right (who would soon call for the Church to more emphatically oppose abortion). His stands on these issues did not make his job any easier. Bernardin would have a hard time earning his reputation as an ecclesial peacemaker in the decade to come.

6

A New Elite

Wearied by disputes over Vietnam, civil rights, and a host of specifically Catholic issues ranging from liturgical reform to birth control, by the 1970s many bishops were wary of making public pronouncements. Most bishops were content to cede public policy formulation and commentary to USCC experts who were adept at dealing with government officials and the news media. It was in the seventies that clerical and lay leaders within the USCC completed the egalitarian reorientation of the hierarchy's social teaching they had begun the previous decade. USCC leaders and staff became the new elite of the American Catholic Church, setting the agenda and defining social doctrine more and more for the bishops so that the concerns and ideology of the USCC secretariat became indistinguishable from that of the American hierarchy.

RADICAL RHETORIC AND PRAGMATIC POLICY

By the early 1970s, the Thomism of the NCWC was no more. Instead Catholic radicalism struggled with a more pragmatic liberalism for control over Catholic social thought. Catholic radicals, who were deeply pessimistic about American capitalism and liberal democracy, sought to use the Church as a megaphone for social criticism. Liberal Catholics, on the other hand, accepted the permanence of bourgeois democracy but generally agreed with their radical brethren that technology (and its misuse) had replaced ideology as the gravest threat to humanity.

Although most bishops did not consciously choose sides in this contest of worldviews, virtually all their advisors at the USCC accepted liberal or radical premises to some degree. NCCB-USCC leaders like John Cardinal Dearden and Bishop Joseph Bernardin belonged more or less to the liberal camp; they worried about the dangers wrought by modern technology but had no intention of squandering the moral authority of the Church—or its tax exemptions—through gratuitous partisanship. With some difficulty, liberal leaders in the bishops' conference and its secretariat linked the egalitarian rhetoric used by more radical Catholic social thinkers to pragmatic policy goals acceptable to Washington political and media elites. This accommodation allowed liberals and radicals within the secretariat to cooperate, for the most part, on domestic issues. Staff members assumed the mantle of modern prophets, reminding Catholics and policymakers that social inequality in America and the world was so severe as to threaten the nation's ability to continue the dialogue that was the basis of its communal existence.

Justice Redefined

An important conceptual change, which occurred at the same time, was the transformation of the concept of justice from a vision of order to the perpetual willingness to level social inequalities. USCC statements began to view modern problems as arising more from reified economic systems and misapplied technology than from flawed social ideas. A few years earlier, the new "political" theology had provided guidelines for revising the NCWC's teaching on the Church's God-given wisdom. The NCCB did preserve the older view of the teaching mission of the Church in their major pastoral letters, such as "To Live in Christ Jesus" (1976), but the USCC secretariat preferred an approach ostensibly based on the documents of the Second Vatican Council.[1] Vatican II's *Gaudium et Spes* described the Church as a force for justice and peace that would illuminate the world from within by the power of its example. "Political" theologians in the 1960s made this insight the core of a new conception of the Church's political responsibility—a vision that satisfied all factions within the USCC secretariat because it allowed them to step back from traditional and controversial Catholic positions on sexual morality while encouraging ever-greater activism for social and political change.[2]

In 1970, the USCC's new Assistant General Secretary, Father James Rausch, proffered this notion of justice to a gathering of the National Council of Catholic Women. Starting with Pope Paul VI's encyclical letter *Populorum Progressio,* he argued:

> Social justice is not a static notion of human relationships that is locked in by a conservative view of civil order where the rights of current possessors of power and wealth are guaranteed against debtors and outcasts. If justice is to exist in the social order it must acknowledge the fallibility, and, indeed, when present, the malicious effects of structures men create which thwart the pursuit of greater humanness for all.

Justice cannot remain a mere concept, said Fr. Rausch; "it must be an act." Rausch insisted, with Pope Paul, that the fruits of the earth are created for all and that no one is justified in keeping property for his sole benefit when others lack the necessities of life. This logic, Rausch claimed, destroyed the comfortable ethic of occasional charity practiced by many Americans, and demanded that Christians provide the poor with access to power.[3] The views expressed by Fr. Rausch were well on their way to being adopted by the bishops' advisors, and more gradually, by the bishops themselves. Rausch's tenure as assistant general secretary saw a marked departure from the traditional Catholic approach to social justice.

The older notion of the organic society, which had understood justice as a proper ordering of relations of unequal parts to the common good, was discarded. The new social ethic, as announced by Fr. Rausch, regarded *all* inequalities of wealth and power that were not *immediately* tied to some greater service for the common good as oppressive. It distrusted even these benefits if their recipients tended to be white males—the dominant wielders of power in America. Following this logic, Rausch regarded the leveling of suspect social distinctions as *by definition* the perpetual and primary task of justice. But Rausch attacked inequality without showing—as the NCWC had done—what equality would look like. This new conception of justice banished the traditional notion of a natural social order and, consequently, the older distinction between justice and charity. Indeed, Fr. Rausch seemed to say that it was arrogant to believe, as Catholics once had, that alms-giving was in any way generous or noble.[4]

Social Sin

Rausch's sentiments were not his alone. By 1970 the bishops' staff had come to view society as an aggregate of groups differentiated by their relative needs—instead of by their contribution to the common good. The manifest inequality between social groups in America led USCC staffers to conclude that the nation pushed certain groups, particularly blacks, Hispanics, Indians, women, youth, farmers, the elderly, and the disabled, to the "margins" of national life. By 1979, the bishops had collectively adopted this view of American society, a classic expression of which was the pastoral letter "Brothers and Sisters to Us." Inequality, the letter explained, was partly the fruit of racism, which had been "part of the social fabric of America since the beginning of European colonization." While overt racism was largely a thing of the past, "Brothers and Sisters to Us" nevertheless detected racist attitudes behind "the triumph of private concern over public responsibility, individual success over social commitment, and personal fulfillment over authentic compassion."[5]

"Brothers and Sisters to Us" also suggested that the sins of those who had created these patterns of mastery and marginalization were compounded by a generalized social indifference that amounted to another sin, in and of itself. Bishops and USCC staffers repeated this notion during the 1970s. Speaking before a congressional committee in 1973, John Cardinal Dearden explained that individuals bore responsibility for society's violations of human rights even when those individuals had managed to "mask" their involvement in some "neutral" social structure or institution.[6] Some USCC statements implied that citizens participated in "social" sin even without knowledge of any particular immoral act.[7] The USCC's Father J. Bryan Hehir defined social sin as an organization or structure that systematically works to the detriment of groups or individuals; the sin redounded to those who constructed the inequitable structure *or permitted it to exist.*[8]

PROPHETIC WITNESS

This new understanding of sin led some bishops and USCC staff members to denigrate the ordinary social contributions made by lay groups and individuals through their daily participation in the community. The NCWC notion of an organic society had understood and stressed that justice was fostered by people perfecting their everyday activities—for instance, by working harder and more efficiently, by hiring employees on the basis of merit, or by establishing and enforcing standards of conduct and practice in their various professions. The USCC now began to suggest that these quotidian practices had actually reified the injustices of American society and the global order; even the virtuous pursuit of private happiness marginalized entire segments of society. USCC logic questioned the good will of those not directly active in promoting redistributive policies and programs.[9]

In the face of widespread social inequality, USCC staffers contended that the social mission of the Church was to serve as a prophetic witness—to highlight patterns or "structures" of marginalization and to create a "community with a conscience" to attack those injustices. James Rausch (by 1973 a bishop and successor of Joseph Bernardin as USCC general secretary) explained the importance of this notion in an address to the Crosier Fathers. Citing the 1971 worldwide Synod of Bishops in this matter, Rausch concluded:

> The function of the Church in the social order is consistently to raise 'the forgotten factor' in human affairs, to highlight the human dimension of issues, which gets lost or subordinated to more pragmatic or concrete concerns.[10]

Clerical Activism

This new emphasis on the Church as public advocate for justice was coupled with a stress on the clergy's duty to shape and lead the faithful in their activities. The Church was not merely to impart the faith and set an example of justice; its clergy and religious would work directly for justice. In a 1970 symposium, Msgr. George Higgins contrasted the old and new approaches to social justice. "The Ryans and the McGowans of the NCWC," he said, had emphasized the layman's role as a citizen and a member of secular organizations in solving social problems, whereas the new Catholic activists stressed the political role of the hierarchy and of the Church as an institution.[11]

Unlike the NCWC, which had usually left the lobbying of officials and lawmakers to the individual bishops or to their Washington secretariat, the USCC called for political activism at all levels of the institutional Church. A typical document of the time was the USCC proposal "Reform of Correctional Institutions in the 1970s" (1973), which contained numerous and detailed proposals. The USCC promised to develop various programs to further prison reform; state Catholic conferences were to lobby state legislatures and governors; dioceses were to "highlight the moral considerations involved in correctional reform and urge action"; parishes were to maintain contacts with correctional institutions and "work to overcome neighborhood resistance to community-based institutions." Finally, religious orders were to use their expertise to work for better prisons and "bring special assistance to administrative and custodial officials."[12]

Influential USCC staff members argued that clerical activism augmented the traditional teaching ministry of the Church. An interviewer for *Sign* magazine once pressed Father J. Bryan Hehir to comment on the fact that Christ spoke of saving souls but made no mention of reforming society. Fr. Hehir was ready. He patiently explained that the "totality" of Church life could not be organized by a literal reading of the Gospels. The social mission of the Church remained the formation of consciences, said Hehir, but the Church could perform this task in many ways. "A picket line can be a teaching instrument"; indeed, the clergy could teach even by angering people, if that anger resulted in reflection on social issues.[13]

Father Hehir formally defended clerical activism in an article in the *New Catholic Encyclopedia*. In his view, the weakness of pre-Conciliar Catholic social teaching stemmed from its sketchy understanding of the distinction between the Church's nature (or mission) and its social ministry. The Second Vatican Council and the 1971 worldwide Synod of Bishops had dispelled this confusion. By identifying social activism as a "constitutive" dimension of the preaching of the gospel, Hehir claimed, the synod had made social ministry central to the Church's mission. Hehir suggested the synod's text could be read as establishing social activism as a *clerical duty*, on a par with preaching and administering the sacraments; he admitted, however, that this understanding of the synod's meaning remained controversial. Nevertheless, Hehir endorsed this interpretation himself and suggested others should as well.[14]

Msgr. Francis Lally of the USCC did just that, in stronger language, at a 1979 conference of the St. Vincent de Paul Society. Lally, the USCC Secretary for Social Development and World Peace, noted that some Catholics believed the task of their clergy and religious was merely to inspire others to do the work of justice. Catholics who believed this, he suggested, would have the Church retreat from the world's challenges. Preaching and principles had their place, but seeking refuge in them alone "must be seen as the empty shell it is."[15]

What amounted to a usurpation of the lay role in society and politics by the clergy was largely an American innovation. The 1971 worldwide Synod of Bishops in Rome—often cited by Americans to justify clerical activism—had actually circumscribed such clerical partisanship. With Pope Paul VI's approval, the synod's statement "Justice in the World" asserted that the fullness of Christian witness to the gospel exists only where Christians commit themselves to fostering justice. "Action on behalf of justice and participation in the transformation of the world," wrote the bishops, is thus "a constitutive dimension of the preaching of the gospel." But this passage, which discussed the vocation of the Church as a whole, agreed with earlier popes in assigning to the laity the primary responsibility for action on behalf of justice, while upholding the clergy's right and duty to teach the principles of justice:

> Of itself it does not belong to the Church, insofar as she is a religious and hierarchical community, to offer technical solutions in the social, economic and political spheres for justice in the world. Her mission involves defending and promoting the dignity and fundamental rights of the human person.[16]

Scattered Objections

Given this reiteration of the clergy's traditional, extra-political calling by the 1971 synod, it was not surprising that some American bishops resisted the new activist role envisioned for them by the USCC—although this resistance remained passive and unorganized. While bishops such as Thomas Gumbleton and John Dougherty prodded the NCCB to speak out on political matters, others grumbled about the pressure to take stands on controversial issues. The *New*

York Times noted the lack of enthusiasm among the bishops in 1976 for a draft resolution that stopped just short of urging Washington to restore the Panama Canal to Panamanian control. John Cardinal Carberry of St. Louis complained that he knew "nothing at all" about Panama and felt silly voting on such a resolution. After the measure nevertheless won approval, Bishop Joseph McNicholas (Springfield, Il.) complained that "the staff people want us to take positions on everything under the sun."[17] Archbishop Bernardin, then president of the NCCB, explained to the *National Catholic Reporter* that the bishops felt "more comfortable when it comes to a document . . . where they don't get into specifics too much."[18] The complaints of scattered objectors during the 1970s were, however, submerged under a torrent of USCC statements and press releases. By 1979, liberal policy prescriptions had become the norm, reflecting the insistence of USCC leaders like Bernardin, Rausch, and Hehir that the USCC adopt the pragmatic goals of secular liberalism and maintain its standing and influence in the Washington policy community.

MORALITY AND PROGRESS

Papal social teaching has always stressed that human dignity advances only when progress is linked with virtue. Paul VI in *Populorum Progressio* had explained that all true progress is for the good of the person, for "the development of each man and of the whole man." Each person "bears the responsibility both for his own development and for his salvation"; he is the "chief architect of his own fortune." The noble harmony of man's nature as a creature endowed with intellect and will obliges him to "direct his life to God, the first truth and the highest good." But each person is also a member of society, and thus "all without exception are called to promote the full development of the whole human society" (14-17). "Truly human conditions" have been achieved when men have attained four things: necessities and culture; a respect for the dignity of others and for the common good; recognition of God as their highest end and bestower of all their blessings; and, finally, faith and unity in the love of Christ (21).

The new American Catholic notion of justice as equal access and power—as opposed to the traditional conception—took a rather different approach to social progress. American Catholic thinkers set aside the older anthropomorphic analogies of the social order. Having done so, they found it harder to generalize about the normative connections between virtue and social progress. While USCC staffers and their allies among the bishops had little trouble explaining how crimes of violence, for example, eroded the anonymous trust essential for communal life, they became hesitant and vague when confronted with "personal" or supposedly victimless phenomena such as promiscuity or pornography. This indecision manifested itself in a reluctance to offend secular and non-Catholic political allies by linking Catholic teachings on vice to public policy in matters of "personal" morality.

A curious inconsistency soon appeared in the secretariat's policy applications of morals. USCC statements, for instance, waxed eloquent concerning the guilt of the rich and powerful and society's obligation to provide for the disadvantaged. But the USCC's liberal leadership feared the absolutism implied in any political claim to moral truth and consequently hesitated to hold all persons, rich and poor, to traditional Catholic teachings on morality. Statements by the NCCB and USCC reversed earlier teachings on morality by attributing vice to social problems rather than to sin or individual moral failure. The USCC statement "Violence in the Family," for example, found "forced competitiveness and the sacrificing of human development for material goods" at all "socio-economic levels," and concluded "the fact that resolving serious problems by violence is part of our American society, and culture supports abusive behavior."[19] Indeed, after 1970, the bishops and their staff rarely repeated the NCWC argument that full human and social development advanced only when individual citizens learned to control their baser desires.[20] This separation of virtue from social progress marked one of the most significant developments in the social teaching of the American bishops since 1919.

Public Policy Concerns

At least one influential adviser to the bishops, Father J. Bryan Hehir, publicly suggested that actions which would be sinful for the faithful could be publicly tolerated, and even subsidized by the taxes of Catholic citizens, if committed by non-Catholics. Hehir promoted this position in a pair of articles on the relationship between population growth and economic development. Working from the assumption that the obsolete "rhythm method" was the only means of birth control condoned by the Church, Hehir argued that Catholics could tolerate policies that promoted the use of contraceptives by non-Catholics; Catholics were not bound in matters of public policy by a literal reading of Pope Paul VI's *Humanae Vitae* (which prohibited artificial birth control) because Catholic moral theologians discerned a certain ambiguity in that encyclical. In addition, Fr. Hehir alleged that Paul VI's ban on contraception applied to *personal* morality, not public policy, and that the traditional, natural law teaching had maintained a distinction between these two realms. Citing what he insisted was the logic of the late John Courtney Murray's argument for religious liberty, Hehir concluded that political prudence sometimes dictated the tolerance of vice for the sake of the common good when a rigorous enforcement of "personal" conceptions of morality would foster evils greater than they were meant to cure.[21]

These and other considerations, said Hehir elsewhere, permitted the Church to oppose abortion and sterilization while maintaining a discreet silence on other policies designed to slow population growth, i.e., the distribution of contraceptives. Indeed, Hehir proposed that the building pressure of population growth exposed "the need to stress systemic over personal values." Echoing the view put forth by Chicago lay activist Edward Marciniak twenty years earlier, Fr. Hehir stated that the Church's "sectarian" opposition to contraception had cost it potential allies. Hehir also warned that continued opposition by the Church to policies which promoted contraception could even reduce the moral force of Catholic opposition to abortion and compulsory sterilization.[22]

Hehir's recommendations were not officially adopted by the bishops, but his concern that a strict application of Catholic sexual mores in matters of public policy would cost the Church valuable allies was echoed by the secretariat's quiet efforts to "broaden" the bishops' opposition to legalized abortion. These efforts, in turn, would produce such controversy within the NCCB and the USCC secretariat that the weary leaders of the conference would gradually demote abortion from its place as the most pressing public policy matter affecting American life.

ROE V. WADE

Overall, the NCWC had paid scant attention to abortion, which was not a salient national issue until the late 1960s. The NCCB, however, grew alarmed as various groups campaigned for a relaxation of legal prohibitions against the practice, and they repeatedly decried the liberalization of state abortion laws. A typical statement, released in April 1970, argued that abortion flouted the right to life and weakened social inhibitions against other forms of killing; the bishops also pledged action to ameliorate the social problems that often pressured women to seek abortions.[23]

The nation's legal barriers to abortion collapsed altogether in 1973 with the Supreme Court's ruling in *Roe* v. *Wade*. USCC leaders immediately denounced this de facto legalization of abortion as an affront to Catholic teaching and conscience. Conference President John Cardinal Krol called it an "unspeakable tragedy." Msgr. James McHugh of the USCC Family Life Division likened it to the 1857 *Dred Scott* decision, which held that blacks were not protected by the U.S. Constitution.[24] Three weeks later, the NCCB's Administrative Committee branded *Roe* v. *Wade* "erroneous, unjust, and immoral" for condoning a practice in violation of God's law. The committee called for "unified and persistent efforts" to instill a new reverence for life in America, and warned that any Catholic who underwent, performed, or assisted at an abortion was thereby excommunicated.[25]

Led by John Cardinal Krol and Archbishop Joseph Bernardin, the NCCB subsequently made abortion its primary policy concern.[26] Mary Segers has noted that the bishops, instead of attacking abortion on more narrowly "Catholic" grounds as one more form of illicit contraception, attacked it as a violation of human rights.[27] In March 1974, four American cardinals — Krol, Medeiros, Manning, and Cody — testified before the Senate on behalf of a proposed constitutional amendment that would protect the unborn child's right to life.[28] In November that year, Cardinal Cody's NCCB Committee for Population and Pro-Life Activities wrote to Congress, wondering whether U.S. vice-presidential nominee Nelson Rockefeller would use the office "to promote a personal viewpoint on permissive abortion."[29] Cardinal Krol also told the bishops that he saw no more urgent or meritorious task for social action than that of "guaranteeing to infants for generations to come the sacred God-given right to life."[30]

Beyond a "One-Issue" Church

Staffers and officials at the USCC secretariat unanimously opposed legalized abortion and defended Church activism, but many indirectly questioned Cardinal Krol's political strategy and his commitment of the Church's moral resources to this issue. Bishop Rausch, discomfited by the moral fervor of the emerging anti-abortion movement, called for a "consistent" moral theory of rights in a speech to the National Assembly of Catholic Laity in late 1973. He suggested that some Catholics had so stressed the right to life that they ignored the quality of life. Rausch explored the link between the two:

> . . . our very necessary concern for the right to life of the unborn in America today must be linked to a vital concern for the quality of life of the very poor, the aged, and the minority members of the American community.[31]

Msgr. George Higgins complained that Catholics were placing too much emphasis on "the legal aspects" of abortion and not enough on moral suasion. Even the legal aspects, he added, "can't be resolved by heavy-handed pressure on legislators." Higgins noted many Catholics were "out of sympathy" with the Church's position on abortion, and recommended shoring up Catholic support "before we launch an all-out attempt to go public on this issue."[32]

Whatever they felt about abortion's relative priority, the bishops and their advisors, according to Mary Hanna, sought to demonstrate that the Church was not a "one-issue" body despite its focus on abortion.[33] For example, the bishops' "Pastoral Plan for Pro-Life Activities" (1975) called on Catholics to form independent lobbying groups in every congressional district to work for the election of pro-life candidates, and added that "the program must extend to other issues that involve support of human life: there must be internal consistency in the pro-life commitment." These other issues included poverty, war, population control, euthanasia, and problems facing the family, youth, the elderly, and the mentally retarded.[34]

Nevertheless, abortion was still at the top of the NCCB's agenda —at the insistence of the NCCB leadership—specifically a constitutional amendment to restrict the practice or to allow the states to do so. In August 1976, as NCCB president, Archbishop Bernardin released a statement aimed at critics of the NCCB stand on the issue. As a direct assault on defenseless human life, abortion demanded priority over all other issues: ". . . if we become insensitive to the violation of the basic human right to life, our sensitivity to the entire spectrum of human rights will ultimately be eroded." Bernardin called it a disservice to accuse pro-lifers of indulging in "single-issue" politics.[35]

The 1976 Election

Within days of Bernardin's statement, however, Catholic disagreement over the centrality of abortion moved toward open confrontation. Bernardin had unwittingly set himself in opposition to Democratic presidential nominee Jimmy Carter, whose campaign aides badly wanted to win the traditionally Democratic Catholic vote. Carter had told Jim Castelli of the USCC's National Catholic News Service that he opposed abortion; he further complained that the Democrats' permissive plank on the issue did not completely reflect his views. (The platform recognized the concerns of pro-lifers but declined to support a constitutional amendment protecting the unborn.) Despite these assurances, on August 13, 1976, Bernardin publicly criticized Carter's "inconsistency" in refusing to support an amendment. Five days later Bernardin praised the Republican party platform for "clearly and forthrightly" endorsing a constitutional remedy.[36]

Carter's staff did not lose hope. His advisors calculated that the other planks of the Democratic Party platform, together with Carter's personal opposition to abortion, could favorably impress the bishops and ease concerns about Carter among Catholic voters. Not wanting to see the USCC obsessed with the abortion issue, Bishop Rausch of the USCC had come to the same conclusion. Rausch, according to Eugene Kennedy, "liked Carter and wanted to help him cope with the strong anti-abortion climate that the American bishops were rapidly generating."[37] He spoke informally with Carter and his aides about conciliating the NCCB leadership. It was finally decided that the Carter campaign should formally approach the reluctant Bernardin with a request for an interview, which ultimately took place at the Mayflower Hotel in Washington, D.C., on August 31. Afterward,

Bernardin read a prepared statement to waiting reporters, indicating that while the session was cordial, he was still "disappointed" with Carter's opposition to amending the Constitution.[38] Two weeks later the same bishops met with the Republican nominee, President Gerald Ford. Although Ford parried their concern about recent increases in federal funding for abortions, the bishops nonetheless pronounced themselves "encouraged" by his support for an amendment.[39]

The bishops' diverse remarks about Carter and Ford struck many observers as an NCCB endorsement of the Republican candidate. This rankled USCC staff members and many bishops; Jim Castelli later noted that more than a few bishops privately complained.[40] George Higgins also criticized the bishops' apparent support of Ford's candidacy. Higgins argued the matter with Msgr. James McHugh, needled Bishop Rausch over meals at the USCC staff house, and complained by letter to Archbishop Bernardin. The bitterness of the dispute greatly distressed Bishop Rausch, who at one point angrily told Higgins to drop the matter because it was engendering hatred within the secretariat.[41]

The NCCB Administrative Committee clarified the situation on September 16, rejecting the impression that Bernardin had endorsed Gerald Ford. While defending the bishops' "profound concern" over abortion, the committee urged Catholics to consider the entire range of positions taken by the presidential candidates.[42] Indeed, the USCC staff—with no formal authorization or clearance from the bishops' leadership—sought to ensure that Catholics did just that by publishing a comparison of secretariat positions with the Democratic and Republican party platforms. The Democratic platform came far closer to reflecting the USCC positions listed in the comparison: they essentially matched on nineteen issues. The Republican platform reflected USCC concerns on only three issues (abortion, television programming, and aid to higher education), but on two other issues —capital punishment and illegal aliens—the Republican platform flatly opposed USCC positions. The lesson was clear: Jimmy Carter's platform reflected the USCC's version of Catholic social teaching far better than Gerald Ford's did.[43]

After this quarrel, Archbishop Bernardin and the bishops' conference shied away from political controversy on abortion and refrained from publicly calling abortion the foremost policy concern of the

Church. Abortion was effectively deemphasized either by omission, or, when it was addressed, by situating it in the context of other issues.[44] For instance, the NCCB's 1976 pastoral letter "To Live in Christ Jesus"—which the hierarchy presented as a definitive statement on moral and social ethics—called abortion an "unspeakable crime" but listed it with seven other domestic policy concerns, including housing, employment, and discrimination. In 1978 another statement, "To Do the Work of Justice: A Plan of Action for the Catholic Community in the U.S.," called life "a most fundamental human right," which would remain "the object of priority efforts." However, the single paragraph devoted to this topic failed to mention whose life was threatened or how, and was followed by several paragraphs outlining strategies to fight discrimination on the basis of race, sex, age, and disability.[45] Abortion was omitted altogether from the USCC study guide "Concerns of Poor Women" (1979) by Barbara Stolz. Neither did the bishops offer any concerted reaction when the Democratic party reiterated and strengthened its pro-abortion platform plank in 1980.

In addition to deemphasizing abortion, Archbishop John Quinn of San Francisco (who in 1977 succeeded Bernardin as NCCB president) admonished opponents of abortion to prove their commitment to life. In his statement marking the fifth anniversary of *Roe* v. *Wade*, Quinn said that anyone who desired credibility in halting abortions "must also defend human life in all other areas." Anti-abortion activists should work for economic justice and support the rights of the oppressed and disadvantaged.[46] Quinn's use of this logic marked a victory for USCC staffers who had advocated such an approach since 1973, and also set the stage for the debate of the following decade over the "consistent ethic of life."

DOMESTIC POLICIES AND POLITICS

Despite the gradual withdrawal of the bishops from the forefront of the abortion conflict, the secretariat's new emphases on social inequality and clerical activism within the American Church translated rather easily into an expanded lobbying role for the USCC. The 1960s had sensitized the staff to social crises—especially to racism and poverty in America's inner cities and marginalized rural areas. USCC lobbyists had set aside the papal vision of a natural social order—with its Aristotelian view of a benign and universally beneficial social inequality—and largely adopted the policy goals of secular liberalism while attempting to apply the "scriptural" norms of a new social analytic. One problem for the USCC (although never acknowledged as such) was that relatively few Americans could be called poor by biblical or even Third World standards. Poverty, in America, had become largely relative.

Fixing Inequality

How could poverty be such an important factor in America's social crises? The secretariat adopted the secular liberal answer: the real problem in America was not dire need but *inequality,* or rigid inequities in the distribution of wealth. But this answer created another problem. How to attack inequality? American society had no use for socialism (nor did any bishops). The only available remedy in America's mixed economy was one already suggested by secular liberals: to use government to redistribute wealth gradually but substantially.

This logic manifested itself in a predictable pattern of premises, arguments, and conclusions in policy recommendations, as the USCC cast the Church in the role of advocate for the voiceless and disadvantaged. Staff personnel took as their starting point shocking inequalities which remained in America, despite its obvious wealth and freedom. These inequities affected public order and human dignity, and thus constituted a *moral* problem for America and a challenge to Catholic teachings on faith and morals. The bishops' advisors viewed America as a microcosm of the world's extremes of wealth and poverty. One USCC statement argued (ignoring evidence to the contrary) that America's senior citizens could not compete "with well-financed interest groups for national resources," and thus needed help from Catholics and activists who would speak out as "advocates for the elderly on public policy matters."[47] "Hunger and malnutrition," concluded another statement, were symptomatic of "basic failures" in American social and economic structures.[48]

According to the USCC scenario, the American legal system operated by a "double standard," which afforded the powerful better counsel than the poor and allowed prosecutors to use legal powers "against government critics, political opponents and even leaders of churches."[49] Giant corporations concentrated wealth and power among a comparative handful of people.[50] American society simply could not continue to ignore its "vast disparities of income and wealth."[51] Social problems in America and the world were simply getting out of control. In congressional testimony and public statements, Catholic bishops and lobbyists frequently argued that various social problems had reached crisis proportions. They referred to a worldwide food crisis in 1974 and 1975.[52] Another document, "The Right to a Decent Home," declared "the housing crisis is overwhelming."[53] The USCC's Msgr. Francis Lally told a House subcommittee in early 1977 that current unemployment figures represented "an economic and human crisis of enormous consequences."[54]

The Federal Preference

Unlike their predecessors in the NCWC, spokesmen for the USCC preferred a direct federal role in resolving many social problems. While hardly defending every government initiative, Catholic spokesmen usually sought to replace ineffective interventions with new federal programs instead of advocating renewed efforts by private groups or local governments. Catholic leaders recommended central economic and social planning or, as Fr. Hehir chastely described it, "coordination and direction of complex social systems."[55]

Father Hehir deduced the principle of "socialization" as an explanation for the USCC's preference for governmental remedies. He cited Pope John XXIII's use of this term in the encyclical *Mater et Magistra,* which had examined the increasing centralization and interdependence of modern society and cautiously approved the state's increasing role. Hehir believed this affirmation allowed contemporary Catholics to use socialization as a balancing principle to counteract what he called the "conservative" and decentralizing bias of the traditional emphasis on subsidiarity. The two principles "ought to be understood in a relationship of tension," he wrote, and Catholics should apply both to their analyses of social issues.[56] A subsequent article by Hehir in the *New Catholic Encyclopedia* retreated somewhat from this position, presenting a similar argument but acknowledging that susidiarity remained the dominant principle.[57]

Examples abound of the USCC's preference for an increased federal role in solving social problems. The federal program Aid to Families with Dependent Children (AFDC), for instance, had met with criticism from the USCC as early as 1970; the bishops alleged that AFDC weakened families and failed to provide recipients with a decent standard of living. The USCC preferred the proposed Family Assistance Act of 1970, which offered a minimum family income paid by the federal government.[58] An appraisal of welfare policy published in 1977 by the USCC's Department of Social Development and World Peace reiterated the earlier criticism of AFDC, but again advocated a national income assistance program "substantially funded by the federal government" to assure uniform benefit levels.[59] A USCC statement on the elderly likewise advocated sweeping federal involvement, including "a national policy guaranteeing full employment, a decent income for those unable to work, equitable tax legislation and comprehensive health care for all."[60] Another statement on prison reform advocated "national standards" for regulating treatment of inmates and suggested that Washington withhold grants to states that refused to adhere to these voluntary guidelines.[61] In 1975 the USCC Administrative Board called for federal loans to financially-stricken New York City—without mentioning a role for New York State.[62] Bishop Rausch of the USCC urged the White House to sign legislation creating public works jobs during the 1975-76 recession.[63] Although the bishops' pastoral letter on moral life, "To Live in Christ Jesus," urged businesses, professions, and workers to show that the common good could be promoted "without intrusion by the state into ever more areas of life," spokesmen for the bishops rarely discussed any domestic problems that were not amenable to increased federal control.

USCC spokesman reiterated these calls. Bishop Thomas Kelly, O.P., who succeeded Bishop Rausch as general secretary in 1977, looked to the federal government to facilitate full employment through "sustained economic planning" and job creation programs.[64] Msgr. Lally testified before Congress in favor of a "comprehensive planning process," including legislation to guarantee full employment and presidential consideration of a "voluntary program of wage and price guidelines."[65] A USCC statement on housing suggested that key decisions regarding the sale and development of land "can no longer be left to the private market alone to resolve."[66]

The Social Order

The decline of the traditional notion of an organic society and the corresponding preoccupation with social inequality lessened the bishops' concern about philosophical and ideological attacks on the principles of social order. The bishops, and especially their staff, were more reluctant than their NCWC predecessors to confront ideologies at home and abroad. The NCCB still indicted secularism as the root of individualism and collectivism, but Catholic social commentary muted what the NCWC had perceived as secularism's corrosion of virtue in America and its manifestation in totalitarianism overseas. In addition, the bishops' conference worried that lingering Cold War attitudes in America had taken on a dangerously absolutist character. The secretariat replaced the NCWC's attacks on intellectual error with critiques of whatever the bishops and their advisors regarded as expressions of moral fervor and nationalism of any stripe. In the years to come, the American episcopacy would become especially distrustful of anti-communism.

Throughout the 1970s, the bishops continued their critique of the "materialism" of American society. A 1974 NCCB review of American life noted the widespread rejection of religion and moral values for a secular, humanistic worldview. The polarization and cynicism engendered by the Vietnam War and the Watergate scandal had produced a state of moral "malaise"; the weakening of national consensus and leadership had reinforced collective and individual selfishness. The willingness of Americans to sacrifice for the common good and the good of other nations had eroded. This same document noted that the preceding years had seen "radical changes in individual moral values" wrought by the sexual revolution, including acceptance of promiscuity, divorce, and abortion for reasons of "convenience." The individualism that found fetal life inconvenient was also advancing "humane" arguments for the euthanasia of those "whose age, illness, or incapacity renders them burdensome. . . ." In all, the NCCB thought it ironic that individualism was wrecking American society while the desire for community was never "more urgent or widespread."[67]

The bishops' attack on individualism concentrated on the problem of avarice more than any other sin or error, a focus that fit with the

American Church's concern over inequality and social sin. The NCCB's 1975 "Pastoral Plan for Pro-Life Activities" noted

> a tendency for individuals to give primary attention to what is personally rewarding and satisfying to them, to the exclusion of responsible concern for the well-being of other persons and society.[68]

The USCC Family Life Division also noted that Americans seemed preoccupied with material satisfactions and warned that the pursuit of material goods tended to dull "our sensitivity to the demands of justice and equity."[69]

AMERICA AND THE WORLD

During the 1960s there was widespread Catholic interest in promoting worldwide social and economic development. In *Mater et Magistra*, John XXIII had outlined the Church's approach to the problem of continuing imbalances between the industrialized nations and their poorer neighbors. Paul VI's *Populorum Progressio* added details and emphasis to this message.

The bishops left foreign policy concerns to their staff at the USCC, which not surprisingly tended to analyze world affairs as patterns of dominance and marginalization, and to prescribe redistribution as the remedy of choice. James Jennings, of the Division for World Justice and Peace, demonstrated this parallelism between domestic and foreign policies when he explained that "the culture of poverty" in America was "only a scale model of the global problem." Both sets of problems made up "the same garment of social justice":

> Just as the complicity of affluent Americans in the causes of poverty on the domestic scene calls upon them to become involved in liberating the powerless here, so too, their complicity in the causes of poverty worldwide calls upon American Catholic citizens to become involved in liberating the powerless nations out there.[70]

The USCC's analysis of international affairs reflected a conviction among Catholic leaders that modern social problems were different not just in degree but in kind from previous social ills. It also seems as though they believed America and its citizens capable of ameliorating and solving not only domestic problems, but international poverty. The traditional Catholic critique of ideological error was set aside in the global war against inequality.

Following the lead of Paul VI, USCC staffers and their allies among the bishops routinely described the international economic order as unjust. Fr. Hehir referred to the "structural injustice" of global economic relations; Archbishop Peter Gerety of Newark, speaking to the U.S. Senate on behalf of the USCC, noted "the existing maldistribution of wealth."[71] The Americans went further than the Vatican, however, by attributing complicity to the United States for this situation. For instance, a USCC Division for World Justice and Peace list of "discussion questions" on international affairs included the claim that Americans, "representing 6 per cent of the world's population," benefitted from structures that allowed them to consume "about 40 per cent of the planet's economic production."[72] Later documents echoed this complaint.[73] These statements, however, failed to mention America's production of a disproportionate share of the world's goods. Indeed, in testimony before the Senate, Archbishop Gerety summarily dismissed just such an observation as "not acceptable in a Christian critique."[74]

The Concept of Interdependence

Bishop Rausch and Father Hehir sought to systematize USCC analyses and explain America's duty to the developing nations by using something they called the concept of interdependence. Interdependence held that inequality and technology had superseded the ideological divisions of the Cold War as the world's leading problems. Fr. Hehir believed that, as a world power, the United States was obligated to strengthen humanity's moral and political bonds by enforcing through material imperatives the Christian duty of love.[75] Hehir applied this concept in one instance to his response to the "world food crisis," arguing that aid should not be viewed as charity but as a duty of justice.[76] A few months later he explained, "We have moved from being asked to share our surplus (the traditional definition of charity) to being asked now to share our scarcity."[77]

The USCC constantly reminded citizens and public officials of the American taxpayer's obligation to correct global injustices. Secular academic analyses of underdevelopment at the time paid little attention to the problem of inducing Third World elites to reform their legal and regulatory structures to encourage investment and entrepreneurship, and the USCC readily adopted the statist approach to development. Its preferred remedy was government-to-government assistance, or, sometimes, U.S. aid to private non-profit groups. Unlike the NCWC, which had advocated private investment over "governmental" aid, the USCC distrusted corporate investment in the Third World.[78] In fact, the USCC statement "Development-Dependency: The Role of Multinational Corporations," accused American companies of cooperating with tyrannies such as Nazi Germany in the past, and Chile in the present, to create "an international market strategy which is of primary benefit to the controlling power and not to the development of peoples."[79] Archbishop Gerety and the USCC's James Jennings later reiterated this message, publicly questioning whether multinational enterprise could truly contribute to Third World development.[80]

MEASURED INDIGNATION

USCC statements on human rights reflected the conviction that inequality—not ideology—was the greatest threat to peace and human dignity. With an attention to ideology rarely seen in documents issued by the bishops' conference after 1965, the NCCB in a 1980 "Pastoral Letter on Marxist Communism" explained that secularism was a worldwide influence, and implied that a social analytic that eschewed eternal moral norms was bound to lapse into relativism because it had no principled objection to policies which destroyed human rights in the name of progress. Nevertheless, the pastoral letter quickly passed over the behavior of actual Marxist regimes—none of which were named. Indeed, to bring about peace and eliminate poverty, the bishops believed that in many countries it had become necessary for Catholics to collaborate with Marxists. They added that restraining America's own rampant consumerism would do more to dissuade poorer nations from Marxism than any volume of anti-communist propaganda.[81]

Circumspection marked the rare criticisms of actual communist regimes in USCC-NCCB statements. A 1974 USCC teaching guide on human rights offered no examples of communist oppression in its three country "case studies." In fact, during the 1970s, the bishops devoted only one statement to human rights violations in communist nations, and that statement concentrated on attacks on religion and did not discuss violations or repression of civil and economic rights.[82] None of the hierarchy's statements on Vietnam after 1970 suggested that a communist victory could result in human rights problems, although in 1978 the NCCB Administrative Board denounced, in passing, the communist oppression that resulted in the Vietnamese and Cambodian "boat people."[83] The NCCB denounced the genocide in neighboring Cambodia in the same quiet manner. Late in 1979— almost a year after the Vietnamese had chased Khmer Rouge dictator Pol Pot from power—the bishops lamented the "starvation and devastation" of the Cambodian people but did not mention the massacres that Pol Pot had perpetrated. The bishops also warned the U.S. government against putting "politics" above human lives when considering aid to Cambodia.[84]

Right-wing dictatorships received more vocal and persistent criticism from the bishops and their staff. The USCC issued two statements on the Rhodesian imprisonment of Catholic clergymen, and elsewhere denounced the racist government of South Africa. In congressional testimony, USCC spokesmen criticized Marxist guerrillas for murdering Catholic missionaries in Rhodesia.[85] USCC indignation over events in Africa was almost totally directed at the continent's white-ruled states. The USCC also decried repression in Latin America, criticizing Argentina, Chile, Brazil, Paraguay, El Salvador, Ecuador, Nicaragua and Bolivia.[86] Because of the NCCB's traditionally close ties to the Latin episcopal conferences, however, the statements on Latin America—while strong in their criticisms—were more knowledgeable and nuanced than USCC commentary on human rights abuses in Asia and Africa.

The USCC's endorsement of economic sanctions against repressive regimes was, again, done selectively. For example, Father Louis Colonnese of the USCC in 1969 opposed the American trade embargo against Cuba and charged the U.S. government—but not Fidel Castro—with stifling the self-determination of the Cuban people.[87]

The Latin America Division of the USCC followed Colonnese's lead in 1972, arguing that the U.S. embargo of Cuba strengthened Havana's ties to Moscow, caused hardship for Cuba's poor, and fueled Latin admiration of Fidel Castro as an embattled David fighting the American Goliath.[88] Not all economic embargoes, however, were judged futile. In 1976, then General Secretary Bishop Rausch argued in a letter to Secretary of State Henry Kissinger that Washington should discourage continued American investment in South Africa and Rhodesia, since such investment constituted tacit approval of those repressive regimes.[89]

Critics challenged the USCC-NCCB's selective criticism of oppressive regimes, citing the focus on right-wing dictatorships to the neglect of communist repression. USCC staffers defended themselves by claiming their rationale was not ideological but practical. According to J. Brian Benestad, Father Hehir believed the American Church was obligated to scrutinize rightist regimes more closely because the United States usually had more influence over them.[90] USCC Latin American expert Thomas Quigley suggested that ideology offered yet another basis for judgment. Addressing Congress on aid to the right-wing Somoza regime in Nicaragua, Quigley explained that his criteria for judging the observance of human rights included social and economic rights as well as civil and political liberties. He suggested that he might endorse aid for a hypothetical society "where there is a certain amount of repression" but also a "serious kind of popular development of enabling people to take more control of their lives and develop the kind of economic systems that are necessary." Quigley refused to name any such society, although he hinted that Cuba might fit his criteria.[91] The USCC's preference for redistribution had influenced its views on human rights, making the bishops' advisors less judgmental of left-wing regimes, which at least paid lip service to egalitarian ideals.

THE NEW COURSE

The USCC secretariat, enjoying more security than the old Social Action Department, held very different ideas about society and politics than its institutional predecessor. Through the 1970s, the USCC's liberal leadership, primarily Bishops Rausch and Bernardin with their new advisor Father Hehir, co-opted the radical Catholic left. They did this by setting a new agenda that advocated redistribution both at home and abroad, and which rejected anti-communism as a motive for American foreign policy. Bishop Rausch and Fr. Hehir labored to ground these policy goals in principles which could be defended as deriving from papal encyclicals or other authoritative Roman statements. The secretariat set aside the older, Thomistic natural law philosophy for what they claimed was a scripturally based social ethic.

The secretariat succeeded in the early 1970s in formulating social policies agreeable to mainstream liberalism, but a new focus for and challenge to Catholic activism had emerged with the legalization of abortion. The Supreme Court's decision in *Roe* v. *Wade* entrenched in constitutional law the secularist argument that religion (or indeed any conception of ultimate truth) is tangential to democratic governance and potentially dangerous to it. Many Catholics (most of them politically conservative) wanted the Church to discipline Catholic public officials who supported legalized abortion. Most bishops and their advisors in the secretariat believed this course too drastic; they feared the loss of all influence and credibility in Washington.

Having abandoned hope of converting America in the wake of Vatican II's *Declaration on Religious Freedom,* the USCC's liberal leadership tried to minimize the friction with its secular allies by muting its own statements on what Father Hehir called "personal" morality. Secretariat leaders expended much energy and effort in the mid 1970s to convince influential prelates (such as NCCB President Joseph Bernardin) that inequality and injustice—reified by technology and impersonal social structures—were the root of problems like abortion and thus the real threats to life in the modern world. The controversy over Archbishop Bernardin's seeming endorsement of Gerald Ford in 1976 marked the turning point in the ultimately successful campaign to ensure that the abortion issue would no longer impede Catholic cooperation with liberal policy elites.

But the fragile coherence of the USCC's policy platform would be challenged anew—this time over the morality of nuclear deterrence. Pacifist bishops and commentators urged the NCCB to condemn the American strategic arsenal as immoral, a step that conference leaders knew would be futile and divisive.

Testing the New Ethic: War, the Economy, and Abortion

The bishops' need to clarify their social teaching led to the formulation of new rubrics for applying the insights that had emerged in conference statements since the 1960s. During the Reagan era, the NCCB issued its two lengthiest and most controversial pastoral letters — "The Challenge of Peace" (1983) and "Economic Justice for All" (1986)—which enunciated the main concepts which have since governed most policy statements by the American Catholic Church. "The Challenge of Peace" applied the criteria of just-war theory with "biblical" pacifism to U.S.-Soviet relations; "Economic Justice for All" judged American society in light of the "preferential option for the poor." The USCC used both these approaches to evaluate American policies in Central America. A third important notion came from Joseph Cardinal Bernardin, who hoped that his "consistent ethic of life" would be compelling enough to halt the drift of politically moderate Catholics toward Republican ideas and candidates.

Leaders of the NCCB hoped to hold together an increasingly centrifugal church. By 1980, American Catholics concerned with social action were arguing over issues like abortion and arms control. The Catholic peace movement, which had emerged during the Vietnam War, again challenged the more moderate foreign policy assumptions of the NCCB and USCC. The policies of the new president, Ronald Reagan, served as a lightning rod for what were becoming diverging constituencies in the Catholic Church: opponents of abortion were encouraged and mobilized by Reagan, while pacifists were alarmed by Reagan's militant opposition to Moscow's "evil empire."

The bishops were under great pressure, both inside and outside of the American Church, to craft some sort of compromise to preserve the credibility of Catholic social teaching.

Any compromise, however, sacrifices something. The bishops modified the social teaching of the Church, but at a price. Politically conservative American Catholics—temperamentally and doctrinally some of the Church's most loyal subjects—were alienated. More importantly, the American bishops preserved unity in their own house by lessening their reliance on papal social teaching.

RELUCTANT WISDOM

The three dominant concepts which pervaded NCCB and USCC social teaching in the 1980s were hardly a radical turn. Each of the NCCB's ruling concepts or themes—the modified just-war doctrine of "The Challenge of Peace," the option for the poor in "Economic Justice for All," and Cardinal Bernardin's consistent ethic of life— summarized and codified ideas expressed in statements from the bishops since the Second Vatican Council. Each of these governing concepts has been used by the bishops and their advisors in analyzing subsequent policy choices. Unfortunately, each rubric has remained ambiguous enough to authorize divergent and even contradictory applications of its principles to concrete political and social issues.

The major statements issued by the conference during the 1980s offered an ad hoc wisdom instead of developing the Church's natural law tradition as enunciated by pontiffs in the modern era from Leo XIII on. "The Challenge of Peace"—in stating that there were *two* rival truths about the morality of war (i.e., just-war doctrine and biblical pacifism)—could hardly insist on the Church's special insight into the natural law. Rather than claiming the Church possessed a unique wisdom, the pastoral urged the Church to be an example of God's peace in history and a sign that that peace was becoming ever more visible in the world.[1] Likewise, "Economic Justice for All" made only the most modest claims for the Catholic understanding of the truth about man's place in creation; it described the Church's educational mission in a way that suggested Catholics had as much to learn from the world as vice versa.[2]

These formulations have not been adopted by Pope John Paul II or the other national episcopal conferences. Indeed, subsequent statements by John Paul—particularly his recent encyclicals *Centesimus Annus* and *Veritatis Splendor*—have moved in a different direction, emphasizing the participation of the acting person in the natural law and presenting Christian morality and sacraments as profoundly liberating. By comparison, the NCCB seemed to craft new rules to serve primarily political purposes, easing internal stresses in the American Church and rendering Catholic social teaching more critical of Reagan administration policies. The semantic compromises and politically nuanced phrases of the NCCB's major statements in the 1980s could hardly be called "prophetic" in the biblical sense of that term.

THE COLD WAR

The collapse of the Soviet Union in 1991 and of the communist ideal itself offers a rare opportunity to compare the relative accuracy of the analyses proposed in recent years by clerical and lay authorities in Rome with those in the United States. John Paul II explained in 1982 that Christians must concern themselves with all "human initiatives in favor of peace," but must also regard those hopes with "realism and humility." "Deceptive hopes lead straight to the false peace of totalitarian regimes." Peoples have a right and duty "to protect their existence and freedom by proportionate means against an unjust aggressor." John Paul clearly implied that the West's reliance on nuclear deterrence was morally tolerable in Cold War circumstances. He added, however, that modern war made it imperative to develop "effective means of negotiation" and "the institutions necessary for building up justice and peace."[3] The philosophical contrast between American Catholic churchmen and the Vatican is most sharp in their clearly divergent analyses of the Cold War. Rome focused on the ideological dimension of the Cold War; the American hierarchy emphasized its technological aspects. Happily, Rome prevailed on policy prescriptions, since the Vatican's analysis of the "nuclear crisis" has proven more accurate.

John Paul II has traced the roots of capitalism and communism to the common error of "economism," but he has never equated the historical manifestations of these schools in a facile moral symmetry.[4] As a university student and later as a seminarian, Karol Wojtyla survived the Nazi occupation of his country, the devastation of world war, and the imposition of Soviet-style communism. As a priest and a bishop, he persevered under the long night of communist rule. As pope, he recognized that communist ideology was the motivating force behind Moscow's foreign policies and that those policies—and not some colossal misunderstanding or mutual provocation—was the true cause and engine of the Cold War.

Gaudium et Spes, published at the close of Vatican II in December 1965, contained a comprehensive discussion of war and peace, applying to contemporary conditions the traditional "just-war" doctrine developed by St. Augustine and later Christian thinkers as a template for judging the morality of conflicts and limiting their violence. John Paul II's statements on modern war have reiterated the teaching of the Second Vatican Council on this matter.

Gaudium et Spes locates the origin of war in man's sinful nature; only vigilant lawful authority and the mastery of passions will produce peace. The causes of war are age-old; what was new was war's destructiveness. The proliferation of "scientific" weapons and the holocaust they threatened compelled man "to undertake an evaluation of war with an entirely new attitude" (80). *Gaudium et Spes* endorsed a right of national self-defense within the bounds of natural law, gave qualified approval to the policy of strategic deterrence using nuclear weapons, and urged progress toward disarmament. It also asked for more humane provisions by which conscientious objectors to military service could serve without bearing arms, and it praised those who renounced "the use of violence in the vindication of their rights," provided they did so "without injury to the rights and duties of others or of the community itself" (78).[5]

The Council Fathers came to this endorsement, however, only after heated debate. Bishops from several countries advised a ban on nuclear weapons, but they were joined by only one American prelate, Joseph Cardinal Ritter of St. Louis. With strong representations against such a ban by the British and American delegations, the council eventually upheld a qualified right of armed deterrence that allowed possession of nuclear weapons. Conscientious objection to military service proved to be another bone of contention. Francis Cardinal Spellman of New York sought to have the council impose a duty of military service upon Catholics, but, in the end, other Americans, and the council itself, heeded the advice of Catholic pacifists and in the final draft of *Gaudium et Spes* inserted qualified praise for conscientious objection.[6]

Looking Back

Events have moved so fast in the last fifteen years that we can already read statements on these matters from the NCCB and USCC with a depth of insight denied to us on most public policy issues. At least one architect of the bishops' teaching has publicly hinted that the time is right to examine the bishops' teaching on war and peace. Father J. Bryan Hehir claims that the bishops' recent activism admirably heightened public understanding of the moral issues surrounding modern war.[7] He is surely correct, but it is also fair to note an omission on his part: that raising the citizenry's consciousness was only part of what the bishops—with Hehir's advice—set out to accomplish in the early 1980s. The NCCB not only offered specific policy prescriptions and goals, but opposed U.S. government policies that contributed to the end of the Cold War and the diminution of the nuclear peril. To understand how this opposition developed, we must survey the bishops' statements on war and peace since Vatican II.

The bishops first treated nuclear strategy in "Human Life in Our Day" (1968). Unfortunately, media attention focused on the document's carefully nuanced defense of Pope Paul VI's official ban on artificial birth control. "Human Life in Our Day" repeated Vatican II's condemnation of total war and its qualified endorsement of deterrence; but it also misstated the declaration of *Gaudium et Spes* on weapons of mass destruction, which had unequivocally condemned the destruction of entire cities, but had not banned all conceivable uses of nuclear weapons per se.[8] "Human Life in Our Day" inaccurately stated that the council had "condemned the use of weapons of mass destruction." The letter also, in effect, adopted the "Mutually Assured Destruction" doctrine implied in U.S. defense policy, urging that American deployment of a strategic defense anti-ballistic missile system would destabilize the strategic equation, inciting Moscow to increase its offensive nuclear forces and to build defenses of its own.[9]

These two ideas laid the rhetorical foundation for pastoral letters to come.

In 1976 one paragraph in a new pastoral letter, "To Live in Christ Jesus," complicated the matter even further. USCC advisors Russell Shaw and J. Bryan Hehir collaborated in drafting language that seemed to abandon Vatican II's toleration of nuclear deterrence: "we must also be aware that not only is it wrong to attack civilian populations but it is also wrong to threaten to attack them as part of a strategy of deterrence."[10]

By this time the USCC had been persuaded of the legitimacy and utility of non-violence. In 1978 the Administrative Board of the USCC endorsed the notion that the Catholic tradition offered two co-equal teachings on peace. It urged the American Church to become "a prophetic voice" and encourage reasonable risks for peace and disarmament. Catholic resources for this task were rich, the board explained. Both pacifism and the traditional just-war teaching were rooted in the gospel, and the Administrative Board promised to draw from each in commenting on defense policy.[11] Another statement that same year suggested that the relation of America to its allies was analogous to the Soviet Union's management of its Eastern European vassals, rhetorically equating American arms sales to its NATO allies with the Soviet arming of the Warsaw Pact.[12]

The board's compromise statement did not settle the Catholic debate over nuclear morality. The ambiguity of "To Live in Christ Jesus," combined with the two parallel "traditions" of moral analysis, left ample room for contradictory interpretations of American defense strategy. For example, Fr. Hehir cited "To Live in Christ Jesus" as a mandate for continued Catholic tolerance of nuclear deterrence.[13] At roughly the same time, however, Bishop Thomas Gumbleton cited the same passage as evidence that Catholics had no business giving even tacit approval to America's immoral possession of nuclear weapons.[14]

John Cardinal Krol's 1979 testimony on the SALT II treaty for a time raised expectations among Catholic pacifists that Church leaders were ready to challenge the moral legitimacy of nuclear deterrence. Krol held that the proclaimed intent to use nuclear weapons against civilian targets constituted a moral evil. Nonetheless, he said, actually using nuclear weapons against civilian targets was obviously the greater evil, and thus the threat to use nuclear weapons was defensible as part of a policy of deterring attack *and* ultimately ending the possibility of nuclear war. Father Hehir, who drafted Krol's testimony for the SALT II hearings, had once considered himself a "nuclear pacifist" (even though he had long considered the just war tradition a useful analytic tool).[15] He was moving away from nuclear pacifism even before the SALT II debate, however, and with the ominous turn in the Cold War at the end of the decade, he became the bishops' key adviser in their effort to defend Church teaching on modern war while updating it to reflect the new political and international situation.

The Reagan Era

As the 1980s began, bishops and staffers at the USCC were shaken by the election of Ronald Reagan as president of the United States, and by the revival of U.S.-Soviet tensions following the Soviet invasion of Afghanistan. The bishops' infrequent reflections on nuclear weapons before 1980 had revealed a growing unease about the morality of nuclear deterrence in view of Catholicism's just-war tradition. Although the Catholic peace movement had lost some of its intellectual and organizational momentum after the Vietnam war, it began to rebound in the late 1970s as it focused on the nuclear arms race. Timothy A. Byrnes believes that the reaction to Reagan's policies was shared by many bishops who considered themselves part of the conference's moderate center. These bishops were distressed by the ability of Reagan and his fellow conservative Republicans to portray themselves as guardians of traditional American values and criticize the Democrats over their libertarian stance on "family" issues, particularly abortion. Several bishops believed that the NCCB should criticize certain Reagan administration policies in part to show that the hierarchy had other concerns besides abortion.[16]

Concerns over nuclear arms and American military power surfaced during the NCCB's annual meeting in November 1980. Francis P. Murphy, an auxiliary bishop of Baltimore, called for the American Church to reassess its teaching on war and peace in light of the new world situation. Several bishops endorsed this call. Bishop Thomas Gumbleton, formerly a leader of Catholic opposition to the Vietnam war, spoke last and most forcefully, denouncing the dangerous over-confidence in American power he saw in the Reagan team. America, he said, had just elected "a president who has sincerely stated that we can have superiority with nuclear weapons, and a vice president who has said we can fight a nuclear war and win it." Gumbleton sat down to the applause of many of his colleagues, and the bishops voted to issue a new study on war and peace in the nuclear age.[17]

THE POLITICS OF "THE CHALLENGE OF PEACE"

In 1981 the American bishops were ready to begin work on what would become one of the most controversial documents issued by the NCCB—"The Challenge of Peace." The NCCB usually delegated the preparation of such documents to its secretariat, but this time the NCCB's new president, Archbishop John Roach (of Minneapolis-St. Paul) appointed a team of bishops to clarify and update earlier NCCB and USCC statements on nuclear arms. A small committee chaired by then Archbishop Joseph Bernardin drafted the pastoral, with help from a team of clerical and religious advisors led by Father Hehir.[18] Archbishop Bernardin set one marker for the committee's work from the outset. The finished pastoral, he decided, would not call for unilateral nuclear disarmament.[19] Pope John Paul II's conditional toleration of nuclear deterrence—which the pontiff voiced in January 1982—set another marker for the deliberations of the drafting committee.[20] Within these boundaries, the practical problem for the drafters was to defend the broad outline of American nuclear strategy without providing aid and comfort to the Reagan administration.

The drafting committee itself came under intense scrutiny as it solicited expert testimony and prepared drafts for the bishops' perusal. After Bishop Gumbleton leaked the committee's first draft to the press in June 1982, Bernardin and other observers were encouraged that the controversy surrounding the committee's progress increased political pressure on the White House and ensured that Catholic thought on modern war would be broadcast to every corner of the land.[21]

The draft documents certainly caused controversy in America. Catholic intellectual Michael Novak, for instance, argued that the bishops' evident desire to uphold the possession of nuclear arms but not the intention to use them, could, if implemented, undermine nuclear deterrence by tempting Moscow to probe America's will in a possibly dangerous manner.[22]

Overseas, concerns and misgivings about the pastoral among European bishops prompted the Holy See to convene a meeting in Rome in January 1983 to discuss the early drafts of the letter. Cardinal-designate Bernardin and the NCCB's president, Archbishop John Roach, with Msgr. Daniel Hoye and Fr. Hehir of the USCC, met with European bishops and Vatican officials, including Secretary of State Agostino Cardinal Casaroli and the Prefect of the Congregation for the Doctrine of the Faith, Joseph Cardinal Ratzinger. Only a carefully worded synopsis of that meeting has found its way to the public, but even its guarded language conveys the tension that marked the discussion. Vatican officials and the Europeans seemed to agree with one another that the pastoral's latest draft came close to imposing contingent prudential judgments as morally binding teachings, and misrepresented Scripture (and distorted Church history and teaching) by juxtaposing a new pacifist tradition alongside the just war teaching. (Pope John Paul II later endorsed these criticisms in a private audience with Bernardin.) For their part, the Americans admitted there were flaws in the drafts, but defended the substance of "The Challenge of Peace"; they promised to clarify the pastoral letter and the levels of authority of its various statements.[23]

The National Conference of Catholic Bishops formally approved "The Challenge of Peace" in May 1983. Even before its endorsement, the pastoral had become the best-known and most controversial statement issued to date by the American bishops. In its final form, "The Challenge of Peace" marked a compromise between the pacifism of Bishop Gumbleton and the liberal pragmatism of Fr. Hehir, who believed it more responsible to maintain nuclear deterrence, within strict limits, and a firm commitment to arms control.

Just-War Principles

"The Challenge of Peace" based its analysis of nuclear weapons on the classic just war principles of "proportionality" and "discrimination," which held special significance "because of the destructive capability of modern technological warfare" (101). *Proportionality* dictated "that the damage to be inflicted and the costs incurred by war must be proportionate to the good expected" (99). *Discrimination* demanded that force "be directed against unjust aggressors, not against innocent people caught up in a war not of their making" (104).[24] The bishops' elaboration of these criteria raised a crucial question: Could any use of nuclear weapons be limited in such a way that the damage remained "proportionate" and civilian casualties were minimized? In brief, could nuclear war, once initiated, be "controlled" by those engaged in it?

The bishops answered no, despite their avowed reluctance to "adjudicate the technical debate" over the possibility of limiting a nuclear exchange. Any use of nuclear weapons, the pastoral implied, endangered both proportionality and discrimination. "The Challenge of Peace" thus prohibited any "first use" of nuclear weapons because of the possibility that a major nuclear exchange would escalate beyond just-war guidelines. The experts cited by the pastoral letter, however, did not restrict their verdict to "major" exchanges; they believed that *any* use of nuclear weapons would escalate out of control (144). The bishops finally concluded that "a nuclear response to either conventional or nuclear attack could cause destruction which went far beyond 'legitimate defense.' Such use of nuclear weapons would not be justified" (160).

This excruciatingly nuanced language deliberately clouded what was meant by banning all "destructive" uses of nuclear weapons; and its subtlety apparently eluded many of the bishops. At the May 1983 NCCB meeting to amend and approve the final draft of the letter, the bishops actually passed an amendment to ban outright all uses of nuclear weapons. Archbishop Bernardin's drafting committee— believing that a strict condemnation of deterrence would place the pastoral outside the mainstream of American debate over strategic nuclear policy—quickly informed the assembly what was at stake and persuaded the bishops to set aside their motion.[25] In its final version, "The Challenge of Peace" implied that there might be moral uses of nuclear weapons, but refrained from discussing or listing any.[26] It seems clear that the bishops believed the very existence of the powerful U.S. arsenal would engender enough uncertainty in Moscow to deter any direct threats to American security.[27]

Opposing the Arms Race

Despite the pastoral's stress on discriminate use and proportionality, the bishops' concern for arms control—and their judgment that American restraint was the most promising avenue toward this end —led them to oppose virtually every proposed modernization of American weapons and strategy.

The Reagan administration called for the deployment of several new weapons, such as the MX and Trident nuclear missile systems, and implemented various changes in strategic doctrine. Virtually all of these developments—which were intended to improve the ability of American commanders to strike Soviet military targets—threatened less collateral harm to civilians. Nevertheless, "The Challenge of Peace" rejected most of the Reagan administration's deployments —particularly the MX and Pershing II missiles—because they appeared to unnamed experts to endanger Soviet nuclear forces.[28] Cardinal Bernardin subsequently explained that the MX and similar weapons could only encourage Moscow to build up its own arsenal, thereby threatening "crisis stability" and increasing the danger of war.[29] Archbishop John Roach, president of the NCCB, used similar logic in questioning the Reagan administration's 1981 decision to deploy the enhanced radiation warhead (the "neutron bomb").[30]

A halt to building ever more devastating weapons, the bishops believed, would end the absurdity of a deterrent strategy that increased the risk of disaster by seeking some technological breakthrough that would make deterrence foolproof. In the bishops' view, the superpowers were trapped in a fiendish cycle: while Soviet and American planners sought greater security through new weapons systems, they made themselves and the world less secure. The bishops observed that deterrence had "become the centerpiece of both U.S. and Soviet policy," and that "certain aspects" of both U.S. and Soviet strategies failed the criteria of the Catholic just-war tradition (144, 163). The bishops also feared that Western anti-communism jeopardized prospects for arms control; indeed, they warned against a simplistic anti-Sovietism which ignored "the common interest both states have in never using nuclear weapons" (257). This judgment that technology was more important than ideology in Soviet-American relations paralleled the approach taken in earlier years by Fr.

Hehir. Hehir had repeatedly cited papal warnings about the need to bring the expanding capabilities of modern weapons under moral control, but rarely mentioned papal emphases on the danger of totalitarian ideology.[31]

In reaching these conclusions, "The Challenge of Peace" made two key assumptions: that any "exchange" of nuclear weapons would rapidly escalate out of control, and that the best way to restrain the arms race was through Soviet-American dialogue, arising from unilateral American restraint. The bishops knew that their resistance to modernizing the American nuclear arsenal opened them to the accusation that they were weakening the nation's defenses. To counter this allegation, "The Challenge of Peace" expressed a willingness to consider an enhanced conventional military capability. Other statements by the NCCB and USCC, however, consistently rejected concrete proposals to strengthen the conventional arsenal. NCCB President John Roach told the bishops at their 1981 annual meeting that the Reagan administration's projected five-year defense budget stood "in stark contrast to budget cuts which threaten the food, the health care and the education of the poor."[32] The bishops' subsequent pastoral letter on economic justice alleged that the defense budget created "a massive drain on the U.S. economy"; later statements on social issues called for tax increases and cuts in defense spending.[33]

THE U.S. AND USSR: MORAL PARITY

The bishops' reluctance to endorse increased military spending fit their assumption that the Reagan administration had exaggerated the Soviet challenge to America's security. "The Challenge of Peace" assumed that the foreign and defense policies of the Soviet Union mirrored those of the United States—regardless of the disparities between the two societies. The safest and thus morally correct policy for the United States, according to the NCCB, was to refrain from new deployments for as long as it took the Soviets to respond in kind and begin a real dialogue about disarmament. Regarding the intentions and motivations of the Soviet leadership, the bishops apparently assumed the best, while saying otherwise—a position which put them at odds with the Reagan administration on a matter of prudential judgment. Ironically enough, the bishops admitted to having no special expertise in "Kremlinology."

"The Challenge of Peace" noted the existence of two views of the Soviet Union: one held it to be expansionist and dangerous; the other saw it as heavily armed but essentially defensive. The bishops declined to judge which depiction was closer to the truth, but took care to reject any sort of "romantic idealism about Soviet intentions" (257), eschewing

> the invidious comparisons made at times . . . between our way of life, in which most basic human rights are at least recognized even if they are not always adequately supported, and those totalitarian and tyrannical regimes in which such rights are either denied or systematically suppressed. (251)

Despite this acknowledgment of the internal differences between the superpowers, the bishops subtly but repeatedly indicated that they believed the Soviet Union was primarily a defensive power. George Weigel has noted that the pastoral's exposition of the Soviet threat appeared only after a lengthy discussion of the dangers of modern weaponry; he cited this as evidence that the NCCB was engaged in the "relativizing of the totalitarian dimension" of the superpower rivalry.[34] This approach minimized the ideological dimension of the Cold War and distrusted Soviet and American intentions almost equally. As history has shown, the revolutions in Eastern Europe and the collapse of the Soviet Union knocked the supports out from under both these notions.

"The Challenge of Peace" could easily—but mistakenly—be portrayed as a victory for the traditional just-war teaching over the pacifism advocated by bishops such as Thomas Gumbleton. Certainly the pastoral letter elicited complaints from American Catholic pacifists unhappy that it both upheld the morality of nuclear deterrence and declined to endorse non-violence as an option for governments as well as individuals.[35] Notwithstanding these complaints, the drafters of "The Challenge of Peace" consistently opposed the build-up of American forces and U.S. military aid and intervention abroad. Indeed, in criticizing Reagan administration defense policies almost across the board, the bishops and their advisors arrived at essentially pacifist recommendations. NCCB and USCC statements on the conflicts in Central America make an interesting case study of this dynamic at work.

OUR OWN BACKYARD

The bishops' secretariat expanded its analysis of Third World issues to include a focus on regional conflicts, particularly those in Central America. Working with a handful of interested bishops, staff advisors developed their earlier concerns for human rights and the international redistribution of wealth into a new analytic which held that violence and armed conflict were primarily symptoms of the deeper problems of underdevelopment. In concrete terms, the source of these ills was the repression, by armed elites, of popular aspirations for economic and political power.[36] The USCC secretariat regarded the Reagan administration as almost immoral in its support for reactionary Central American elites and its seeming preference for military solutions that avoided the structural causes of regional conflicts.

Evenhanded Recommendations

The USCC secretariat began paying close attention to events in Central America in 1977. In 1981 the bishops had grown sufficiently concerned to issue their own statement, which argued that

> . . . the dominant challenge is the internal conditions of poverty and the denial of basic human rights which characterize many of these societies. These conditions, if unattended, become an invitation for intervention. . . . Any conception of the problems in Central America which is cast principally in terms of global security issues, military responses, arms transfers, and preservation of a situation which fails to promote meaningful participation of the majority of the population in their societies is, in our view, profoundly mistaken.[37]

The bishops and the USCC secretariat were fairly evenhanded in apportioning blame for regional conflicts, particularly in Nicaragua and El Salvador. They repeatedly denounced repression by the Salvadoran government, and readily admitted that the Marxist revolutionaries there committed their share of atrocities.[38] Nicaragua enjoyed only a brief reprieve from USCC criticism after the left-wing Sandinista rebels ousted dictator Anastasio Somoza in 1979. The USCC initially held high hopes for the Sandinistas. Archbishop of Washington, D.C., James Hickey, testifying before Congress on the secretariat's behalf, noted that the Sandinista revolution's "original goals" had been social justice, political pluralism, and a mixed economy.[39] In 1981, however, the bishops began to criticize the increasingly repressive Sandinista junta for causing the human rights situation in that country to deteriorate.[40] The bishops likewise criticized human rights abuses by the U.S.-supported *contras* who soon took up arms against the Sandinista regime.[41] USCC statements generously advocated humanitarian aid for all sides in the region's conflicts, urging humanitarian and economic assistance to the governments of El Salvador and Nicaragua despite their human rights records.[42] In 1985, Archbishop Hickey even accepted, on behalf of the USCC, President Reagan's request for $14 million in humanitarian aid to the *contras*.[43]

The only morally acceptable way out of the conflicts in Central America, according to the bishops and USCC officials, was dialogue in conjunction with a negotiated, multilateral cutoff of arms sales. The USCC repeatedly characterized the Reagan administration as preoccupied with military solutions, and they warned that a "victory" won by arms would only precipitate further bloodshed. This policy underwent a certain degree of modification as it became clearer that the Reagan administration had not simply invented out of whole cloth its claims that the rebels in El Salvador were taking arms and support from the Soviet bloc. In his 1981 testimony to Congress, Archbishop Hickey voiced the USCC's disbelief that U.S. military advisors would influence the security forces of El Salvador to respect human rights; in fact, he argued, the continuing involvement of the United States might just confirm in Latin minds the suspicion that Washington meant to dominate the region by force.[44] Two years later, the USCC reversed itself and grudgingly endorsed military assistance to El Salvador, as long as that aid was part of a larger diplomatic strategy.[45]

Bishops and USCC officials denounced U.S. military aid to the Nicaraguan *contra* rebels as soon as rumors of this covert program began to circulate in Washington. Archbishop Hickey told Congress that covert destabilization of another government undermined "the very values a democratic nation should support," and complained that American arms for the *contras* only worsened Nicaragua's human rights situation.[46] The NCCB later argued that the *contra* aid program was a disproportionate response to the dispute between the United States and Nicaragua; the bishops condemned what they saw as Washington's resort to armed struggle before all diplomatic avenues had been exhausted.[47] While the USCC later noted the national election that swept the Sandinistas from power in 1990, the bishops drew no connection between the military pressure created by the *contras* and the Sandinista's final acquiescence in a democratic solution.[48]

The bishops' analyses of the region's troubles always assumed that the United States and the Soviet Union were equally to blame. In 1987, the bishops contended that both superpowers vied with one another "in adding fuel to the flames of an already burning house." "We should not use Central American lives as pawns in a superpower struggle."[49] The USCC's Fr. Hehir wanted Washington to dissuade the Soviet Union and Cuba from arming the Sandinista regime and the Marxist rebels in El Salvador, but neither he nor other Church representatives explained how the halting of American deliveries of military aid would win Soviet and Cuban cooperation.[50]

Central American Exasperation

The inclination of the American Catholic hierarchy to blame both Marxists and democrats (or at least America's allies) for the troubles of the region occasionally exasperated the episcopacy of Central America, whose painful experiences at the hands of various tyrants had encouraged a more appreciative view of American diplomacy.

The American bishops at first advertised their rejection of military aid to El Salvador as reflecting the wishes of the Salvadoran church, particularly those of the martyred Archbishop Oscar Romero (whom USCC staffer Thomas Quigley curiously hailed as a brilliant popular leader like Pope John XXIII or Mao Tse-Tung).[51] The bishops and their secretariat—who usually coordinated USCC foreign policy statements with the bishops of the country in question—seemed more embarrassed than enlightened when representatives of the Salvadoran bishops' conference visited Washington in late 1981 to ask their American brothers to support U.S. military aid to their nation.[52] Several years later, Nicaragua's bishops were annoyed by what they regarded as insensitivity. For example, a spokesman for Nicaraguan Archbishop Obando y Bravo protested the conduct of Thomas Quigley to General Secretary Daniel Hoye in 1984. (Quigley had made statements to the Sandinista-controlled media that, when aired, seemed critical of the Nicaraguan bishops.)[53] Bishop Joseph Sullivan of Brooklyn also got an earful when he met with a group of Central American bishops in 1987. They told him—apparently to his surprise —that the Sandinistas were totalitarians and that the NCCB should pay more attention to the region's bishops and less to North American activist clerical and religious groups that claimed to be bringing social justice to the region.[54]

"Economic Justice for All"

The bishops' counteroffensive against President Reagan's policies and ideas had begun within weeks of his election in November 1980. The annual gathering of the bishops in Washington, D.C., that year authorized the drafting of "The Challenge of Peace" and approved another pastoral letter: a lengthy theoretical analysis of communism. As the committee considered the final draft of this latter document, however, several bishops worried aloud about the "damage" such a statement might do to the public image of the Church. Bishop William Weigand of Salt Lake City warned that the statement would be badly received, especially in Central America, unless the NCCB promised "a future document on the evils and aberrations of capitalism." Peter Rosazza, an auxiliary bishop in Hartford, Conn., likewise urged that the Marxism letter be amended to address capitalism's successes and injustices as well.[55] Although Bishop Rosazza's request came too late to affect the pastoral letter on Marxism, his and similar concerns persuaded the bishops to authorize a sequel study which was destined to become the NCCB's second major social statement of the decade: the pastoral letter "Economic Justice for All."

The bishops' unease over domestic policy grew into deep anxiety as the drafting committee of the letter on capitalism, headed by Archbishop Rembert Weakland of Milwaukee, began work in 1981. The federal budget cuts proposed by the Reagan administration particularly alarmed USCC staff and spurred the bishops' advisors to resist such initiatives with every measure at their disposal.[56] The USCC's 1981 Labor Day statement put the struggle in perspective:

> Do we want a government that is a protector and promoter of human dignity and human rights. . . . Or do we want a government that is a protector of the wealthy and a producer of greater inequality — a government of the rich, by the rich and for the rich?[57]

The secretariat's analysis of the Reagan program was harsh and showed little originality; USCC spokesmen told Congress that the administration's plans to cut or trim the growth of various social programs would hurt the poor because local programs and private charity were stretched to the limit by the demand for services. Bishops and staffers carried the same text to Capitol Hill again and again, varying their illustrative anecdotes to suit whichever social program was under discussion.[58]

Weakland's committee shared these concerns and acted on them by unilaterally reinterpreting its mandate from writing a letter on capitalism in general to writing a letter on the American economy. The committee worked slowly, holding many hearings with experts and ethicists and taking far longer than Archbishop Bernardin's committee had in producing "The Challenge of Peace." After three years, Weakland explained to the NCCB at its November 1983 meeting that his committee had changed the focus of its research. From the outset, his panel had foreseen that a theoretical examination of capitalism would be difficult, given the various forms of capitalism and its lack of a "coherent philosophical worldview." Instead, Weakland and his colleagues decided instead to study the American economy, especially its performance in the areas of jobs, poverty, trade, and planning.[59] Archbishop Weakland hinted in 1985 that the committee's true focus was much broader. Conceding that the U.S. economy performed well in relative terms, he worried that its healthy statistics obscured less savory aspects of American life. The American economic system was perhaps the worst in the developed world at distributing the wealth it created.[60] "It is fair enough to judge an economic system by economic standards," he wrote in another context, "but that is not a sufficient criterion for judging a *society*" (Weakland's emphasis).[61]

Weakland implied his committee would produce a broad critique of American institutions, drawing together the NCCB's and USCC's various analyses of policies and ideas. The committee's first draft was submitted to the bishops and the public in November 1984, a second in 1985, and a third, which the bishops approved, in November 1986. The finished product reflected the changing focus of Weakland's drafting committee, and it lengthily expounded the criticism of American economic performance that Weakland had hinted at in 1985.

Taking the Option Further

The central assumption of "Economic Justice for All" was the notion that the ostensibly rational functioning of the free market— the basis of the American economy—produced great wealth, but also left many people powerless:

> The concentration of privilege that exists today results far more from institutional relationships that distribute power and wealth inequitably than from differences in talent or lack of desire to work. These institutional patterns must be examined and revised if we are to meet the demands of basic justice. (76)

"Economic Justice for All" argued that Catholics, government, and society in general were obligated by Scripture to remedy this situation, calling this obligation the "preferential option for the poor." American Catholic intellectuals had borrowed this phrase from the 1979 conference of Latin American bishops at Puebla, Mexico, which had spoken of "preferential options" for the poor and for youth in the Church's evangelizing activity.[62] NCCB and USCC spokesmen discreetly omitted the option for young people and removed the "option for the poor" from its evangelical context when they used the phrase as a call for social justice.[63] This approach diverged somewhat from the papal interpretation of the Puebla message.

Roman documents in the 1980s tried to steer Catholics back toward the original, broader meaning of the option for the poor.[64] John Paul II himself treated the issue as part of his effort to narrow the gap between the virtues of justice and charity while preserving the distinctiveness of each. His encyclical letter *Sollicitudo Rei Socialis* (*On Social Concern*, issued in late 1987, a little over a year after "Economic Justice for All") identified the virtue of "solidarity," defining it as a "firm and persevering determination to commit oneself to the common good" (38).[65] Solidarity should be practiced by all persons and social groups, as well as by nations on a global scale. This virtue, said John Paul, is closely related to the "option" for the poor that is part of Christian charity. Although this preference for the poor is distinctly Christian, John Paul urged national leaders to bear in mind the immensity of modern poverty and the "special form of poverty which consists in being deprived of fundamental human rights, in particular the right to religious freedom and also the right to economic initiative" (42).

Notwithstanding Vatican misgivings about an expansive use of the concept of the option for the poor, Archbishop Weakland took the option further still, deriving from it a characteristic of justice itself that dovetailed with the new definition of social justice that the late Bishop Rausch in the 1970s had given the USCC.[66] His primary target was not poverty but *inequality*. In *America,* Weakland wrote that the option for the poor was meant to challenge all Americans to reduce social inequality by allowing everyone to participate in society.[67] Speaking at a symposium a few months later, Weakland defined what he meant by participation. Because man is a social animal, injustice could be defined as the exclusion, or marginalization, of a person or group from the moral community of the human race. Justice, on the other hand, meant "the establishment of minimum levels of participation for all persons." He found this implied in Scripture: "the biblical concept of justice suggests strongly that the justice of a community is measured by how it treats the powerless in society."[68]

Despite the argument of "Economic Justice for All," the Old and New Testaments provide scant warrant for the idea that the poor as such have some pre-eminent claim on government policies and resources. Both Scripture and papal encyclicals have consistently urged statesmen and believers to remember society's weakest members, but this is not quite the same injunction delivered by Archbishop Weakland. If the American formulation of the "option for the poor" arose from neither Scripture nor Church documents, from whence did it come? As with many other things, it actually came from Harvard; the option for the poor in "Economic Justice for All" is really Harvard philosopher John Rawls's "difference principle" pronounced with a Spanish accent. Rawls declares that "the social order is not to establish and secure the more attractive prospects of those better off unless doing so is to the advantage of those less fortunate"; in other words, inequality can only be tolerated if it works to the advantage of society's bottom rung.[69]

Subsidiarity Redefined

The finished pastoral letter reflected the bishops' long-standing concern with a better distribution of the fruits of the American economy, but like many other USCC statements in the 1980s, it looked to one of society's least participatory structures—the state— to equalize access to the benefits of modern society. Although the bishops faintly echoed the NCWC in their hope for cooperative planning by all economic sectors, they wanted government to move from its alleged role as social referee to a commitment to reducing social inequality. "Economic Justice for All" endorsed the consolidation of decision-making power for every part of the economy. It advocated, among other things, national standards for welfare benefits, a higher minimum wage, increased public sector employment, gender pay equity, affirmative action, government subsidies for private job formation and training, broader crop-production control programs, and more steeply progressive taxes on incomes and farm acreage. Subsequent USCC statements on a variety of domestic problems continued this stress on federal remedies.[70]

The bishops' preference for governmental action reflected the logic of their option for the poor as well as their reliance on liberal commentators and analyses. Government's new obligation to "assist and empower" society's weakest members allowed the bishops to advocate a great variety of "social" policies and programs not directly intended to ameliorate poverty (92, 123). The bishops justified this preference for government action by citing studies by liberal groups such as the Childrens' Defense Fund, the National Urban League, and the Council on Economic Priorities. The writings of Daniel Patrick Moynihan, Richard Barnet, Gar Alperovitz, and other liberal and progressive commentators also received respectful mention in "Economic Justice for All." On the other hand, the pastoral cited only a handful of politically conservative thinkers. University of Chicago economist Milton Friedman's negative-income-tax scheme received a mild endorsement, as did the idea of creating "enterprise zones" to redevelop blighted inner cities. By and large, however, works containing conservative arguments were either ignored or, like Charles Murray's controversial book, *Losing Ground,* buried in footnotes.[71]

Critics Respond

Critics had rapped the Weakland committee for its political bias years before approval of the pastoral's final draft in 1986. Although conservative Catholics formed the best orchestrated opposition, they were not the letter's only opponents. After reviewing the pastoral's first public draft, Chicago priest and sociologist Andrew Greeley accused the bishops of neglecting the Church's traditional social teaching and accepting the centralization of economic power wrought by both socialism and modern capitalism. "I think the basic failure of the pastoral," said Greeley, "is that neither the bishops nor their staff are aware of the theory of the organic society."[72]

Conservative Catholic laymen, led by Michael Novak, devised a rather different critique of the bishops' work. Novak's group (which included former Reagan administration cabinet secretaries William Simon and Alexander Haig along with academics such as James Q. Wilson and public figures like J. Peter Grace and Clare Booth Luce) held its own hearings with expert witnesses and presented its conclusions in a lengthy alternative statement. Where Archbishop Weakland had focused on the American economy's treatment of the poor, Novak and his colleagues emphasized the proven performance of the American economy in lifting people from poverty. The Novak committee statement, titled "Toward the Future," was released a few days before the initial draft of "Economic Justice for All." It claimed to be based on traditional Catholic social teaching, and Novak and his collaborators refrained from proposing many concrete programs or initiatives.[73]

Novak's stress on subsidiarity struck the Weakland committee and its advisers as warmed-over Social Darwinism; they simply could not understand how ostensibly well-meaning Catholics could believe such arguments. One of the Weakland committee advisors, David Hollenbach, S.J., debated Novak while the bishops put the finishing touches on "Economic Justice for All." Interestingly enough, the Novak-Hollenbach dispute was more over conclusions than principles. Both men were critics of papal social teachings, but they disagreed over what status to assign to "economic rights."[74]

Novak argued that the first responsibility for securing economic rights belonged with individuals and that social disregard of this truth opened the door to statism. He charged Hollenbach and, by implication, the NCCB, with forgetting this truth.[75] Hollenbach admitted that individuals bore a great responsibility for their welfare, but argued that the principle of subsidiarity (as taught by Leo XIII) implied that the state is duty-bound to intervene when persons and groups can no longer provide for their own welfare. He highlighted what he perceived as a contradiction in Novak's argument: Novak had admitted that the state should intervene in "emergencies" despite his own stress on non-intervention.[76] But Hollenbach either missed or ignored one of Novak's key points, remaining silent on what the principle of subsidiarity recommends in cases where the state itself fails to deliver the goods it has promised when it intervenes in hitherto private spheres of activity.

Archbishop Weakland seemed to take public criticism of the pastoral letter personally and was still bothered by it years later. He denounced the charge that the economic pastoral was endorsing what wags called "the preferential option for the state." Speaking at Georgetown University in 1985, he defended the bishops' willingness to insist that government guarantee the provision of economic necessities. He also defended the interventionist state, because charity "provides often only a more degrading help that ultimately causes more deeply seated problems."[77] Later, Weakland publicly worried that neoconservative "advocates of free enterprise in its Enlightenment form" would "seduce" the American Church; he also told an interviewer that Novak and Simon—who discussed the pastoral with him in 1984—had reminded him of "high-ranking Mafia leaders."[78]

Trickle-Down Morality

"Economic Justice for All" reflected the bishops' new-found hesitancy to link social progress to "personal" morality, although its statements in this field gained little attention in comparison with the NCCB's subsequent public musings on abortion and AIDS. The bishops recognized that some poor people engaged in destructive behavior, but they blamed this on society as a whole—or the economic system—and rejected "actions, words, or attitudes that stigmatize the poor." "Economic Justice for All" had no patience with notions such as "the poor are poor by choice or through laziness, that anyone can escape poverty by hard work, [or] that welfare programs make it easier for people to avoid work" (194). The pastoral suggested that problems which disproportionately affect the poor, such as divorce and illegitimacy, were spread by "false values" trickling down from society's upper classes:

> The constant seeking for self-gratification and the exaggerated individualism of our age, spurred on by false values often seen in advertising and on television, contribute to the lack of firm commitment in marriage and to destructive notions of responsibility and personal growth. (345)

This was not an admission that lethargy or immorality can cause poverty, but rather a depiction of the poor as passively molded by social mores. The possibility that some poor people could have become self-destructive on their own, or that a poorly ordered soul could lead even a wealthy individual to vice, was not discussed.

Archbishop Weakland seemed to suggest that the pastoral letter's "biblical" approach to social justice fit poorly with the traditional Catholic emphasis on the conversion of hearts. Social attitudes and moral conduct, he readily admitted, had to be changed, but he complained that critics of the bishops who wanted to "restrict the kingdom [of God] to the hearts of people" failed to show "how such a change then affects peoples' conduct or especially how such a conversion should lead to the construction of a just society."[79]

THE "CONSISTENT ETHIC OF LIFE"

The bishops' third major concept of the 1980s was the "consistent ethic of life." Archbishop Weakland's suggestion that vice is a symptom (and not a cause) of evil structures and social inequality represented the intellectual core of the "consistent ethic of life"—Joseph Cardinal Bernardin's attempt to codify the internal logic of the new social teaching of the American Catholic Church.

As Timothy A. Byrnes has noted, political candidates in the 1970s began to co-opt parts of the Catholic agenda while ignoring others.[80] Cardinal Bernardin had been pondering this problem since the nasty dispute within the bishops' secretariat over his "endorsement" of President Ford in the 1976 election. He was stung by the caricature of the Church as having a "one-issue" political program (i.e., a single-minded focus on abortion), and he worried that the pro-life movement might be taken over by its right wing unless Catholics defended human dignity in all its facets. Bernardin also hoped to make the abortion issue more appealing to those Catholic activists in welfare advocacy and the peace movement who ordinarily shunned the pro-life cause.[81]

After finishing work on "The Challenge of Peace," Cardinal Bernardin enlisted the bishops' leading theoretician, Father J. Bryan Hehir, to help him formulate a new way of linking the "life issues" stressed in Catholic social teaching.[82] Bernardin, by now the newly named chairman of the bishops' Committee for Pro-Life Activities, offered his new synthesis in a speech at Fordham University in December 1983. Calling for a "consistent ethic of life," he challenged critics—especially politically conservative Catholics—to support a public ethic based on the right to life and human dignity. Abortion, he said, is only one of many threats to life and human dignity in the modern world. Such an ethic should be presented in civil and non-religious terms in order to maximize its influence on America's pluralist culture.[83] The bishops' conference as a whole officially adopted the phrasing and concept of the consistent ethic of life in revising its comprehensive "Pastoral Plan for Pro-Life Activities" in November 1985.[84]

The Seamless Garment

This "seamless garment" had been presented before, although not quite in the same cut. It reiterated several themes that had appeared in NCCB and USCC statements since the 1970s. Cardinal Bernardin perceived the primary danger to life in "the careening development of technology," which was creating "a qualitatively new range of moral problems." He theorized that modern technology and economic systems had created structures which held masses of people in powerlessness, and which in turn produced despair and vice. Bernardin also implied that the most effective counter to the moral evils denounced by traditional Catholic morality was to attack the structures that produced poverty and desperation.[85]

Most bishops shared Cardinal Bernardin's belief that widespread acceptance of abortion was primarily a symptom of the structural and economic failures of modern life. This inclination occasionally caused tension between the bishops' conference and pro-lifers in the 1980s —a tension which undermined the stated goal of the consistent ethic: to strengthen the pro-life movement by broadening it. In his Fordham speech, Cardinal Bernardin seemed to imply that many of the people who opposed abortion wanted to have it "both ways": to support the right to life while neglecting "the specific political and economic positions" that upheld the quality of life.[86] Although Bernardin amended these remarks in subsequent statements to avoid giving offense to pro-lifers, other leaders of the bishops' conference publicly complained about the political conservatism of the pro-life movement.[87] Archbishop Weakland later suggested that Catholic pro-lifers needed "a laxative. And a hug."[88]

THE NEW ORTHODOXY

During the 1980s, the leaders of the NCCB and the USCC consciously resolved to play a "prophetic" role in confronting the errors of the Reagan administration. Attacking President Reagan's nuclear deployments as reckless and morally bankrupt, they implied there was no real moral difference between the strategies of the Reagan administration and those of the Soviet Politburo. The bishops and their advisors collectively treated Reagan's economic policies—and public supporters of these policies—as beyond the pale of reasoned debate, suggesting that many American Catholics who did not agree with the conclusions of "Economic Justice for All" were not quite orthodox.

In response to the Reagan presidency, the NCCB and USCC demonstrated that their consistent ethic of life—particularly in its stress on the quality of life—was an unwieldy analytic tool which allowed its users to cloak policy preferences as scripturally based moral judgments. The NCCB diligently attacked as a threat to life every incremental policy that "increased" the risk of nuclear war, while muting their teaching on promiscuity and contraception, both of which have been recognized by the Church as precursors to a greater societal acceptance of abortion. The USCC and NCCB would soon endorse statements which argued, with only a slight simplification, that the gospel tradition of respect for human life could tolerate the use of condoms to prevent AIDS, but not the deployment of defensive systems to protect American lives from nuclear missiles. Even when the bishops cited traditional, natural law principles, they did not apply them coherently. To put it bluntly, the consistent ethic of life, so trumpeted by the NCCB and USCC, was not applied consistently, and far from fulfilling its expectations, it was not the glue to hold together what seemed at times a splintering Church.

8

The Status Quo

In recent years the bishops have applied the just war criteria, the option for the poor, and the consistent ethic of life to a host of issues and problems, from immigration reform and poverty programs to U.S. military peacekeeping missions. NCCB and USCC publications are read by chanceries and seminaries across Catholic America; officials and volunteers in diocesan and parish "justice and peace" offices follow the bishops' official pronouncements, using the concepts and phrasing of these statements as guidelines for state and local Catholic activism. Indeed, the social witness of the Catholic Church in America has never been more consistent across hierarchical, institutional, and geographic boundaries. Today what is said and written in Catholic offices in Washington, D.C., echoes to every corner of America.

A PACIFIST STANCE

The course of world events since the late 1980s kept the bishops and their advisors busy applying the principles enumerated in "The Challenge of Peace." The applications reveal a consistent pattern. On the one hand, the bishops have specifically criticized plans to modernize U.S. conventional and nuclear forces. On the other, statements by the NCCB and USCC, while employing just-war criteria, have taken pains to avoid either condemning or endorsing the deployment of American troops in combat. The traditional just-war teaching has effectively been used to defend a consistently pacifist orientation.

Arms Control

The bishops have also reiterated the ascription in "The Challenge of Peace" of nearly equal blame to the U.S. and the former USSR for the excesses of the arms race. In a 1988 review of "The Challenge of Peace" and the world situation, a new ad hoc committee of bishops —once again led by Cardinal Bernardin—portrayed the Reagan administration and the Soviet regime as equally narrow and reactive:

> When "The Challenge of Peace" was written in the early 1980s, there was virtually no serious discussion between the superpowers, there were no prospects for serious arms control and the defense expenditures of both the United States and the Soviet Union were rising sharply.[1]

Cardinal Bernardin's committee hailed bilateral steps to "renew" the arms control process as "the *beginning* of responsible statesmanship" (emphasis added), and chastised both sides for the earlier impasse; each superpower had supposedly made unreciprocated gestures of restraint, and each had developed weapons contrary to the spirit of "The Challenge of Peace." The bishops neglected to mention that the most troublesome Soviet systems were deployed years before the United States responded with new missiles such as the MX, and they criticized the Reagan administration for wanting to end American compliance with the SALT I and Anti-Ballistic Missile (ABM) treaties. Bernardin's committee ignored the contention of the White House that previous Soviet treaty violations had made such steps necessary.[2]

A salient feature of the NCCB review—impossible to ignore in view of the astonishing events which concluded the 1980s—was its inability to entertain anything other than its own approved "means" toward peace. The NCCB and USCC never credited the possibility that the expansion of America's qualitative military and economic power, coupled with Washington's insistence on meaningful arms reductions, might convince Moscow of the futility of the Cold War. In short, the bishops' pronouncements on arms control in the 1980s suggested that the United States should honor its obligations to the letter and pursue new treaties regardless of Soviet actions and deployments. This was the only morally licit way to convince the Soviets to change their goals and behavior according to the NCCB and USCC.

The bishops deployed this logic in opposing the Reagan administration's ambitious plans for the Strategic Defense Initiative (SDI). While conceding the moral appeal of defending civilians (as opposed to MAD, the strategy of "mutually assured destruction"), and conceding that SDI should continue as a research program, Cardinal Bernardin's 1988 review of deterrence worried that an actual strategic defense system would destabilize the superpower relationship. "The more compelling moral case," concluded the study, "presently rests with those who specify the likely risks of an aggressive SDI program at this time." These risks were three: such a program could impede arms control, it could be used offensively, and it might prompt Moscow to create a destabilizing "pre-emptive" nuclear strategy. These uncertainties seemed to increase the risk that nuclear weapons might one day be used. For this reason, along with the expense of deploying strategic defenses, the bishops judged that "proposals to press deployment of SDI do not measure up to the moral criteria outlined in this report."[3] Strategic defense, for Cardinal Bernardin, was more a moral challenge than a prudential dilemma, and thus it could not be left to the discretion of the Reagan White House.

A Sea Change

The bishops applauded the democratic revolutions of 1989 in Eastern Europe and the demise of the Soviet Union in 1991. In 1990 the USCC Administrative Board expressed thankfulness and even awe: "we are witnesses to a time of special grace. We see signs of a deeper movement of the Spirit; a reassertion of the transcendent, of a deeper understanding of the full meaning of what it is to be human."[4] The board subsequently called on the West to help speed the transition to market economies and democracy in the former communist states.[5] Curiously, however, the USCC never analyzed at length what caused the break-up of the Soviet empire. The "more open political climate ushered in by [Soviet] President Mikhail Gorbachev's policies" received major credit in the board's 1990 statement, which also noted, in passing, that Pope John Paul II had worked strenuously for change in the East.[6] American (or Western) policies and actions were not mentioned.

The bishops continued through the late 1980s to comment on

regional conflicts, but with less overt criticism of U.S. diplomacy once Ronald Reagan finished his final term as president. For instance, the bishops' analysis of American policy toward Israel paralleled its critique of U.S. relations with El Salvador in that it portrayed both nations as American clients with records of human rights violations. The bishops seemed more lenient toward Israel, however, perhaps because it was more democratic than El Salvador, and because the bishops took more seriously the external threat to Israel's security. The NCCB regarded Israel's human rights problems as stemming from the thorny but comparatively limited dispute over Palestinian self-determination. Nonetheless, the NCCB's only major statement on the Arab-Israeli conflict laid roughly equal blame on both sides, portraying each as almost passive victims of anonymous violence, and calling on both to recognize the rights of the other, since both Jews and Palestinians deserved their own homelands.[7]

Shortly before the 1991 Persian Gulf War, NCCB President Daniel Pilarczyk, Archbishop of Cincinnati, politely warned President George Bush that force could not substitute for the "frustrating work of searching for political solutions to the deep-seated problems in the Middle East which have contributed to this current crisis." Offensive military action "could well violate" just-war criteria, especially the principles of proportionality and "last resort." Archbishop Pilarczyk condemned Iraqi aggression against Kuwait, and allowed that U.S. and allied troop deployments might strengthen American diplomatic efforts to resolve the situation. Nevertheless, the archbishop seemed not to have considered the possibility that Iraqi strongman Saddam Hussein might interpret a unilateral Western disavowal of offensive action as a sign of weakness and as proof that international pressure on Iraq would eventually subside.[8]

The Persian Gulf War did, however, occasion some second thoughts among the bishops about their critical stance toward American foreign policy. At a conference on Catholic social teaching in Washington, D.C.,—which convened as the American-led ground offensive drove the Iraqi army out of Kuwait in February 1991— Cardinal Bernardin stated that, while he had opposed the war and had not endorsed the U.S. led counter-offensive, the U.S. and its coalition partners had essentially fulfilled just-war tests of moral legitimacy.[9] Bernardin's thoughts on the war indicated that opinion on the use of force among the bishops and the USCC had begun to shift toward greater acceptance of American military intervention abroad.

Recent USCC statements on China, post-war Iraq, the former Soviet Union, and the Balkan conflict have demanded respect for human rights and democracy. The bishops consistently urged Washington to use diplomatic and economic persuasion—in concert with the United Nations—to defuse conflicts and promote reform.[10] Operation Restore Hope, the deployment of U.S. troops to halt starvation in the African nation of Somalia in late 1992, received a cautious USCC endorsement.[11] Concerning Haiti, the American bishops noted the Haitian hierarchy's virulent opposition to a restoration of ousted President Jean-Bertrand Aristide (a former priest whose followers had publicly humiliated the papal nuncio).[12] The USCC limited itself to denouncing Haiti's military junta and criticizing the harshness of the international economic embargo against that nation; the bishops did not endorse U.S. military intervention.[13]

The USCC's fine line between pacifism and the strictest possible application of just war criteria has sometimes blurred toward meaninglessness. For instance, USCC spokesmen, appalled by the savagery of the conflict in the former Yugoslavia, and following the lead of Pope John Paul II, came perhaps even closer than they had in the Persian Gulf War to endorsing the use of force. In one statement, Archbishop John Roach, chairman of the USCC Committee on International Policy, wrote Secretary of State Warren Christopher, urging the deployment of American peacekeeping troops to help end the bloodshed in Bosnia. When publicly asked whether he had advised the Clinton administration to commit U.S. forces to combat, Roach hastily insisted he had not.[14] The USCC hinted that the Bosnian case had met just-war criteria for the use of force, but acknowledged that it might still be unwise to commit American lives to the conflict. This deference to the prudential judgment of the Clinton administration represented a change from the USCC's insistence, throughout the 1980s, on the relative moral superiority of the American hierarchy's judgments on foreign affairs.

Rich and Poor

The bishops have also maintained their advocacy of American aid to developing nations to redress unbalanced international development. NCCB and USCC statements have continued to blame Western "overconsumption" for underdevelopment—as well as for global environmental degradation—and to advocate the state-centered remedies tried in the 1970s.[15] "The temptation to withdraw, to build new walls and even to lash out against foreigners is great," warned the USCC's Committee on International Policy in 1992. Nevertheless, American Catholics should "renew their commitment to the good of the whole human family."[16]

John Paul II's social encyclicals have endorsed this sentiment but advocated a different means toward its attainment, exhorting both rich and poor nations to foster the full development of all persons by promoting cultural and religious attainments alongside material prosperity. *Sollicitudo Rei Socialis* criticized the international trading system and the Cold War for perpetuating the gap between rich and poor (16, 20). Nevertheless, the encyclical also blamed the recipient nations for allowing selfish elites to impede development by oppressing other social groups and suppressing private initiative (44). John Paul's subsequent social encyclical *Centesimus Annus* restated this analysis:

> Stronger nations must offer weaker ones opportunities for taking their place in international life, and the latter must learn how to use these opportunities by making the necessary efforts and sacrifices and by ensuring political and economic stability, the certainty of better prospects for the future, the improvement of workers' skills, and the training of competent business leaders who are conscious of their responsibilities (35).[17]

VIRTUE AND VICE

Joseph Cardinal Bernardin's consistent ethic of life released a flood of scholarly and partisan commentary during the 1980s. The cardinal's proposal resonated with many Catholics, although it did not, as he had hoped it would, enlist substantially new Catholic resources in the fight against abortion. While statements by the NCCB and USCC on abortion have repeatedly invoked the consistent ethic of life, the bishops have not applied the consistent ethic to other issues of sexual morality, particularly homosexuality and contraception.

In December 1987, the USCC's Administrative Board issued a

statement on the Acquired Immune Deficiency Syndrome (AIDS) which, like the NCCB's consistent ethic of life, examined the structural (as opposed to the personal or ideological) sources of vice:

> When people think their lives are devoid of meaning or when they find themselves in oppressive and despair-inducing poverty, they may turn to drugs or reach out for short-term physical intimacy in a mindless effort to escape the harsh conditions in which they live.

The board affirmed Church teachings that sex is licit only within marriage, and that the best check to the spread of disease is an authentic understanding of sexuality. Nevertheless, the Administrative Board failed to address the causes of what—besides poverty—was engendering despair and meaninglessness. The document undermined its reiteration of Church teaching on marriage, moreover, by suggesting that Catholic health counselors could advise unmarried individuals who would not abstain from sex to use condoms to prevent or slow the spread of AIDS. To justify this curious position, the Administrative Board argued from the principle of "toleration": That the Catholic moral tradition permits a certain toleration of a lesser moral evil in order to prevent a greater evil. (This echoed Fr. Hehir's stance a decade earlier, which defended the distribution of contraceptives in the Third World.)[18] The Vatican—and even some defenders of the board's AIDS statement—subsequently criticized the board's use of the principle of toleration. Joseph Cardinal Ratzinger, prefect for the Congregation of the Doctrine of the Faith, implied that the Administrative Board's statement had gone beyond mere toleration of moral evil to actually condoning the facilitation of immorality.[19]

The ensuing controversy over the AIDS statement prompted rumors that the bishops would retract the document. Although the rumors soon died down, Archbishop Francis T. Hurley of Anchorage publicly faulted the USCC Administrative Board for not coordinating the statement with all the bishops, saying that the board should have known that reporters would seize on whatever was controversial in the statement and portray it as the latest declaration by the American hierarchy.[20] At the bishops' semi-annual retreat in June 1988, Joseph Cardinal Bernardin extinguished any lingering possibility that the NCCB might retract the AIDS document. Speaking to the assembled bishops, and knowing that some wanted to repudiate the AIDS statement, Bernardin insisted that retraction would be "disastrous," leading people to believe that "the entire Administrative Board was in serious error." The AIDS statement had to stand as it was, he persuasively insisted, but the bishops could still write a new statement that would complement and clarify it.[21]

Almost two years later, the bishops approved a sequel statement on AIDS, which neither repudiated nor superseded the earlier document by the USCC Administrative Board, according to Archbishop Roger Mahony of Los Angeles (who chaired the drafting committee for the new statement).[22] The NCCB's sequel statement more strongly attacked the immediate circumstances of vice, especially drug abuse. The bishops now advocated expanded government and private educational efforts, counseling, treatment, and interdiction to halt the spread of drug abuse and salvage the lives it blighted. The NCCB, however, declined to treat homosexuality in the same manner in its statement, noting instead that AIDS had devastated "the homosexual community." The bishops repeated earlier calls for "a special degree of pastoral understanding and care" that would urge homosexuals to form "chaste, stable relationships."[23]

Revisiting Abortion

In late 1989, New York's John Cardinal O'Connor succeeded Cardinal Bernardin as chairman of the Committee for Pro-Life Activities, an appointment that suggested the NCCB might once again make abortion its top public policy issue, as it had during the mid-1970s. That November the bishops lauded the recent Supreme Court decision in *Webster* v. *Reproductive Health Services,* which had allowed greater state regulation of abortion. In a brief but widely publicized statement, the bishops called abortion "the fundamental human rights issue for all men and women of good will."[24]

Some had hoped that the NCCB might take a harder line against Catholic politicians who voted in favor of liberalizing access to abortion. But this was never likely. NCCB leaders feared that ecclesial sanctions on public figures would backfire; indeed, only a handful of individual prelates imposed any such penalties on members of their flock.[25] The NCCB offered no new guidance to individual bishops dealing with this "overriding concern"; instead, the conference "Pastoral Plan for Pro-Life Activities," a decade-old program of education and activism updated in 1985 with a mention of the "consistent ethic of life," was thought sufficient.[26] In early 1990, the NCCB launched a new program of anti-abortion activities and educational publicity, but its several million dollars-worth of surveys and advertisements had no decisive effect on the correlation of political forces on the issue. One lasting achievement of the 1990 effort was the hiring of a young, articulate attorney, Helen Alvaré, as NCCB pro-life spokesperson: an effective counterpoint to the feminist domination of the abortion debate in the national media.

Since the reaffirmation of *Roe* v. *Wade* by the Supreme Court in its 1992 decision in *Planned Parenthood* v. *Casey,* the bishops and their secretariat have remained largely on the defensive, opposing congressional and executive branch efforts to make abortions more common. Helen Alvaré has conceded that the *Casey* decision prompted a reevaluation of strategy; the bishops would now work harder to publicize alternatives to abortion for women in "crisis" pregnancies.[27] Statements by NCCB leaders and committees still blast abortion and the rationalizations used to defend it.[28]

Some in the USCC secretariat now seem to regard the abortion fight as unwinnable and, indeed, an obstacle to common action on other problems. General Secretary Robert Lynch, for example, lent his name and the prestige of the USCC to a 1993 statement, "The Common Good: Old Idea, New Urgency," issued in conjunction with the National Council of Churches and the Synagogue Council of America. USCC officials involved in the drafting of "The Common Good" easily persuaded their co-authors to cite the "option for the poor" in the joint statement, but they also agreed to leave out all mention of abortion in the document's enumeration of the problems troubling American life.[29] On the whole, the bishops and their advisors appear reluctant to fight the abortion battle unless forced to do so in the context of some other issue, such as health care reform.

LIVING CONSISTENTLY

In late 1990, the bishops' conference approved a summary of Catholic social teaching in commemoration of the hundredth anniversary of

Pope Leo XIII's *Rerum Novarum*. The document, entitled *"Rerum Novarum:* A Century of Social Teaching: A Common Heritage, A Continuing Challenge," once again put the "option for the poor" at the center of conference teaching on domestic economic issues.[30] Unfortunately, "the poor" were not defined with any precision, nor was it explained how material poverty itself conferred a privileged claim on society's conscience or on state resources. The bishops' commemoration of *Rerum Novarum* mentioned the principle of subsidiarity only in a footnote, but took care to reiterate earlier suggestions that redistribution of wealth was the best means of helping the unfortunate.

Hints of a different approach to poverty did emerge in the NCCB pastoral letter "Putting Children and Families First" (1991). The pastoral decried the polarization of the debate over morality and progress, limply conceding a measure of truth to both liberals and conservatives. "The undeniable fact is that our children's future is shaped *both* by the values of their parents and the policies of our nation" (emphasis added). Unfortunately, the pastoral letter offered sympathetic suggestions but no central message apart from an anodyne plea for society to care for America's children. Here again, the "biblical" approach to social justice proved limited and inconsistent. "Putting Children and Families First" cited Church experience in social activism but offered little reason to believe that the insights of the Church were any deeper than those of non-Catholic lobbies and activists. The bishops invoked various scriptural passages to illustrate that children are a gift from God to the world as a sign of His goodness, and a call to familial and social duties; but the pastoral letter offered no reasons why anyone should prefer the Church's insight into Scripture as an entry-point for thinking through family policy.[31]

One critique of this pastoral letter noted that the bishops had conflated the plight of families that were poor for reasons beyond their control (the proverbial "widows and orphans") with those families impoverished because of parental immorality or selfishness.[32] While not completely fair to the pastoral, this critique hit close to the truth in one respect. The bishops had declined to choose sides in the policy debate between liberal and conservative theories of poverty. Instead, they tried to split the difference between the two contending theories. Although the pastoral decried immorality and the social changes abetting it (such as permissive divorce laws), the NCCB's refusal to adjudicate the theoretical debate between liberals and conservatives suggested that the bishops had not really pondered the intellectual and ideological errors that had done so much to create the culture of poverty.[33]

Clinton and Health Care

During the 1992 presidential campaign, the USCC closely tracked the growing national debate over health care reform. Bill Clinton's victory in November 1992 soon placed health care near the top of the nation's domestic agenda, raising the possibility that some form of national health insurance—advocated by the bishops for more than four decades—might soon become a reality. But there was a catch. The Clinton administration was determined to include abortion as a mandated "service" in the new health care system. The bishops badly wanted to support comprehensive health care reform, but they were just as determined to oppose any requirement that Catholics subsidize or be required to perform abortions.

The bishops' opposition to an abortion mandate played itself out before a backdrop of wide agreement with President Clinton's policies and priorities. USCC spokesmen made no secret at the beginning of the Clinton administration of their happiness with the likelihood of a new president finally addressing what the bishops considered some of the basic problems of American life. Auxiliary Bishop John Ricard of Baltimore, chairman of the USCC's Domestic Policy Committee, chose the afternoon before President Clinton's first State of the Union address to issue a statement echoing Clinton campaign rhetoric on the need for America to "invest in our people and communities."[34] The June 1993 NCCB-USCC-Synagogue Council of America statement on the common good, signed by General Secretary Robert Lynch, judged the political moment especially promising for a renewal of the nation's general welfare, given the recent "return of our national confidence."[35]

The bishops entered the coalescing health care reform debate while meeting in New Orleans later that summer. The stakes were high: The Catholic Church in America controlled 600-odd hospitals and another 1,500 specialized care centers. All told, Catholic health care facilities served more than 20 million people a year, many of them indigent or uninsured. The first priority of health care reform, said the bishops in a published resolution, should be to ensure "universal access" to health care, with priority consideration given to "the vulnerable and the poor" in the allocation of resources. The NCCB conceded that "real" reform would be impossible without increased governmental, particularly federal, intervention to hasten universal access, ensure "quality care," and "contain" costs. Abortion, euthanasia, and assisted suicide were not "health care," however, and the bishops warned that it would be "morally wrong and counterproductive to compel individuals, institutions or states to pay for or participate in procedures that fundamentally violate basic moral principles and the consciences of millions of Americans."[36]

The bishops' statement went on to make a strategic mistake by accepting the Clinton administration's premise that the American health care system was in crisis. "We have the best health care technology in the world," explained the bishops, "but tens of millions have little or no access to it and the costs of the system are straining our nation, our economy, our families and our Church to the breaking point."[37] By endorsing this hyperbole—which USCC spokesmen and Catholic activists would repeat countless times over the following year—the bishops made it easier for the Clinton administration, and members of Congress busy drafting reform plans of their own, to overlook the bishops' dissent from the inclusion of abortion, euthanasia, and assisted suicide in a national health care reform plan.

As the climax of the health care debate in Congress neared in the summer of 1994, the bishops faced the real possibility of having to support or reject a health care bill that mandated abortion coverage. "We have not been listened to," complained Helen Alvaré. "It was our hope that by now we would have been able to impress on members of Congress the dramatic violation of our conscience that inclusion of abortion would be." In sadness and frustration, the bishops decided they would not compromise their opposition to abortion even to win sweeping health care reform. NCCB president Archbishop William Keeler of Baltimore, joined by Bishop Ricard and Roger Cardinal Mahony (now chairman of the NCCB's Pro-Life Committee), sent a letter to thirty congressional leaders in July warning them to expect the Church's "vigorous opposition" to any reform package that required all health insurers to include abortion coverage.[38]

Why had no one listened? Probably because the bishops had applied the "option for the poor" in a rigid and unconvincing manner. They failed to explain what they meant by "access" to health care, but still demanded that the entire health-care reform effort be redirected toward providing this vague "access" for "the poor"—a group of Americans that the bishops had spent even less time defining and identifying. The bishops thus offered neither a coherent philosophical defense of their complicated stand on health care nor any meaningful sanctions against Catholics who defied the NCCB on this issue. It was not surprising that the bishops were not heard.

9

A Prognosis

Is Christianity compatible with social progress? This has been the fundamental question driving Catholic social teaching since the end of the nineteenth century. Can the Catholic faith be kept entire in the modern world, or has science—as manifested in modern modes of organization and criticism—forced the rational Christian to suspend his belief in certain Christological and moral doctrines? If, on the other hand, the novelty of modernity is primarily ideological rather than scientific, then how can the fallen world really be improved, in its laws and institutions, through Christian remedies?

A century ago, Pope Leo XIII affirmed Christianity's compatibility with progress, declaring that the faith was even conducive to the betterment of social conditions—if progress were defined as the closer attainment of man's true goals: virtue and salvation. The Church teaches the truth; this is its gift to society. Since *Rerum Novarum*, papal social encyclicals have proclaimed salvation as man's ultimate goal, urged the practice of virtue as the proper means not only to eternal salvation, but as one of the essential components of ameliorating class conflict, and warned of the dangers of modern ideology. The core of the social doctrine of the Catholic Church is still to be found in *Rerum Novarum*. We should remember, however, that papal social theory is relatively young as Church teachings go —barely more than century old. It has yet to be fully illuminated and tested by history; Pope John Paul II's recent clarifications and extensions of the Leonine doctrine testify to the comparative novelty of a Catholic social teaching.

165

The Leonine vision of the social order informed the social teaching of America's bishops before the Second Vatican Council. Advised by experts such as Msgr. John A. Ryan, the bishops insisted that Catholics could be patriotic Americans and still preserve their faith whole and entire. The virtue demanded by Catholic social teaching could be best understood as man's rational, social participation in the universal order of nature. After 1931, NCWC statements advocated a restructuring of the nation's economy, and addressed the dangers posed by totalitarianism abroad and secularism at home. The reforms the NCWC outlined were to be facilitated by prudential judgments of the laity based on natural law principles.

By the time of the Second Vatican Council, however, the NCWC prescriptions no longer seemed satisfactory to many American Catholics. "Liberal" Catholics, impatient with the response of the Church to the civil rights struggle and the global crisis of inequality, worried that the traditional emphasis on virtue—with its Thomistic emphasis on norms of social and moral order—actually impeded Catholic social action. Traditional Catholic social teaching, they complained, could diagnose social ills, but could offer little practical advice for choosing among licit policy options. Furthermore, the focus of the American church on anti-communism and sexual probity seemed unwisely confining to some Catholics who sought greater cooperation with non-Catholic reformers.

The Second Vatican Council transcended these concerns by reformulating the ancient debate over the relative primacy of freedom and truth. The mission of the Church was to show man and society the truth, which each man must seek in freedom. Only in truth, said John XXIII and the Council Fathers, does man maximize his freedom and find himself in his true authenticity. Popes Paul VI and, to an even greater degree, John Paul II, have reiterated and developed this message for Christians and for society as a whole.

The language of Vatican II, however, sounded strange to many American ears. A series of coincidences in the 1960s contributed to the bishops' hesitation in presenting the council's message to America in its full integrity. In particular, the battle over birth control and the collapse of Thomism among American Catholic intellectuals eliminated the possibility of an organic development of NCWC social teaching. By 1970, the policy statements and pastoral letters issued by the NCCB and USCC sounded significantly different from those written by the NCWC only a few years before.

The bishops' reorganization of the NCWC into the NCCB and USCC brought in new personnel, processes, and ideas. Vatican II had formally endorsed national bishops' conferences, giving the bishops' Washington secretariat considerably more institutional clout than the Social Action Department of the NCWC had enjoyed. In the late 1960s, the reformed and expanded USCC secretariat took in new advisors who reoriented the message of the bishops' conference. Inspired by European notions of a "political theology," the USCC staff prompted the bishops to take critical stands on newly designated "moral issues," particularly poverty and the Vietnam war. The new Political Theology was not a true reading of Vatican II, however, and when USCC staffers applied it to American issues and problems it tended to tip the council's delicate balancing of freedom and truth. America's bishops in the NCCB now hesitated to assert that the Catholic faith holds truths for all society. They were even more reluctant to criticize the ideological sources of error and vice, or to insist that true social progress has its source and end in Christ.

The American Church at the time felt beset by galloping secularism in society and internal theological doubt about the existence of absolute moral norms. Working within this social and ecclesial context, bishops such as James Rausch and USCC advisors such as Father J. Bryan Hehir tried to ground the new policy prescriptions of the NCCB and USCC in principles which could be defended as deriving from Scripture and from papal and conciliar texts. The new teaching that they had developed in the 1970s would grow by 1984 into Joseph Cardinal Bernardin's "consistent ethic of life." Fearing the politicization of Church social action, Cardinal Bernardin and many other Catholics understood the "consistent ethic of life" as a carefully balanced concept that enabled the bishops to resist demands from partisans on both sides of the political spectrum. Balanced as that teaching might have been, however, it could not be called either Thomistic—in the Leonine tradition—or phenomenological, in the way the Second Vatican Council and Pope John Paul II used the new philosophical methods and language to illuminate Leo XIII's social teaching.

New procedures implemented by the bishops' conference since the 1960s widened the influence of the USCC staff over the bishops' agenda and social statements. If modern social science has shown anything, it has demonstrated that "process" is never neutral—that any set of organizational procedures fosters certain policy outcomes while discouraging others. The process employed by the USCC and NCCB in drafting social statements is no exception to this rule. Bishops perforce rely on their staff for expert advice about complicated public policy issues. As the NCCB and USCC spoke out on more and more social issues in the 1970s, the Washington secretariat exerted increasing influence over the selection of issues that came before NCCB meetings, as well as over the drafting of statements for consideration by the USCC Administrative Board or by the bishops collectively. The bishops, when assembled for biannual meetings, rarely debated the substance of their own social statements. The sheer mechanics of running a meeting of 250-plus bishops placed a premium on compromise and semantics, and reduced "prophecy" to parliamentary procedure.

Since the formation of the NCCB and USCC, the bishops have never really explained *how* the Catholic faith presents the truth to society. The old NCWC had promoted Catholic social doctrine as the fulfillment of reason—as the full and true exposition of the natural law that was attainable only in the light of Christ. The NCCB, however, with its qualms about any brand of collective moral fervor, has regarded the Church's God-given wisdom more as a "resource" than an imperative. Church social teaching became a well of valuable insights, a filter with which to screen out bad arguments, and—if used carefully—a spur to motivate Christians into socially beneficial action. Conference statements after the 1960s only rarely tried to show how the truth revealed by Jesus Christ benefits all society; instead they emulated the policy pronouncements of secular lobbies and interest groups by criticizing current policies, advocating new ones, and calling generally for cooperation, planning, and peace.

Costs and Benefits

The developments of the last generation suggest that a national conference of Catholic bishops that takes specific stands on public policy issues risks dividing Catholic citizens against one another and diminishes the Church's moral authority. The Church becomes, in the public mind, just another interest group. This impression becomes more prevalent and more lasting—for Catholics as well as for non-Catholics—as Church leaders pronounce their opinions on matters that admit of alternative morally licit responses and complex prudential considerations.

The bishops and their advisors should remember this hard truth and anticipate the inevitable collateral effects of their statements on political and social issues. The duty of the Church to defend human dignity must be exercised with prudence, and prudence demands a balance between the benefits and the costs of political "prophecy." I would suggest the following rule: Do no harm. Bishops should not speak out collectively unless the issue they plan to address directly and significantly affects Church interests as such, or if it is truly of grave national moment. A proposal to repeal the tax-exemption for religious organizations would qualify under the former heading. Abortion and genocidal warfare would fit the latter. Other examples could obviously be adduced in both categories, but, needless to say, many of the "crises" addressed by the NCCB and the USCC in recent years can hardly be said to meet either test.

Pope John Paul II has deliberately and systematically taken a different route. He has elucidated the relationship between freedom and truth as these goods were analyzed anew by Vatican II's *Declaration on Religious Freedom*. John Paul's moral and social encyclicals have reaffirmed the obligation of the Church to proclaim the truth to all mankind and have insisted that truth derives from and points to Christ. John Paul has not outlined detailed prescriptions for American society—or for any other society—in those same encyclicals. Here is a challenge for America's bishops: explain John Paul II's teaching to the nation, a people unaccustomed—at least in recent years—to hearing that their inalienable rights derive from "the laws of Nature and Nature's God." Imagine a bishops' conference explicitly devoted to teaching all Americans about the central dynamic of the natural law: that the truth dictates certain imperatives for human freedom, and that denial of truth does not affirm but actually erodes that freedom.

On the present evidence, it seems as if the Catholic Church in the United States will continue toward more comprehensive accommodation to the main cultural currents of modern American life (although the Church will, assuredly, remain counter-cultural on the life issues of abortion and euthanasia). But the social magisterium of John Paul II provides an alternative model: one that transcends the sterile options of cultural accommodation or "pragmatic" compromise with modern ideological error. By focusing the social doctrine of the Church on the moral and cultural foundations of democracy and the free economy, the pope has diagnosed the pathologies that afflict American liberty, and threaten its capacity to promote justice for all.

All Americans bear witness to the daily testing of the proposition that a self-governing people, lacking both official creed and established church, can summon the virtues essential for liberty. The Catholic Church in America, led by its bishops, bears another sort of witness: to the truth as revealed by Jesus Christ and illuminated by reasoned reflection on history. Remember that a witness testifies to the truth; he is free to change his expressions according to the questions asked of him, but the truth does not change, and neither does the obligation of the witness to tell it. Pope John Paul II has reminded the Church and the world of these realities. He is deeply interested in that American witness and more familiar with its possibilities and defects than any of his predecessors; his successors are likely to share his interest and concern. Thus what is taught by our nation's bishops—if that teaching fully articulates John Paul's reflections on freedom and truth —could echo throughout Christendom as more peoples confront the dilemmas familiar to the American experience of ordered liberty.

Notes

CHAPTER 1

1. Rodger Charles, S.J., with Drostan Maclaren, O.P., *The Social Teaching of Vatican II: Its Origin and Development; Catholic Social Ethics: An Historical and Comparative Study* (San Francisco: Ignatius Press, 1982). See his discussion on "The Divine Eternal Law as the Ultimate Moral Norm: The Teaching of the Scriptures," 48-60.

2. *Catechism of the Catholic Church* (Washington, D.C.: United States Catholic Conference, 1994). Roman documents, such as encyclical letters and this catechism, and some statements from the NCWC and NCCB-USCC, are numbered by paragraphs or sections in a more or less standard fashion, and, where helpful, these numbers will be cited in the text instead of page numbers.

3. For a succinct exposition of the natural law tradition, see John Paul II, *Veritatis Splendor (The Splendor of Truth)* (Washington, D.C.: United States Catholic Conference, 1993), pars. 31-44. See also Russell Hittinger, "The Problem of the State in *Centesimus Annus*," *Fordham International Law Journal* 15 (1991-92): 963.

4. Leo XIII, "Rerum Novarum," in The Papal Encyclicals, ed. Claudia Carlen (Wilmington, N.C.: McGrath Publishing, 1981), 2:241-59.

5. Kevin A. McMahon offers an interesting discussion of this wisdom in his "Economics, Wisdom and the Teaching of the Bishops in the Theology of Thomas Aquinas," *Thomist* 53 (January 1989): 91-106.

6. Congregation for Catholic Education (William Cardinal Baum), "Guidelines for the Study and Teaching of the Church's Social Doctrine in the Formation of Priests," *Origins* 19 (August 3, 1989): 173-74.

7. Vatican II, "Declaration on Religious Freedom" *(Dignitatis Humanae),* in *The Documents of Vatican II,* ed. Walter M. Abbott, S.J., and trans. Joseph Gallagher (New York: America Press, 1966), 675-96.

8. See John Paul II, *Sollicitudo Rei Socialis (On Social Concern)* (Washington, D.C.: United States Catholic Conference, 1988), par. 41.

9. Vatican II, "Declaration on Religious Freedom," as quoted by Rodger Charles, *Social Teachings of Vatican II,* 11.

10. Charles, *The Social Teachings of Vatican II*, 9-11, 15.

11. Thomas Gumbleton, "The Bishop as Social Activist," *Origins* 12 (September 30, 1982): 249-56.

12. Rembert G. Weakland, "How Medellin and Puebla Influenced North America," *Origins* 18 (April 13, 1989): 758-59.

13. National Conference of Catholic Bishops (NCCB), *Economic Justice for All* (Washington, D.C.: United States Catholic Conference, 1986).

14. The thesis of "Economic Justice for All" drew its main scriptural support from Isaiah 3:14-15 and 10:2. Both passages warn judges and officials that God will punish them for oppressing the poor. Avery Dulles's discussion of the scriptural foundations of this "Church as servant" model is also useful in this context; see *Models of the Church* (New York: Image Books, 1987), 99-102.

15. Rembert G. Weakland, "Church Social Teaching and the American Economy," *Origins* 13 (December 8, 1983): 447-48.

16. Weakland, "The Economic Pastoral: Draft Two," *America* 153 (September 21, 1985): 132.

CHAPTER 2

1. Rodger Charles, S.J., with Drostan Maclaren, O.P., *The Social Teaching of Vatican II* (San Francisco: Ignatius Press, 1982), 236-43.

2. Ernest L. Fortin, "'Sacred and Inviolable': *Rerum Novarum* and Natural Rights," *Theological Studies* 53 (June 1992): 210-11.

3. Thomas Bokenkotter, *A Concise History of the Catholic Church* (New York, N.Y.: Doubleday, Image Books, 1979), 345-48.

4. Leo XIII, "On Christian Philosophy" *(Aeterni Patris)*, in *The Church Speaks to the Modern World: The Social Teachings of Leo XIII*, ed. Étienne Gilson (Garden City, NY: Doubleday, 1954), 31-51, pars. 27-29.

5. Quoted in Carl Braaten, "Protestants and Natural Law," *First Things* 19 (January 1992): 20. The principal drafter of *Rerum Novarum* was Italian Jesuit economist Matteo Liberatore; see Fortin, "'Sacred and Inviolable,'" 211.

6. St. Paul, I Cor 12:12-30. See also Rom 12:4-5.

7. See also Hubert Jedin, Konrad Repgen, and John Dolan, eds. *History of the Church* (New York: Crossroad, 1989), 10:246.

8. For more on the organic analogy, see Oswald von Nell-Breuning, *Reorganization of Social Economy: The Social Encyclical Developed and Explained* (New York: Bruce Publishing, 1936), 220-29.

9. Russell Hittinger, "The Problem of the State in *Centesimus Annus*," *Fordham International Law Journal* 15 (1991-92): 956.

10. Aaron I. Abell, "The Reception of Leo XIII's Labor Encyclical in America, 1891-1919," *Review of Politics* 7 (October 1945): 468-73, 493-95. See also Francis L. Broderick, *Right Reverend New Dealer: John A. Ryan* (New York: Macmillan, 1963), 19-21.

11. Abell, "The Reception of Leo XIII's Labor Encyclical," 483-90.

12. F. T. Hurley, "National Catholic Welfare Conference," in Catholic University of America, *New Catholic Encyclopedia* (New York: McGraw-Hill, 1967), 13:225.

13. Joseph M. McShane, *"Sufficiently Radical": Catholicism, Progressivism, and the Bishops' Program of 1919* (Washington, D.C.: Catholic University of America Press, 1986), 148.

14. Broderick, *Right Reverend New Dealer,* 104-105.

15. Ibid., 105.

16. NCWC, "Bishops' Program of Social Reconstruction," in *Pastoral Letters of the United States Catholic Bishops,* ed. Hugh J. Nolan (Washington, D.C.: United States Catholic Conference, 1984), 1:255-71.

17. Elizabeth McKeown, *War and Welfare: American Catholics and World War I* (New York: Garland Publishing, 1988), 172.

18. Austin Dowling, "The National Catholic Welfare Conference," *Ecclesiastical Review* 79 (October 1928): 340-41.

19. Hurley, "National Catholic Welfare Conference," 226.

20. Nolan, *Pastoral Letters,* 1:244.

21. NCWC, "Pastoral Letter," in Nolan, *Pastoral Letters,* 1:272-333.

22. McKeown, *War and Welfare,* 174.

23. William Teeling, *Pope Pius XI and World Affairs* (New York: Frederick A. Stokes, 1937), 160-61.

24. Elizabeth McKeown, "Apologia for an American Catholicism: The Petition and Report of the National Catholic Welfare Council to Pius XI, April 25, 1922," *Church History* 43 (December 1974): 520-21, 527-28.

25. C. Joseph Nuesse, "The National Catholic Welfare Conference," *The Catholic Church, U.S.A.,* ed. Louis J. Putz C.S.C. (Chicago: Fides Publisher, 1956), 142.

26. McKeown, *War and Welfare,* 172.

27. John B. Sheerin, *Never Look Back: The Career and Concerns of John J. Burke* (New York: Paulist Press, 1975), 66.

28. See, for instance, John A. Ryan, "Criticisms of the Social Action Department," *NCWC Bulletin* 3 (July 1921): 17-18.

29. Martin E. Marty, *The Irony of It All,* vol. 1 of *Modern American Religion* (Chicago: University of Chicago Press, 1986), 185-86.

30. John A. Ryan, "The Economic Philosophy of St. Thomas," in *Essays in Thomism,* ed. Robert Brennan (Freeport, N.Y.: Books for Libraries reprints, 1972), 260. See also Ryan, "The Doctrine of Fascism," reprinted in *Commonweal* 99 (November 16, 1973): 157.

31. This was Ryan's so-called principle of expediency; it is crucial to note that Ryan did not mean to imply that efficacious policies are *ipso facto* ethical policies, but rather that, in the long run, efficacious policies and eternal moral principles are in harmony. See Patrick W. Gearty, *The Economic Thought of Monsignor John A. Ryan* (Washington, D.C.: Catholic University of America Press, 1953), 298, 306.

32. Ibid., 298-99, 304.

33. John A. Ryan, *Social Doctrine in Action: A Personal History* (New York: Harper & Brothers, 1941), 80, 266; Broderick, *Right Reverend New Dealer,* 148-50.

34. Joseph McShane, *"Sufficiently Radical,"* 237.

35. Broderick, *Right Reverend New Dealer,* 74; Gearty, *Economic Thought of Monsignor John A. Ryan,* 34, 48.

36. Broderick, *Right Reverend New Dealer,* 138, 160; Gearty, *Economic Thought of Monsignor John A. Ryan,* 42.

37. David J. O'Brien, *American Catholics and Social Reform: The New Deal Years* (New York: Oxford University Press, 1968), 130. Gearty, *Economic Thought of Monsignor John A. Ryan*, 42. Ryan, "The Doctrine of Fascism," 156-58. Broderick, *Right Reverend New Dealer*, 233-34.

38. Gearty, *Economic Thought of Monsignor John A. Ryan*, 310.

39. Broderick, *Right Reverend New Dealer*, 150, 165-70.

40. Ibid., 155-61.

41. Ibid., 137.

42. Ibid., 161-62. See also Francis L. Broderick, "The Encyclical and Social Action: Is John A. Ryan Typical?" *Catholic Historical Review* 55 (April 1969): 3-5.

43. Broderick, *Right Reverend New Dealer*, 155-61.

44. O'Brien, *American Catholics and Social Reform*, 144; Karl Cerny, "Monsignor John A. Ryan and the Social Action Department: An Analysis of a Leading School of American Catholic Social Thought" (Ph.D. diss., Yale University, 1955), 113.

45. Broderick, *Right Reverend New Dealer*, 120-21; Gearty, *Economic Thought of Monsignor John A. Ryan*, 41.

46. Broderick, *Right Reverend New Dealer*, 236.

47. NCWC, "Statement on Federalization and Bureaucracy," in Nolan, *Pastoral Letters*, 1:334.

48. Sheerin, *Never Look Back*, 106.

49. Ibid., 209-210.

CHAPTER 3

1. Pius XI, *"Quadragesimo Anno,"* in *The Papal Encyclicals*, ed. Claudia Carlen (Wilmington, N.C.: McGrath Publishing, 1981), 3:415-44.

2. For an overview of Pius's debt to Pesch and the German Jesuits, see John Cort, *Christian Socialism: An Informal History* (Maryknoll, N.Y.: Orbis Books, 1988), 288-98.

3. Il Duce was not flattered by *Quadragesimo Anno*. Indeed, he seemed to regard it as an attack on his policies, according to Oswald von Nell-Breuning (as cited by Michael Novak in *The Catholic Ethic and the Spirit of Capitalism* [New York: Free Press, 1993], 75).

4. Karl Cerny, "Monsignor John A. Ryan and the Social Action Department: An Analysis of a Leading School of American Catholic Social Thought" (Ph.D. diss., Yale University, 1955), 235-44.

5. Luke E. Ebersole, *Church Lobbying in the Nation's Capital* (New York: Macmillan, 1951), 106-12.

6. Francis Broderick, *Right Reverend New Dealer: John A. Ryan* (New York: Macmillan, 1963), 108-9, 121, 216.

7. Ibid., 196.

8. John B. Sheerin, *Never Look Back: The Career and Concerns of John J. Burke* (New York: Paulist Press, 1975), 177-79.

9. Patrick W. Gearty, *Economic Thought of Monsignor John A. Ryan* (Washington, D.C.: Catholic University of America Press, 1953), 49-52; Broderick, *Right Reverend New Dealer*, 227.

10. Ryan was not speaking for the NCWC in this address; see Sheerin, *Never Look Back*, 188-89. Ryan's broadcast also attacked the proposals of Father Charles Coughlin; see David J. O'Brien, *American Catholics and Social Reform: The New Deal Years* (New York: Oxford University Press, 1968), 139; Broderick, *Right Reverend New Dealer*, 226.

11. Broderick, *Right Reverend New Dealer*, 229.

12. Ibid., 257. John B. Sheerin says that Fr. Burke had issued a similar prohibition in March 1936, an edict that Ryan had skirted that following October by claiming to speak only for himself (*Never Look Back*, 188-89).

13. Gerald M. Costello, *Without Fear or Favor: George Higgins on the Record* (Mystic, Conn.: Twenty-Third Publications, 1984), 172-73.

14. Garry Wills, *Nixon Agonistes: The Crisis of the Self-Made Man* (New York: Houghton Mifflin, 1969), 26-30.

15. John Cronin, S.S., *Catholic Social Principles: The Social Teaching of the Catholic Church Applied to American Economic Life* (Milwaukee: Bruce Publishing, 1950); see also his *Social Principles and Economic Life* (Milwaukee: Bruce Publishing, 1964).

16. Donald F. Crosby, S.J., *God, Church and Flag: Senator Joseph R. McCarthy and the Catholic Church, 1950-1957* (Chapel Hill: University of North Carolina Press, 1978), 83-86, 158. The bishops' criticism is in the pastoral letter "God's Law: The Measure of Man's Conduct," *Pastoral Letters of the United States Catholic Bishops*, ed. Hugh J. Nolan (Washington, D.C.: USCC, 1984), 2:143.

17. Crosby, *God, Church and Flag*, 55-56.

18. Ibid., 199-200. Cronin later wrote that at some point in the early 1950s Archbishop Mooney had "kindly advised" him to "deemphasize the problem [of communism] and to concentrate more upon the general area of Catholic social principles." See "Social Action: Myth or Reality," *Catholic Mind* 65 (December 1967): 42.

19. Crosby, *God, Church and Flag*, 62.

20. Broderick, *Right Reverend New Dealer*, 235, 257.

21. William E. McManus, "Inside the Bishops' Conference," *America* 153 (September 21, 1985): 133-34; Thomas J. Reese, S.J., *A Flock of Shepherds: The National Conference of Catholic Bishops* (Kansas City, MO: Sheed & Ward, 1992), 25-26.

22. NCWC, "A Statement on Man's Dignity," in Nolan, *Pastoral Letters*, 2:165-68.

23. NCWC, "Explosion or Backfire?" in Nolan, *Pastoral Letters*, 2:222.

24. NCWC, "God's Law," 139-45.

25. See NCWC, "A Statement on the Teaching Mission of the Catholic Church," in Nolan, *Pastoral Letters*, 2:207-11.

26. Philip Gleason, "Pluralism, Democracy, and Catholicism in the Era of World War II," *Review of Politics* 49 (Spring 1987): 211-12.

27. Father Burke reconciled his opposition to birth control clinics with his belief in federalism by asking federal officials to close new clinics only when they opened in communities such as Puerto Rico, where the federal government held jurisdiction over matters elsewhere decided by state or local authorities. See Sheerin, *Never Look Back*, 194-96.

28. See NCWC, "Man's Dignity," in Nolan, *Pastoral Letters*, 2:169.

29. NCWC, "Statement on Church and Social Order," in Nolan, *Pastoral Letters*, 1:436-54.

30. Douglas P. Seaton, *Catholics and Radicals: The Association of Catholic Trade Union-*

ists and the American Labor Movement, from Depression to Cold War (Lewisburg, Pa.: Bucknell University Press, 1982), 39.

31. NCWC, "Statement on Secularism," in Nolan, *Pastoral Letters,* 2:74-81.

32. Father Ryan, for instance, angrily declared that Smith would have defeated Hoover were it not for Smith's Catholicism; see Broderick, *Right Reverend New Dealer,* 184.

33. NCWC, "Resolution on Russia," in Nolan, *Pastoral Letters,* 1:335.

34. NCWC, "Statement on Social Problems," in Nolan, *Pastoral Letters,* 1:422-25.

35. NCWC, "To the Spanish Hierarchy," in Nolan, *Pastoral Letters,* 1:416-18.

36. NCWC, "Statement on Tyranny in Mexico," in Nolan, *Pastoral Letters,* 1:408-11.

37. NCWC, "To the German Hierarchy," in Nolan, *Pastoral Letters,* 1:419-21.

38. NCWC, "Victory and Peace," in Nolan, *Pastoral Letters,* 2:38-43.

39. Sheerin, *Never Look Back,* 212-13.

40. NCWC, "A Statement on International Order," in Nolan, *Pastoral Letters,* 2:56-61.

41. NCWC, "Between War and Peace," in Nolan, *Pastoral Letters,* 2:62-65.

42. NCWC, "Man and the Peace!" in Nolan, *Pastoral Letters,* 2:67-73.

43. NCWC, "A Statement on Freedom and Peace," in Nolan, *Pastoral Letters,* 2:214-20.

44. Daniel Callahan, *The Mind of the Catholic Layman* (New York: Charles Scribner's Sons, 1963), 86-90.

45. Garry Wills, *Bare Ruined Choirs: Doubt, Prophecy, and Radical Religion* (Garden City, N.Y.: Doubleday, 1972), 56-57.

46. Daniel Callahan, *The New Church: Essays in Catholic Reform* (New York: Charles Scribner's Sons, 1966), 180.

47. William Oliver Martin, *Metaphysics and Ideology* (Milwaukee: Marquette University Press, 1959), 65-67.

48. Reinhold Niebuhr, "Catholicism in America," *Commonweal* 58 (May 8, 1953): 117.

49. Edward A. Marciniak, "Catholics and Social Reform," *Commonweal* 58 (September 11, 1953): 559-60.

CHAPTER 4

1. John XXIII, *"Humanae Salutis," The Documents of Vatican II,* ed. Walter M. Abbott, S.J., and trans. Joseph Gallagher (New York: America Press, 1966), 703-5.

2. John F. Kobler, *Vatican II and Phenomenology: Reflections on the Life-World of the Church* (Norwell, Mass.: Kluwer Academic Publications, Martinus-Nijhoff, 1985), 7.

3. Vatican II, "Message to Humanity," in Abbott and Gallagher, *The Documents of Vatican II,* 5-7.

4. Kobler, *Vatican II and Phenomenology,* 139-41.

5. Hubert Jedin, Konrad Repgen, and John Dolan, eds., *History of the Church* (New York: Crossroad, 1989), 10:246.

6. John XXIII, *"Mater et Magistra,"* in *The Papal Encyclicals,* ed. Claudia Carlen (Wilmington, N.C.: McGrath Publishing, 1981), 5:59-90.

7. John XXIII, *"Pacem in Terris,"* in Carlen, *The Papal Encyclicals,* 5:107-31.

8. John Paul II has a seemed a little defensive about the Church's tardy endorsement of democracy. In *Centesimus Annus* he attacks the claim that "agnosticism and skeptical relativism" is the only outlook consistent with representative government. See *Centesimus Annus (On the Hundredth Anniversary of Rerum Novarum)* (Washington, D.C.: United States Catholic Conference, 1991), par. 46.

9. See I John 3:17.

10. Ecumenical councils are gatherings convened by the pope of the world's bishops, cardinals, and leaders of religious orders. When speaking in harmony with him, a council is deemed authoritative and even infallible on matters of faith and morals. A council is not, however, the Catholic equivalent of a national legislature, and conciliar teachings are not inherently more authoritative than papal encyclicals. When a pope dies before the completion of a council—as happened during Vatican II —the council is automatically suspended until his successor reconvenes it, if ever. The Church has held twenty-one ecumenical councils; Vatican II was the second to be held in Vatican City. (Vatican I met in 1869 until political disruptions caused by the Franco-Prussian war interrupted it the following year; it is best remembered for having defined the doctrine of papal infallibility.)

11. Jedin, Repgen, and Dolan, *History of the Church,* 10:262-63, 268-69.

12. Kobler, *Vatican II and Phenomenology,* 135, 139-40.

13. Jedin, Repgen, Dolan, *History of the Church,* 10:235.

14. Vatican II, "Declaration on Religious Freedom" in Abbott and Gallagher, *The Documents of Vatican II,* 675-96.

15. John McKenzie, S.J., "Natural Law in the New Testament," *Biblical Research* 9 (1965): 12-13.

16. Michael Novak, *A New Generation: American and Catholic* (New York: Herder and Herder, 1964), 93-97. See also Novak's "How I Have Changed My Mind," *Catholic Mind* 77 (March 1979): 34-39.

17. Robert O. Johann, "Reason, Nature, and Morality," *America* 112 (April 10, 1965): 487.

18. Leslie Dewart, "Soviet-American Diplomacy and *Pacem in Terris,"* *Cross Currents* 14 (Summer 1964): 307-8; Michael Novak, "Bernard Lonergan: A New Approach to Natural Law," *Proceedings* (American Catholic Philosophical Association) 41 (1967): 248.

19. Ernan McMullin, "Who Are We?" *Proceedings* (American Catholic Philosophical Association) 41 (1967): 13-14. William Oliver Martin also addressed this in *Metaphysics and Ideology* (Milwaukee: Marquette University Press, 1959), 58-59.

20. Douglas J. Roche, *The Catholic Revolution* (New York: David McKay, 1968), 41-44.

21. "Häring Joins American Theologians in Swift Critical Response to Pope," *National Catholic Reporter,* August 7, 1968.

22. National Conference of Catholic Bishops (NCCB), "The Government and Birth Control," in *Quest for Justice: A Compendium of Statements of the United States Catholic Bishops on the Political and Social Order, 1966-1980,* ed. J. Brian Benestad and Francis J. Butler (Washington, D.C.: United States Catholic Conference, 1981), 173.

23. NCCB, "Human Life in Our Day," in *Pastoral Letters of the United States Catholic Bishops,* ed. Hugh J. Nolan (Washington, D.C.: USCC, 1983), 3:164-74.

24. "A Disappointing Statement," *Commonweal* 79 (November 29, 1963): 267-68.

25. Peter Riga, "Catholics and Community," *Today* 19 (June 1964): 9-11.

26. David J. O'Brien, "Join it, Work it, Fight it," *Commonweal* 116 (November 17, 1989): 626-27.

27. Richard L. Porter, S.J., "Social Encyclicals Course and the New Theology," *Review of Social Economy* 27 (March 1969): 41-43.

28. Roche, *The Catholic Revolution*, 58, 62.

29. John A. Coleman, *An American Strategic Theology* (New York: Paulist Press, 1982), 61.

30. Avery Dulles, *Models of the Church* (New York, N.Y.: Doubleday & Co., Image Books, 1987), 91-98; Johannes B. Metz, "The Church's Social Function in the Light of a 'Political Theology,'" in *Faith and the World of Politics*, vol. 36 of *Concilium* (New York: Paulist Press, 1968), 5-10.

31. Philipp Herder-Dorneich, "How Can the Church Provide Guidelines in Social Ethics?" in *The Social Message of the Gospel*, vol. 35 of *Concilium* (New York: Paulist Press, 1968), 84-85, 88-90. See also Marthaler, "The New Hermeneutic," 78-80.

32. Bernard Häring, "Man in Search of Liberation in Community," *Human Rights and the Liberation of Man in the Americas*, ed. Louis Colonnese (Notre Dame, Ind.: University of Notre Dame Press, 1970), 249-56. See also Metz, "The Church's Social Function," 17.

33. Coleman, *An American Strategic Theology*, 61-62.

34. Roche, *The Catholic Revolution*, 293-94, 299-302. See also Metz, "The Church's Social Function," 18.

CHAPTER 5

1. Daniel Callahan, *The Mind of the Catholic Layman* (New York: Charles Scribner's Sons, 1963), 96.

2. Vatican II, *"Christus Dominus"* ("Decree on the Bishops' Pastoral Office in the Church"), *The Documents of Vatican II*, ed. Walter M. Abbott, S.J., and trans. Joseph Gallagher (New York: America Press, 1966), 396-429. Despite Vatican II's mandate to teach on social questions, there remains some dispute over the teaching authority of bishops' conferences on social issues. For a persuasive—although by no means compelling—treatment of this question, see Avery Dulles, "Bishops' Conference Documents: What Doctrinal Authority?" *Origins* 14 (January 24, 1985): 528-34.

3. "Mum on High-level Study by Bishops," *National Catholic Reporter,* May 5, 1965.

4. Thomas J. Reese, S.J., *A Flock of Shepherds* (Kansas City, Mo.: Sheed & Ward, 1992), vii.

5. George Dugan, "Catholic Bishops Say U.S. Coerces Poor Over Births," *New York Times,* November 15, 1966.

6. Tom Roberts, "The Legacy of Cardinal Dearden," *Washington Post,* August 6, 1988.

7. Eugene Kennedy, *Cardinal Bernardin: Easing Conflicts—and Battling for the Soul of American Catholicism* (Chicago: Bonus Books, 1989), 37, 69, 92.

8. James F. Andrews, "New USCC Head Wants an Arbitration Board," *National Catholic Reporter,* April 17, 1968.

9. Joseph L. Bernardin, "Are Changes in the Church a Threat or a Challenge?" *Catholic Mind* 67 (February 1969): 46-51. See also Kennedy, *Cardinal Bernardin,* 284.

10. NCCB committees, on the other hand, were staffed only by bishops. Thomas Reese explains the structure, purposes, and processes of NCCB and USCC committees in *A Flock of Shepherds,* 105-42.

11. Marciniak left unstated the direction in which the bishops were to lead their people; see "Catholic Social Action: Where Do We Go From Here?" *America* 123 (December 12, 1970): 511, 515-16.

12. Reese, *A Flock of Shepherds,* 324.

13. John F. Cronin, S.S., "Social Action: Myth or Reality," *Catholic Mind* 65 (December 1967): 41-44.

14. Russell Shaw, "John F. Cronin: Activator," *National Catholic Reporter,* April 26, 1967. Fr. Cronin was beginning to express such doubts a few years earlier; see his *Social Principles and Economic Life* (Milwaukee: Bruce Publishing, 1964), 136.

15. John F. Cronin, S.S., "Social Responsibility and the New Theology: Comment," *Review of Social Economy* 27 (March 1969): 63.

16. Gerald M. Costello, *Without Fear or Favor: George Higgins on the Record* (Mystic, Conn.: Twenty-Third Publications, 1984), 67, 108, 276. See also Reese, *A Flock of Shepherds,* 295-96.

17. Costello, *Without Fear or Favor,* 142.

18. George Higgins, "Random Observations on My 50 Years as a Priest," *Origins* 20 (June 7, 1990): 62-64.

19. Author's telephone interview of Marvin Bordelon, July 26, 1994.

20. Marvin Bordelon, "Development Decade: A Disaster?" *Priest* 25 (May 1969): 265.

21. Jeremiah O'Leary, "Colonnese New Latin America Bureau Head," *National Catholic Reporter,* May 29, 1968. Louis M. Colonnese, "The Church in Latin America: Imperialism or Servanthood?" *American Ecclesiastical Review* 161 (August 1969): 109-11.

22. Author's telephone interview of Marvin Bordelon, July 26, 1994.

23. "USCC Official Fired," *Origins* 1 (September 16, 1971): 211-12.

24. Joseph Gremillion, ed., *The Gospel of Peace and Justice: Catholic Social Teaching Since Pope John* (Maryknoll, N.Y.: Orbis Books, 1976), ix.

25. Reese, *A Flock of Shepherds,* 85-89.

26. Charlotte Hays, "The Voice in the Bishops' Ear," *Washington Post Magazine,* April 3, 1983.

27. J. Bryan Hehir, "Non-Violence, Peace and the Just War," *Worldview* 12 (June 1969): 20.

28. NCWC, "Discrimination and Christian Conscience," *Pastoral Letters of the United States Catholic Bishops,* ed. Hugh J. Nolan (Washington, D.C.: USCC, 1984), 2:201-06.

29. NCWC, "On Racial Harmony," in Nolan, *Pastoral Letters,* 3:18.

30. Garry Wills, *Bare Ruined Choirs: Doubt, Prophecy, and Radical Religion* (Garden City, N.J.: Doubleday, 1972), 146-47.

31. NCWC Social Action Department, "1966 Labor Day Statement," *Catholic Mind* 64 (October 1966): 58; also Costello, *Without Fear or Favor,* 152-53.

32. "Episcopal Leadership," *America* 111 (September 12, 1964): 249.

33. Social Action Department, "1966 Labor Day Statement," 58.

34. Costello, *Without Fear or Favor*, 154-56.

35. NCCB, "Race Relations and Poverty," *Quest for Justice: A Compendium of Statements of the U.S. Catholic Bishops on the Political and Social Order, 1966-1980,* ed. J. Brian Benestad and Francis J. Butler (Washington, D.C.: USCC, 1981), 356.

36. John F. Cronin, S.S., "Must We Have Race Riots?" *Sign* 46 (April 1967): 17-19.

37. "U.S. Bishops Tooling Up Riot Study Responses," *National Catholic Reporter,* March 13, 1968.

38. Douglas J. Roche, *The Catholic Revolution* (New York: David McKay, 1968), 63.

39. NCCB, "The National Race Crisis," in Benestad and Butler, *Quest for Justice,* 361-63.

40. USCC Division for Urban Life, "USCC's 1969 Labor Day Statement," *Catholic Mind* 67 (September 1969): 1-4. Higgins customarily wrote the Labor Day statement, but he told the author on September 2, 1992, that he did not write this one.

41. NCCB, "Resolution on Crusade Against Poverty," in Nolan, *Pastoral Letters,* 3:214-15.

42. NCCB, "Resolution on the Campaign for Human Development," in Nolan, *Pastoral Letters,* 3:273-74.

43. Social Action Department, "1966 Labor Day Statement," 57. See also John F. Cronin, S.S., *The Catholic as Citizen* (Baltimore: Helicon, 1963), 142-48.

44. House Committee on Education and Labor, "Economic Opportunity Amendments of 1969," 91st Cong., 1st Sess., 1969, 1586-87, 1591-92.

45. Paul VI, *"Populorum Progressio," The Papal Encyclicals,* ed. Claudia Carlen (Wilmington, N.C.: McGrath Publishing, 1981), 5:183-202.

46. For an example of NCWC thinking on the relative priority of spiritual versus "socio-economic" needs, see Harry W. Flannery's interview of Fr. John J. Considine, director of the Latin America Bureau of the NCWC in "The Pope's Plan for Latin America," *Catholic World* 193 (July 1961): 235-36.

47. Ivan Illich, "The Seamy Side of Charity," *America* 116 (January 21, 1967): 88-89.

48. Joseph Manton, "Moving the Latin American Glacier," *Ligourian* 55 (April 1967): 26-27.

49. Colonnese, "The Church in Latin America," 109.

50. Mary T. Hanna, *Catholics and American Politics* (Cambridge, Mass: Harvard University Press, 1979), 45.

51. NCWC, "Statement on Compulsory Peacetime Military Service," in Nolan, *Pastoral Letters,* 2:106.

52. Higgins explained a month later that this was not meant to be seen as a binding moral judgment on the war; see Costello, *Without Fear or Favor,* 234-35. Eugene Kennedy says Bishop Bernardin helped draft the 1966 statement, modelling it on a pastoral letter for the Atlanta archdiocese; see *Cardinal Bernardin,* 36-37.

53. NCCB, "Peace and Vietnam," in Benestad and Butler, *Quest for Justice,* 51-54.

54. George G. Higgins, "The Need for Catholic Awareness and Commitment," *National Catholic Educational Association Bulletin* 62 (1965): 302.

55. John F. Cronin, S.S., "Pacifism and America," *Sign* 46 (August 1966): 17-18.

56. John F. Cronin, S.S., "Clergymen and the Conflict in Vietnam," *Catholic Mind* 65 (April 1967): 7-9.

57. NCCB, "Human Life in Our Day," in Nolan, *Pastoral Letters,* 3: 190-91. Much of part two of the pastoral letter was drafted under the supervision of Msgr. Marvin Bordelon by a State Department official named Edward Doherty, who went on to work at the USCC full-time in the 1970s. See Jim Castelli, *The Bishops and the Bomb: Waging Peace in a Nuclear Age* (Garden City, N.Y.: Image Books, 1983), 76.

58. Ronald G. Musto, *The Catholic Peace Tradition* (Maryknoll, N.Y.: Orbis Books, 1986), 254.

59. Author's telephone interview of Marvin Bordelon, July 26, 1994.

60. USCC, "Declaration on Conscientious Objection and Selective Conscientious Objection," in Nolan, *Pastoral Letters,* 3:285. NCCB, "Human Life in Our Day," 193.

61. All three of these events were covered by the National Catholic News Service in its dispatches to Catholic press subscribers. The dispatches are currently on file at the United States Catholic Conference. See "Catholic Officials Comment on Vietnam Peace Moratorium," October 3, 1969, 13-14; Margaret M. Carlen, "U.S., Soviet Churchmen Back Arms Control," October 4, 1969, 1-4; "Congressman Asks Investigation of USCC Tax-Exempt Status," June 13, 1969, 17.

62. Costello, *Without Fear or Favor,* 229-30; Musto, *Catholic Peace Tradition,* 252.

63. Robert F. Drinan, S.J., *Vietnam and Armageddon: Peace, War and the Christian Conscience* (New York: Sheed & Ward, 1970), 27.

64. USCC, "The Bishops and the War," *Origins* 1 (September 16, 1971): 215.

65. NCCB, "Resolution on Southeast Asia," in Benestad and Butler, *Quest for Justice,* 78.

66. Marvin Bordelon, "The Bishops and Just War," *America* 126 (January 8, 1972): 18.

67. Thomas Gumbleton, "Life After Birth and the War," *Origins* 1 (April 27, 1972): 751-52.

68. Joseph Bernardin, "A Time of War," *Origins* 1 (May 4, 1972): 765.

69. Rick Casey, "Tension at USCC on War," *National Catholic Reporter,* May 26, 1972.

70. "Praise 8 Bishops; Censure USCC Leaders," *National Catholic Reporter,* July 21, 1972.

71. Eleanor Blau, "Catholic Bishops Ask End of Bombing in Vietnam," *New York Times,* November 17, 1972. For more on Gumbleton's endorsement of McGovern, see Castelli, *The Bishops and the Bomb,* 69.

72. USCC, "Statement on U.S. Bombing Operations in Cambodia," in Benestad and Butler, *Quest for Justice,* 82. Also "Bishops Rejected Bombing Statement," *National Catholic Reporter,* April 6, 1973.

73. James Jennings, "World Justice and Peace and American Catholics," *Catholic Mind* 71 (January 1973): 42.

74. Callahan, *The Mind of the Catholic Layman,* 96.

CHAPTER 6

1. The traditional view of the Church's wisdom is expressed in the NCCB's "To Live in Christ Jesus: A Pastoral Reflection on the Moral Life," in J. Brian Benestad and Francis J. Butler, eds., *Quest For Justice: A Compendium of Statements of the U.S. Catholic Bishops on the Political and Social Order, 1966-1980* (Washington, D.C.: USCC, 1981), 27-30.

2. The new formulation of the wisdom of the Church is seen in the USCC Administrative Board's election year messages on political responsibility. The first in the series was published in 1976; see "Political Responsibility: Reflections on an Election Year," in Benestad and Butler, *Quest for Justice*, 15-18.

3. James Rausch, "Development and Justice," *Catholic Mind* 69 (March 1971): 4-5.

4. Bishop Rausch held to this view of charity during his later tenure as NCCB general secretary. In 1975 he argued that defining policy choices in terms of charity distracted Catholics from key national questions; see "Hunger is a Right-to-Life Issue," *Our Sunday Visitor*, December 7, 1975.

5. NCCB, "Brothers and Sisters to Us," in Benestad and Butler, *Quest for Justice*, 373, 377-78.

6. House Committee on Foreign Affairs, "International Protection of Human Rights," 93rd Cong., 1st Sess., 1973, 62.

7. The USCC statement "The Right to a Decent Home: A Pastoral Response to the Crisis in Housing" noted the "*immoral* situation of indecent, inadequate housing" (emphasis added). See Benestad and Butler, *Quest for Justice*, 318.

8. J. Bryan Hehir, "The Just Society," *Chicago Studies* 13 (Fall 1974): 332.

9. This conception of social sin implied a call for direct action by all members of the Church that was not universally accepted. Indeed, in 1977 a group of prominent Chicago laymen complained about the notion, fostered by many priests, that citizens work for justice only by stepping outside of their day-to-day occupations. Such ideas, their statement noted, departed from the mainstream of Catholic social thought. Ironically, the statement's signatories included Edward Marciniak, who a generation earlier had publicly called for far-reaching revisions to the natural law social teaching. See "On Devaluing the Laity," *Origins* 7 (December 29, 1977): 441-42.

10. James Rausch, "Forming America's Conscience," *Origins* 3 (August 16, 1973): 131-32, 143-44.

11. George Higgins, "Historical Résumé of the Teaching, Policy and Action of the Church in 'Social Mission,'" in Philip D. Morris, ed., *Metropolis: Christian Presence and Responsibility* (Notre Dame, Ind.: Fides Publishers, 1970), 147.

12. USCC, "Reform of Correctional Institutions in the 1970s," in Benestad and Butler, *Quest for Justice*, 219-20.

13. J. T. Ryan, "'Render unto Caesar,'" *Sign* 59 (February 1980): 37-38.

14. J. Bryan Hehir, "Ministry of Justice and Peace," *New Catholic Encyclopedia* (New York: McGraw-Hill, 1979), 17:317.

15. "Lally Disputes 'Church, Politics don't mix' Claim," *National Catholic Reporter*, June 15, 1979.

16. Synod of Bishops, "Justice in the World," *The Gospel of Peace and Justice: Catholic

Social Teaching Since Pope John, ed. Joseph Gremillion (Maryknoll, N.Y.: Orbis Books, 1976), 514, 521, 524.

17. Thomas Fleming, "Divided Shepherds of a Restive Flock," *New York Times Magazine,* January 16, 1977. Russell Shaw later explained that Panama's bishops privately had pressed the NCCB to comment; see Joop Koopman, "USCC Finds Itself Focus of Scrutiny," *National Catholic Register,* May 29, 1983.

18. Mark Winiarski, "Bernardin: 'Bishops Ahead of Catholic Mainstream,'" *National Catholic Reporter,* November 12, 1976.

19. Barbara Ann Stolz, *Violence in the Family: A National Concern, A Church Concern* (Washington, D.C.: USCC, 1979), 11-12.

20. For an example of the NCCB's discussion of sin, see "To Live in Christ Jesus," 25. Its list of sins mention only *interpersonal* transgressions.

"To Live in Christ Jesus" had an interesting gestation. It was preceded by a 1974 study done by the NCCB's Ad Hoc Committee on Moral Values, issued that same year as a pamphlet titled *On Moral Values in Society* (see pages 3 and 11 for the tenor of their remarks). This little publicized study was the NCCB's strongest attack on secularism and vice in the 1970s, but many of its criticisms were not incorporated in "To Live in Christ Jesus." In addition, about six months before "To Live in Christ Jesus" was approved, a group of theologians and USCC staff members (represented by Fr. Hehir) tried unsuccessfully to persuade the bishops to consider an "alternative" moral values pastoral that they had drafted; see Richard Rashke, "Bishops Voted on 'Moral Values' Without Seeing Alternative Drafts," *National Catholic Reporter,* November 26, 1976.

21. J. Bryan Hehir, "Development and Population: Policy Perspectives and Catholic Teaching," *Review of Politics* 40 (July 1978): 359, 361-62, 364. Hehir did not cite any passage in Murray's writings that condoned artificial birth control or which suggested that contraception should be overlooked by public authorities.

22. J. Bryan Hehir, "The Church and the Population Year: Notes on a Strategy," *Theological Studies* 35 (March 1974): 75-81. For an earlier view of this issue, see the NCWC's 1959 statement "Explosion or Backfire?" in *Pastoral Letters of the United States Catholic Bishops,* ed. Hugh J. Nolan (Washington, D.C.: USCC, 1984), 2:221-24. In this statement, the bishops argued that the promotion of artificial birth control is ineffective at halting population growth and dangerous for society because it hinders man's higher development by eroding self-discipline.

23. NCCB, "Statement on Abortion" (1970), in Benestad and Butler, *Quest For Justice,* 148-49.

24. John Krol, James McHugh, "Initial Reaction: The Catholic Community," *Origins* 2 (February 1, 1973): 505.

25. NCCB, "Pastoral Message of the Administrative Committee," in Benestad and Butler, *Quest For Justice,* 155-56.

26. Eugene Kennedy, *Cardinal Bernardin: Easing Conflicts—and Battling for the Soul of American Catholicism* (Chicago: Bonus Books, 1989), 146.

27. Mary C. Segers, "The Bishops, Birth Control, and Abortion Policy: 1950-1985," in Segers, ed., *Church Polity and American Politics: Issues in Contemporary Catholicism* (New York: Garland, 1990), 225-27.

28. Senate Committee on the Judiciary, "Abortion," 93rd Cong., 2nd Sess., 1974, 157.

29. "Rockefeller and Abortion," *Origins* 4 (December 5, 1974): 374. This action by Cody's committee was opposed by several bishops; see Sharlene Shoemaker, "Bishops' Meeting—An Analysis," *National Catholic Reporter,* December 6, 1974.

30. John Krol, "The Hunger for Purpose and Truth," *Origins* 4 (November 28, 1974): 357.

31. James Rausch, "Human Rights: Legacy and Challenge in the Church," *Origins* 3 (November 8, 1973): 316. Timothy A. Byrnes notes that other bishops, particularly Thomas Gumbleton, were privately making similar arguments in NCCB councils not long afterward; see his *Catholic Bishops in American Politics* (Princeton, N.J.: Princeton University Press, 1991), 59.

32. George Higgins, "Dialogue: Strictly of the Essence," *Origins* 4 (May 30, 1974): 8-9.

33. Mary T. Hanna, *Catholics and American Politics* (Cambridge, Mass.: Harvard University Press, 1979), 155-56.

34. NCCB, "Pastoral Plan for Pro-Life Activities," Benestad and Butler, *Quest for Justice,* 161-62. For comment on the plan, see Paul J. Weber, "Bishops in Politics: The Big Plunge," *America* 134 (March 20, 1976): 220.

35. Joseph Bernardin, "The Church and Partisan Politics," *Origins* 6 (September 2, 1976): 170.

36. Ibid., 170-73.

37. Kennedy, *Cardinal Bernardin,* 157. Kennedy cites Archbishop Thomas Kelly, who served as USCC general secretary from 1977 to 1981, as his source for Rausch's desire to help Carter "cope" with the pro-life movement.

38. Byrnes, *Catholic Bishops in American Politics,* 72-76.

39. "The Bishops Meet Ford," *Origins* 6 (September 23, 1976): 216-18.

40. Jim Castelli, *The Bishops and the Bomb: Waging Peace in a Nuclear Age* (Garden City, N.J.: Image Books, 1983), 68. See also Byrnes, *Catholic Bishops in American Politics,* 83.

41. Rausch's anger at Higgins's criticism for "endorsing Ford" can well be imagined. Rausch was an old friend of fellow Minnesotan and Democratic vice-presidential candidate Walter Mondale; see "Catholic Conference Says Staff Must Be Nonpartisan," *Our Sunday Visitor,* October 10, 1976.

Rumors of threatened mass resignations at the USCC over the incident were probably exaggerated. Msgr. Higgins had claimed he knew of no staffers who actually threatened to quit the USCC over this affair; see Gerald M. Costello, *Without Fear or Favor: George Higgins on the Record* (Mystic, Conn.: Twenty-Third Publications, 1984), 197-99.

42. NCCB, Administrative Committee, "Bishops Clarify Position," *Origins* 6 (September 30, 1976): 236

43. "Comparing the Party Platforms and USCC Positions," *Origins* 6 (September 30, 1976): 237-41. By my count, USCC positions either paralleled or contradicted both parties on fourteen other issues.

44. For more on the bishops' silence over the 1980 Democratic abortion plan, see Byrnes, *Catholic Bishops in American Politics,* 85.

45. NCCB, "To Do the Work of Justice," in Benestad and Butler, *Quest for Justice,* 203-4.

46. John Quinn, "Taking Up the Role of Prophets," *Origins* 7 (February 2, 1978): 526.

47. USCC, "Society and the Aged: Toward Reconciliation," in Benestad and Butler, *Quest for Justice,* 339.

48. USCC Department of Social Development and World Peace, "Statement on Feeding the Hungry: Toward a U.S. Domestic Food Policy," ibid., 262.

49. USCC Committee on Social Development and World Peace, "Community and Crime," ibid., 229, 242-43.

50. USCC Department of Social Development and World Peace, "Development-Dependency: The Role of Multinational Corporations," ibid., 108.

51. USCC, "The Economy: Human Dimensions," ibid., 267.

52. NCCB Administrative Board, "Statement on the World Food Crisis: A Pastoral Plan of Action," ibid., 104. See also USCC, "Food Policy," *Origins* 5 (September 25, 1975): 216.

53. USCC, "The Right to a Decent Home: A Pastoral Response to the Crisis in Housing," in Benestad and Butler, *Quest for Justice,* 299.

54. House Committee on Education and Labor, "The Full Employment and Balanced Growth Act of 1977," 95th Cong., 1st Sess., 1977, 355. The official unemployment rate that January was 7.3 per cent.

55. J. Bryan Hehir, "Person, Income, Society: Ethical Themes of Catholic Social Teaching," *Social Thought* 1 (Spring 1975): 7.

56. Hehir, "Just Society," 333. Hehir presented this idea to the bishops at their November 1978 meeting; "Church and State: Basic Concepts for an Analysis," *Origins* (November 30, 1978): 380-81.

57. Hehir, "Ministry of Justice and Peace," 319.

58. USCC, "Welfare Reform Legislation," in Benestad and Butler, *Quest for Justice,* 255.

59. USCC Department of Social Development and World Peace, "Welfare Reform in the 1970s," ibid., 273, 277.

60. USCC, "Society and the Aged," ibid., 339.

61. USCC, "Reform of Correctional Institutions," ibid., 216.

62. USCC Administrative Board, "Resolution on New York City," ibid., 270.

63. James Rausch, "Public Works Legislation: USCC," *Origins* 5 (February 12, 1976): 547.

64. Thomas Kelly, "Statistics on Unemployment," *Origins* 7 (September 22, 1977): 222.

65. House Committee on Education and Labor, "Full Employment and Balanced Growth Act," 357-59.

66. USCC, "Right to a Decent Home," 308.

67. NCCB, "A Review of the Principal Trends in the Life of the Catholic Church in the United States," in Nolan, *Pastoral Letters,* 3:456-57, 463. Parts of this statement had been incorporated into the NCCB pamphlet *On Moral Values in Society.*

68. NCCB, "Pastoral Plan for Pro-Life Activities," in Benestad and Butler, *Quest for Justice,* 159.

69. USCC Division of Family Life, "The Family as an Agent of Reconciliation," *Catholic Mind* 73 (June 1975): 4.

70. James R. Jennings, "World Justice and Peace and American Catholics," *Catholic Mind* 71 (January 1973): 41-42, 46.

71. J. Bryan Hehir, "International Affairs and Ethics," *Chicago Studies* 11 (Summer

1972): 200. Peter Gerety, "The Ethics of International Relations," *Origins* 5 (February 5, 1976): 521.

72. USCC Division of World Justice and Peace, "Towards the Synod: Putting Justice in an American Context," *Origins* 1 (August 26, 1971): 174.

73. U.S. Division of World Justice and Peace, *Human Rights: A Question of Conscience* (Washington, D.C.: USCC, 1974), 2-3. See also NCCB, "Brothers and Sisters to Us," 385.

74. Gerety, "The Ethics of International Relations," 525.

75. J. Bryan Hehir previewed this in the summer of 1972; see "International Affairs," 200-202. James Rausch, "Human Rights: Legacy and Challenge in the Church," *Origins* 3 (November 8, 1973): 315.

76. J. Bryan Hehir, "Hunger: The Food Crisis and the Church," *Origins* 3 (January 24, 1974): 359. See also Rausch's foreword in Gremillion, *The Gospel of Peace and Justice: Catholic Social Teaching Since Pope John,* ix-x.

77. J. Bryan Hehir, "The Ministry for Justice," *Network Quarterly* 2 (Summer 1974): 5.

78. For an example of the NCWC's thinking on foreign aid, see "Freedom and Peace," in Nolan, *Pastoral Letters,* 2:217.

79. USCC Department of Social Development and World Peace, "Development-Dependency," 109-10.

80. Gerety, "The Ethics of International Relations," 525. Also James Jennings, "Multinational Corporation: Friend or Foe," *New Catholic World* 218 (September-October 1975): 230.

81. NCCB, "Pastoral Letter on Marxist Communism," in Nolan, *Pastoral Letters,* 4:380-81, 392-99. The pastoral was drafted by Yale professor Louis Dupre; see "Bishops Target Laity, Sexist Liturgy and Marxism," *Our Sunday Visitor,* November 23, 1980.

82. USCC, "Religious Liberty in Eastern Europe: A Test Case for Human Rights," in Benestad and Butler, *Quest for Justice,* 136.

83. NCCB, "Statement on Small-Boat Refugees in Southeast Asia," ibid., 139.

84. NCCB, "Statement on Cambodia," in Nolan, *Pastoral Letters,* 4:356.

85. USCC, "Southern Africa: Peace or War?" in Benestad and Butler, *Quest for Justice,* 129. House Committee on International Relations, "The Rhodesian Sanctions Bill," 95th Cong., 1st Sess., 1977, 25.

86. Senate Committee on International Relations, "Human Rights in Argentina," 94th Cong., 2nd Sess., 1976, 26-27. USCC Administrative Board, "Statement of Solidarity on Human Rights: Chile and Brazil," in Benestad and Butler, *Quest for Justice,* 123. House Committee on Appropriations, "Foreign Assistance and Related Agencies Appropriations for 1979," 95th Cong., 2d Sess., 1978, 160. House Committee on International Relations, "Religious Persecution in El Salvador," 95th Cong., 1st Sess., 1977, 2-5. Joseph Bernardin, "NCCB Protests Ecuadorian Arrests," *Origins* 6 (September 2, 1976): 169. USCC Division for Justice and Peace, "Human Rights in Bolivia," *Origins* 3 (August 30, 1973): 152. Senate Committee on Foreign Relations, "Latin America," 95th Cong., 1st Sess., 1978, 100.

87. "Colonnese Fired in Ideological Split," *National Catholic Reporter,* September 24, 1971.

88. USCC Division for Latin America, "The Human Terms of the Cuban Embargo," *Origins* 2 (June 22, 1972): 82.

89. James Rausch, "African Continent: Threatening Battlefield," *Origins* 5 (May 13, 1976): 753. USCC staffers consistently endorsed economic sanctions against Rhodesia and South Africa: see House Committee on Foreign Affairs, "Economic Sanctions Against Rhodesia," 96th Cong., 1st Sess., 1979, 145.

90. J. Brian Benestad, *The Pursuit of a Just Social Order: Policy Statements of the U.S. Catholic Bishops, 1966-1980* (Washington, D.C.: Ethics and Public Policy Center, 1982), 54. In 1983 Hehir again said that the USCC paid more attention to human rights abuses in nations with close ties to the United States because it was unrealistic to believe American criticism could affect the human rights situation in the Soviet Union; the United States could influence Latin America. See Charlotte Hays, "Hehir, Neuhaus Dispute Human Liberty Agenda," *National Catholic Register,* July 31, 1983.

91. Quigley stated no economic aid should be provided to Nicaragua because even humanitarian assistance would give the Somoza regime a propaganda tool. See Senate Committee on Foreign Relations, "Latin America," 106, 111-12. Quigley's concept of judging regimes by economic and social conditions as well as by their observance of civil liberties was reiterated by Msgr. Francis Lally in testimony before the Senate in 1979: Committee on Foreign Relations, "International Human Rights Treaties," 96th Cong., 1st Sess., 1979, 371, 373.

CHAPTER 7

1. NCCB, "The Challenge of Peace: God's Promise and Our Response," *Pastoral Letters of the U.S. Catholic Bishops,* ed. Hugh J. Nolan (Washington, D.C.: USCC, 1984), 4:493-581.

2. NCCB, *Economic Justice for All: Pastoral Letter on Catholic Social Teaching and the U.S. Economy* (Washington, D.C.: USCC, 1986).

3. John Paul II, "1982 World Day of Peace Message," *Origins* 11 (January 7, 1982): 478.

4. John Paul II, *Laborem Exercens (On Human Work)* (Washington, D.C.: USCC, 1981), pars. 7, 13.

5. Vatican II, *"Gaudium et Spes" (Pastoral Constitution on the Church and The Modern World),* in *The Documents of Vatican II,* ed. Walter M. Abbott, S.J., and trans. Joseph Gallagher (New York: America Press, 1966), 199-308.

6. See Ronald G. Musto, *The Catholic Peace Tradition* (Maryknoll, N.Y.: Orbis Books, 1986), 252-53.

7. J. Bryan Hehir, "American Christians and New World Disorders," *Being Christian Today: An American Conversation,* ed. Richard John Neuhaus and George Weigel (Washington, D.C.: Ethics and Public Policy Center, 1992), 239-40.

8. Vatican II, *"Gaudium et Spes,"* in Abbott and Gallagher, *The Documents of Vatican II,* par. 80.

9. NCCB, "Human Life in Our Day," *Pastoral Letters of the U.S. Bishops,* ed. Hugh J. Nolan (Washington, D.C.: USCC, 1983), 3:185-86, pars. 106, 111.

10. NCCB, "To Live in Christ Jesus: A Pastoral Reflection on the Moral Life," *Quest for Justice: A Compendium of Statements of the U.S. Bishops on the Political and Social*

Order, 1966-1980, eds. J. Brian Benestad and Francis J. Butler (Washington, D.C.: USCC, 1981), 44. See also Patricia McNeal, *Harder than War: Catholic Peacemaking in Twentieth-Century America* (New Brunswick, NJ: Rutgers University, 1992), 247.

11. USCC Administrative Board, "The Gospel of Peace and the Danger of War," in Benestad and Butler, *Quest for Justice,* 84-85.

12. USCC Office of International Justice and Peace, *Arms Exports Policies: Ethical Choices* (Washington, D.C.: USCC, 1978), 22.

13. J. Bryan Hehir, "Catholic Church and the Arms Race," *Worldview* 21 (July-August 1978): 15.

14. Thomas Gumbleton, "Chaplains Blessing the Bombers," *Commonweal* 106 (March 2, 1979): 106.

15. Senate Committee on Foreign Relations, "The SALT II Treaty," 96th Cong., 1st Sess., 1979, 118, 128. John Langan, "Struggling for Moral Clarity about Nuclear Deterrence: David Hollenbach and Michael Novak," *Thought* 59 (March 1984): 94. McNeal, *Harder than War,* 246.

16. Timothy Byrnes, *Catholic Bishops in American Politics* (Princeton, N.J.: Princeton University Press, 1991), 91, 98-99.

17. Patty Edmonds, "U.S. Bishops Assail Death Code; Seek Active Laity," *National Catholic Reporter,* November 21, 1980.

18. Besides Archbishop Bernardin, other members on the drafting committee included Thomas Gumbleton, George Fulcher of Columbus, Ohio, Daniel P. Reilly of Norwich, Conn., and John O'Connor, then an auxiliary bishop in New York City, whose primary duty was to head the U.S. Military Vicariate. Bishops Fulcher and Gumbleton belonged to the Catholic pacifist organization Pax Christi, and Bishop Reilly (as did most bishops) signed Pax Christi's nuclear freeze petition in the spring of 1982; see Phyllis Zagano, "Media Morality: American Catholic Bishops and Deterrence," *Center Journal* 3 (Winter 1983): 181. Advisors to the drafting committee included Fr. Hehir and Edward Doherty of the USCC secretariat, Fr. Richard Warner and Sr. Juliana Casey, representing American religious, and Bruce Russett of Yale, editor of the *Journal of Conflict Resolution,* who did much of the drafting work. See Patricia McNeal, *Harder than War,* 250.

19. McNeal, *Harder than War,* 250.

20. Francis X. Winters, "Did the Bishops Ban the Bomb? Yes and No," *America* 147 (September 10, 1983): 106-7.

21. Joseph Bernardin, "U.S. Bishops Debate War and Peace Pastoral," *Origins* 12 (December 2, 1982): 398. Also J. Bryan Hehir, "The Process & The Product," *Commonweal* 109 (December 17, 1982): 680. See also Eugene Kennedy, *Cardinal Bernardin: Easing Conflicts — and Battling for the Soul of American Catholicism* (Chicago: Bonus Books, 1989), 231. For Gumbleton's leak of the draft, see Patricia Scharber Lefevere, "Bishops' Draft Says Qualified 'No' to Nuke Use, 'Possession OK,'" *National Catholic Reporter,* July 2, 1982.

22. Michael Novak, "Arms & the Church," *Commentary* 73 (March 1982): 40. See also Novak's "counter-letter," "Moral Clarity in the Nuclear Age," *National Review* 35 (April 1, 1983): 354-92.

23. "January Meeting in Rome on the War & Peace Pastoral," *Origins* 12 (April 7, 1983): 692-95. For a report on John Paul II's remarks to Cardinal Bernardin, see Patty

NOTES TO PAGES 132-36

Edmonds, "Bishops Commit Church to Peace," *National Catholic Reporter,* May 13, 1983.

24. Interestingly, the bishops also cautioned against a strategy which targeted *only* nuclear delivery systems, judging that such a "counterforce" doctrine would undermine the stability of deterrence in a crisis and thus make war more likely; par. 184.

25. Thomas J. Reese S.J., *A Flock of Shepherds: The National Conference of Catholic Bishops* (Kansas City, Mo.: Sheed & Ward, 1992), 236.

26. John Cardinal O'Connor afterward told Congressmen that a retaliatory use of nuclear weapons against warships at sea could possibly satisfy the just war criteria; see House Committee on Foreign Affairs, "The Role of Arms Control in U.S. Defense Policy," 98th Cong., 2d Sess., 1984, 174.

27. This was Fr. Hehir's famous "centimeter of ambiguity"; it carefully straddled the line between outright nuclear pacifism and the strictest possible application of the just war criteria. See McNeal, *Harder than War,* 254; see also J. Bryan Hehir, "The Context of the Moral-Strategic Debate and the Contribution of the U.S. Catholic Bishops" in Charles J. Reid, ed., *Peace in a Nuclear Age: The Bishops' Pastoral Letter in Perspective* (Washington, D.C.: Catholic University of America Press, 1986), 150; Winters, "Did the Bishops Ban the Bomb?" 107.

28. NCCB, "Challenge of Peace," par. 190. The MX missile was denounced on several occasions by USCC spokesmen; see House Committee on Armed Services, "Hearings on Military Posture," 96th Cong., 2d Sess., 1980, 168; also James Malone, "U.S. Bishops Urge Rejection of MX Missile," *Origins* 14 (March 28, 1985): 667. In rejecting modernization of the strategic arsenal, the bishops followed Hehir's logic as outlined in J. Bryan Hehir and Robert A. Gessert, *The New Nuclear Debate* (New York: Council on Religion and International Affairs, 1976), 67-69.

29. House Committee on Foreign Affairs, "The Role of Arms Control," 135-36.

30. John Roach, "A Step Closer to Nuclear War?" *Origins* 11 (August 27, 1981): 167.

31. See J. Bryan Hehir, "War and Peace: Reflections on Recent Teaching," *New Catholic World* 225 (March-April 1982): 63. For a more recent example of Hehir's thinking on this topic, see "Papal Foreign Policy," *Foreign Policy* 78 (Spring 1990): 43. John Paul II's teaching on ideology is exemplified in his 1982 "World Day of Peace Message," 474-75.

32. John Roach, "The Need for Public Dialogue on Religion and Politics," *Origins* 11 (December 3, 1981): 393. Fr. Hehir echoed this in 1985; see "Debating Deficits, Debating Deterrence," *Commonweal* 112 (January 11, 1984): 7.

33. NCCB, *Economic Justice for All,* pars. 148, 294. See also "On File," *Origins* 16 (March 26, 1987): 714.

34. George Weigel, *Tranquilitas Ordinis: The Present Failure and Future Promise of American Catholic Thought on War and Peace* (New York: Oxford University Press, 1987), 282.

35. See McNeal, *Harder than War,* 254-57.

36. For a typical statement of this view, see the testimony of Thomas Quigley, the USCC's principal Latin American expert, in Senate Committee on Foreign Relations, "Latin America," 95th Cong., 2d Sess., 1978, 101.

37. NCCB, "Statement on Central America," (1981) in Nolan, *Pastoral Letters,* 4:465-66.

38. House Committee on Foreign Affairs, "U.S. Policy in El Salvador," 98th Cong., 1st Sess., 1983, 242.

39. Ibid., 231.

40. NCCB, "Statement on Central America" (1981), 467.

41. NCCB, "Statement on Central America," *Origins* 17 (December 3, 1987): 443.

42. House Committee on Appropriations, "Foreign Assistance and Related Programs Appropriations for 1982," 97th Cong., 1st Sess., 1981, 250. House Committee on Foreign Affairs, "U.S. Policy in El Salvador," 216. See also House Committee on Foreign Affairs, "U.S. Support for the Contras," 99th Cong., 1st Sess., 1985, 115.

43. House Committee on Foreign Affairs, "U.S. Support for the Contras," 99th Cong., 1st Sess., 1985, 137.

44. House Committee on Foreign Affairs, "U.S. Policy toward El Salvador," 97th Cong., 1st Sess., 1981, 53.

45. House Committee on Foreign Affairs, "U.S. Policy in El Salvador," 199, 210.

46. House Committee on Foreign Affairs, "U.S. Policy in El Salvador," 215-16. See also Daniel Hoye's opposition to contra aid renewal in 1986: "USCC Opposes Military Aid to Contras," *Origins* 15 (April 3, 1986): 694.

47. NCCB, "Statement on Central America," (1987), 444.

48. See, for example, "On File," *Origins* 19 (March 18, 1990): 646. The USCC's Thomas Quigley was still uncomfortable with this hypothesis two years later; see d'Souza, "Viva la Demoracia," 19-20.

49. NCCB, "Statement on Central America" (1987), 443, 445.

50. George Weigel, "How the U.S. Catholic Bishops Missed Their Chance to Be a Force for Peace in Central America," in Michael Scully, ed., *The Best of This World* (Lanham, Md.: University Press of America, 1987), 299-300.

51. NCCB, "Statement on Central America," (1981), 466. See also Thomas Kelly, "U.S. Military Aid: El Salvador," *Origins* 9 (April 3, 1980): 671. House Committee on Appropriations, "Foreign Assistance," 239. Quigley's comment is quoted by Edmund W. Robb and Julia Robb, in *The Betrayal of the Church: Apostasy and Renewal in the Mainline Denominations* (Westchester, Ill.: Crossway, 1986), 166.

52. "Salvadoran Bishop Explains Need for U.S. Arms," *Our Sunday Visitor,* December 6, 1981. See also Reese, *A Flock of Shepherds,* 241-43. The bishops and their staff eventually stopped claiming to speak for the Salvadoran bishops. In 1983 Archbishop Hickey, confronted at a congressional hearing with evidence that Salvadoran Catholics favored American military aid, replied, "I am not here to speak for the Church in El Salvador"; House Committee on Foreign Affairs, "U.S. Policy in El Salvador," 245.

53. Joan Frawley, "Nicaraguan Church Official Says USCC Staffer Hindered Bishops," *National Catholic Register,* September 9, 1984. The same article reported that Quigley had asked a former nun who had worked in Nicaragua not to criticize the Sandinistas because such criticism would only give ammunition to the Reagan administration.

54. Margin note, *Origins* 17 (August 13, 1987): 152-53.

55. Edmonds, "U.S. Bishops Assail Death Code."

56. "Bishops' Body Vows All-Out War on Reagan Budget Cuts," *Our Sunday Visitor,* March 29, 1981. See also Stephanie Russell, "Church Officials Urge Nationwide Opposition to Planned Budget Cuts," *National Catholic Reporter,* April 10, 1981.

57. USCC, "Reviewing and Renewing the Church's Social Teaching: The 1981 Labor Day Statement," *Catholic Mind* 79 (December 1981): 53.

58. Senate Committee on Agriculture, Nutrition & Forestry, "Proposed Reauthorization of the Food and Agriculture Act of 1977," 97th Cong., 1st Sess., 1981, 327-29. House Committee on the Judiciary, "Legal Services Corporation Reauthorization," 97th Cong., 1st Sess., 1981, 483-87. House Committee on the Budget (Task Force on Entitlements, Uncontrollables and Indexing), "Impact of the Omnibus Reconciliation Act," 97th Cong., 2d Sess., 1982, 14-27. House Committee on Banking, Finance, and Urban Affairs, "Housing and Urban-Rural Recovery Act of 1982," 97th Cong., 2d Sess., 1982, 1626-31.

59. Rembert G. Weakland, "Church Social Teaching and the American Economy," *Origins* 13 (December 8, 1983): 447-48.

60. Nat Hentoff, *John Cardinal O'Connor: At the Storm Center of a Changing American Catholic Church* (New York: Charles Scribner's Sons, 1988), 171.

61. Rembert G. Weakland, *All God's People: Catholic Identity After the Second Vatican Council* (Mahwah, N.J.: Paulist Press, 1985), 201.

62. "Final Document: A Preferential Option for the Poor," in John Eagleson and Philip Scharper, eds., *Puebla and Beyond: Documentation and Commentary* (Maryknoll, N.Y.: Orbis Books, 1979), 264-67.

63. For example, the NCCB's 1986 pastoral statement on evangelization, "To the Ends of the Earth," said that the poor of the world help us to critique our own society. Although the overall letter was on evangelization, its brief discussion of the option for the poor was couched almost entirely in social, not spiritual, terms. See *Origins* 16 (December 4, 1986): 464.

64. See, for instance, Congregation for the Doctrine of the Faith (Joseph Cardinal Ratzinger), "Instruction on Christian Freedom and Liberation," *Origins* 15 (April 17, 1986): 723.

65. John Paul II, *Sollicitudo Rei Socialis (On Social Concern)* (Washington, D.C.: USCC, 1988).

66. Bishop James Rausch of Phoenix died in 1981.

67. Rembert G. Weakland, "The Economic Pastoral: Draft Two," *America* 153 (September 21, 1985): 130-31. The NCCB statement on evangelization clarified this point when it noted that the option for the poor entailed a need to "evangelize the powerful" so that they would help build a new society. See "To the Ends of the Earth," 464.

68. Rembert G. Weakland, "Morality and the Economic Life of a Nation," *Origins* 15 (January 30, 1986): 550-51.

69. John Rawls, *A Theory of Justice* (Cambridge: Harvard University Press, 1971): 75. "Economic Justice for All" (par. 69) also noted the need for "fairness" (a classic Rawlsian formulation) in commutative justice; see Rawls, "Justice as Fairness," *Philosophical Review* 57 (1958): 175, 178-79, 182.

70. See, for example, Fr. J. Bryan Hehir's congressional testimony on the homeless: "Homelessness Today—and Tomorrow," *Origins* 16 (February 26, 1987): 656-59.

71. This tendency to accept liberal and left-wing formulations of economic issues continued for years after the publication of the economic pastoral. The NCCB's 1991 statement on the environment, for example, gently criticized certain errors of the environmental movement but accepted without discussion the movement's dire warnings of global warming and atmospheric ozone depletion. See "Renewing the Earth," *Origins* 21 (December 12, 1991): 431.

72. Andrew Greeley, "A 'Radical' Dissent," *America* 152 (January 12, 1985): 19-25.

73. Lay Commission on Catholic Social Teaching and the U.S. Economy, *Toward the Future: Catholic Social Thought and the U.S. Economy* (New York: American Catholic Committee, 1984), 5-7, 19.

74. Novak once explained that the "solidarism" proposed by Pius XI in *Quadragesimo Anno* resembled socialist organizational schemes and "ways of thinking" and was a recipe for authoritarianism and economic stagnation. See Michael Novak, *Freedom with Justice: Catholic Social Thought and Liberal Institutions* (San Francisco: Harper & Row, 1984), 118-22. Hollenbach held that the natural law social teaching was obsolete, or at least in need of overhaul; see "Modern Catholic Teachings Concerning Justice," in John C. Haughey, ed., *The Faith that Does Justice: Examining the Christian Sources for Social Change* (New York: Paulist Press, 1977), 214-21.

75. Michael Novak, "Economic Rights: The Servile State," *Catholicism in Crisis* 3 (October 1985): 10.

76. David Hollenbach S.J., "The Growing End of an Argument," *America* 153 (November 30, 1985): 366.

77. Rembert G. Weakland, "The Issues: Between Drafts of the Pastoral," *Origins* 15 (May 23, 1985): 10-12.

78. Rembert G. Weakland, "How Medellin and Puebla Influenced North America," *Origins* 18 (April 13, 1989), 758. Paul Wilkes, "The Education of an Archbishop," *New Yorker*, July 15, 1991: 50.

79. Rembert G. Weakland, "The Bible and Catholic Social Teaching," *The Bible Today* 24 (November 1986): 352.

80. Byrnes, *Catholic Bishops in American Politics*, 115.

81. Kennedy, *Cardinal Bernardin*, 228, 243.

82. Ibid., 244.

83. "Cardinal Bernardin's Call for a Consistent Ethic of Life," *Origins* 13 (December 29, 1983): 493-94.

84. NCCB, "Pastoral Plan for Pro-Life Activities: A Reaffirmation" (pamphlet) (Washington, D.C.: USCC, 1985), 4.

85. "Cardinal Bernardin's Call for a Consistent Ethic of Life," 492-93.

86. Ibid.

87. Joseph Bernardin, "Enlarging the Dialogue on a Consistent Ethic of Life," *Origins* 13 (April 5, 1984): 708. See also Peter Sheehan, "Bishop James Malone, NCCB President, on the Church in America and Where It's Headed," *Our Sunday Visitor*, March 11, 1984. Hentoff, *John Cardinal O'Connor*, 81-84.

88. Wilkes, "The Education of an Archbishop," 54.

CHAPTER 8

1. NCCB Ad Hoc Committee on the Moral Evaluation of Deterrence, "A Report on 'The Challenge of Peace' and Policy Developments 1983-1988," *Origins* 18 (July 21, 1988): 136, 140.

2. Ibid., 140, 144.

3. Ibid., 141-44.

4. USCC Administrative Board, "New Moment in Eastern and Central Europe," *Origins* 19 (April 26, 1990): 784-85.

5. USCC Administrative Board, "Statement on the Soviet Union and Yugoslavia," *Origins* 21 (September 26, 1991): 258-59.

6. USCC Administrative Board, "New Moment in Eastern and Central Europe," 784-85.

7. NCCB, "Toward Peace in the Middle East: Perspectives, Principles and Hopes," *Origins* 19 (November 23, 1989): 404-09.

8. Daniel Pilarczyk, "Letter to President Bush: The Persian Gulf Crisis," *Origins* 20 (November 29, 1990): 397, 399-400.

9. "Revisiting Five Bishops' Pastorals: Justice For All," *Origins* 20 (March 14, 1991): 653-54. Bernardin reflected again on the Gulf War two years later, while serving on the NCCB's ad hoc committee to draft a statement commemorating the tenth anniversary of "The Challenge of Peace." The Cardinal now doubted that the liberation of Kuwait had met the just-war criteria of "last resort" and "proportionality." The wartime coalition, he suggested, had not exhausted every peaceful means of resolving the crisis, and had used a disproportionate level of violence, devastating Iraq's economic infrastructure and causing "widespread loss of innocent civilian lives"; see Joseph Bernardin, "The Post-Cold War Agenda for Peace," *Origins* 23 (May 20, 1993): 6. Fr. J. Bryan Hehir had made similar comments in the spring of 1991; see "Christians and New World Disorders," *Being Christian Today: An American Conversation,* ed. Richard John Neuhaus and George Weigel (Washington, D.C.: Ethics and Public Policy Center, 1992), 242.

10. John Roach, "According China Most-Favored Nation Status," *Origins* 21 (June 27, 1991): 120. John Roach, "Moral Questions the Iraq Embargo Poses," *Origins* 21 (August 15, 1991): 174-75. USCC, "Statement on the Soviet Union and Yugoslavia," 258-59.

11. Drew Christiansen, USCC, to Archbishop John B. Roach and John Carr, USSC, "Thinking on Somalia Intervention," December 3, 1992.

12. Larry Rohter, "Over Cheers for Aristide, Silence of Haiti's Bishops," *New York Times,* September 28, 1994.

13. USCC spokesmen commented on Haiti several times in 1990s. Shortly before the U.S.-led intervention, NCCB president Archbishop William Keeler issued a joint statement with the heads of the Canadian and Latin American episcopal conferences; see "Urgent Call for Democracy and Dialogue in Haiti," *Origins* 24 (September 22, 1994): 266.

14. John Roach, "On U.S. Intervention in Bosnia," *Origins* 23 (May 27, 1993): 22-23.

15. Drew Christiansen, "Establishing Foreign Aid Priorities," *Origins* 21 (October 24, 1991): 323-24. See also NCCB, "Renewing the Earth," *Origins* 21 (December 12, 1991): 429-30.

16. USCC International Policy Committee, "American Responsibilities in a Changing World," *Origins* 22 (October 29, 1992): 339.

17. John Paul II, *Centesimus Annus (On the Hundredth Anniversary of Rerum Novarum)* (Washington, D.C.: USCC, 1991); see also pars. 16, 20, 44.

18. USCC Administrative Board, "The Many Faces of AIDS: A Gospel Response," *Origins* 17 (December 24, 1987): 486-89. For Fr. Hehir's call for toleration of con-

traceptive programs, see "Development and Population: Policy Perspectives and Catholic Teaching," *Review of Politics* 40 (July 1978): 359-64.

19. Joseph Ratzinger, "Cardinal Ratzinger's Letter on AIDS Document," *Origins* 18 (July 7, 1988): 117. James F. Keenan, S.J., "Prophylactics, Toleration, and Cooperation: Contemporary Problems and Traditional Principles," *International Philosophical Quarterly* 29 (June 1989): 206-7.

20. Francis T. Hurley, "NCCB/USCC/W.I.T.D," *America* 158 (March 19, 1988): 284.

21. Kennedy, *Cardinal Bernardin*, 299-302.

22. Thomas J. Reese, S.J., "Bishops Meet in Baltimore," *America* 161 (November 25, 1989): 369.

23. NCCB, "Called to Compassion and Responsibility: A Response to the HIV/AIDS Crisis," *Origins* 19 (November 30, 1989): 428-29.

24. NCCB, "Resolution on Abortion," *Origins* 19 (November 16, 1989): 395-96.

25. "On File," *Origins* 19 (December 14, 1989): 458.

26. NCCB, "Pastoral Plan for Pro-Life Activities," in Benestad and Butler, *Quest for Justice,* 159-69. The plan was slightly updated and reissued by the NCCB in November 1985.

27. Robin Toner, "The Catholic Hierarchy and Clinton: Already a Complicated Relationship," *New York Times,* February 3, 1993.

28. See, for example, the NCCB Pro-Life Committee's commemoration of the 25th anniversary of the encyclical *Humanae Vitae,* "Human Sexuality From God's Perspective," *Origins* 23 (August 12, 1993): 164-66.

29. Robert Lynch, Joan Brown Campbell, and Henry Michelman, "The Common Good: Old Idea, New Urgency," *Origins* 23 (June 24, 1993): 83. See also Richard John Neuhaus, "Speaking for the Common Good," *First Things* 37 (November 1993): 44-46.

30. NCCB, "*Rerum Novarum:* A Century of Social Teaching: A Common Heritage, a Continuing Challenge," *Origins* 20 (November 22, 1990): 394-96.

31. NCCB, "Putting Children and Families First: A Challenge For Our Church, Nation and World," *Origins* 21 (November 28, 1991): 396-98.

32. Barbara Dafoe Whitehead and David Blankenhorn, "What the Bishops Don't Know About Families," *First Things* 23 (May 1992): 20-22.

33. NCCB, "Putting Children and Families First," 399, 402.

34. John Ricard, "How Fiscal and Human Deficits Intertwine," *Origins* 22 (March 4, 1993): 637, 639-40.

35. Lynch, "The Common Good: Old Idea, New Urgency," 81.

36. NCCB, "Resolution on Health Care Reform," *Origins* 23 (July 1, 1993): 99-101.

37. Ibid., 101.

38. Peter Steinfels, "Bishops Enter Health Battle With a Warning on Abortion," *New York Times,* July 13, 1994.

Index of Names

195